Cootassep
#0
6/88

SO-BDG-958

Currently available :

Socio-economic studies - No. 1. *Evaluating social action projects : principles, methodological aspects and selected examples.*

Socio-economic studies - No. 2. *Socio-economic indicators for planning methodological aspects and selected examples.*

Socio-economic studies - No. 3. *Women and development : indicators of their changing role.*

Socio-economic studies - No. 4. *Planning methods and the human environment.*

Socio-economic studies - No. 5. *Quality of life : problems of assessment and measurement.*

Socio-economic studies - No. 6. *Evaluation manual.*

Socio-economic studies - No. 7. *Applicability of indicators of socio-economic change for development planning.*

Socio-economic studies - No. 8. *Social science methods, decision-making and development planning.*

Socio-economic studies - No. 10. *Evaluation in Latin America and the Caribbean : Selected experiences.* (Published also in Spanish.)

Socio-economic studies - No. 11. *Planning integrated development : methods used in Asia.*

Socio-economic studies - No. 12. *Socio-economic analysis and planning : critical choice of methodologies.*

Socio-economic studies - No. 13. *Women's issues in development planning.*

Socio-economic studies - No. 14. *Innovative approaches to development planning.*

Innovative approaches
to development planning

Unesco

The authors are responsible for the choice and presentation of the facts contained in this book and for the opinions contained therein, which are not necessarily those of Unesco and do not commit the Organization.

Published in 1988 by the United Nations
Educational, Scientific and Cultural Organization,
7, place de Fontenoy, 75700 Paris
Printed by Imprimerie Duculot, Gembloux

ISBN 92-3-102539-2

Preface

This is the fourteenth issue of *Socio-economic studies*, a bi-annual series of the Division of Study and Planning of Development, Bureau of Studies, Action and Co-ordination for Development. This issue is concerned with innovative approaches and methods of development planning, a subject which is increasingly engaging the attention of development planners and policy makers as well as professional social scientists.

Experience over the past years has demonstrated that economic growth is only one aspect of development, albeit an essential one. "Development, in order to fulfil national as well as spiritual aspirations and further the development of the creative capacities of each individual, should encompass all aspects of life" and should be multidimensional.

The elaboration of methods of development planning, encompassing different dimensions of development is in a stage of evolution. Through its programmes and field actions Unesco has emhasized integrated development planning and has contributed towards the elaboration of approaches and methods of integrated planning at the national and subnational levels. It is hoped that the studies included in this volume will be a further contribution.

The present volume *Innovative approaches and methods of development planning* consists of three studies undertaken to contribute to the integration of educational, scientific, cultural, communication and social dimensions in development planning.

The first paper "Systems approach to planning integrated development", by Albert Hajnal, emeritus Adviser, Institute of Economic Planning, National Office of Planning, Budapest, and Istvan Kiss, Director, Bureau of Systems Analysis, State Committee of Technical Development, Budapest, reviews critically the state of the art of planning for integrated development and points out how a systems approach is necessary to take account of the multidimensional nature of development in planning.

The second paper "Integrated development planning using socio-economic and quality of life indicators" by Alex C. Michalos, University of Guelph, Canada, proposes a set of social indicators and statistics of use in integrated planning in Unesco's fields of competence, and suggests a theory for measuring satisfaction - multiple discrepancies theory - to improve understanding of judgments based on the indicators suggested. The study also gives the results of applications of multiple discrepancies theory to university students in 23 countries.

In his paper "Development planning in Sri Lanka - a study of innovative methods and approaches used", Lloyd Fernando, Director,

National Planning, Colombo, describes Sri Lanka's experience in the field of development planning, with special reference to education, science and technology, culture and communications. The paper highlights the role played by the rolling five-year public investment programme in the planning system of the country and how this approach could serve to integrate the different dimensions of development planning.

Comments and suggestions about this issue, and the series in general, as well as requests for copies of this and past issues, may be addressed to :

Division of Study and Planning of Development
Unesco
7, Place de Fontenoy
75700 PARIS
France.

Contents

Systems approach to planning integrated development

Albert Hajnal and Istvan Kiss

INTRODUCTION

This study aims at reviewing and encouraging different methods and approaches to development planning. The audience of this study will be planners and those concerned with methods and techniques to improve the integration of different factors (educational, scientific, technological, cultural, economic) of development in planning. Further, this study discusses the adequacy and special purpose of the systems approach to integrated development. Thus, the study will pay particular attention to the following concepts :

- integrated development,
- systems approach, and
- planning.

These together represent a contextual frame and within this framework the three concepts mutually interpret each other.

One can also identify usages of the three basic concepts in isolation from each other. Again, time series from combined educational and economic statistical indicators might reveal some integrated developmental feature analysed in terms of two combined indicators where neither indicator alone is adequate. To avoid misinterpretations, it seems fruitful to review those usages of the three basic concepts which are compatible with the contextual frame mentioned above, and it seems important to point out usages in which the interpretation of each of the three concepts is compatible with that of the two others. Based on these considerations, the main steps in unfolding the study will be the following :

Part I gives an overview of conceptualizations relating to the contextual frame. It will enquire

- into the nature of development, integrated societal development,
- into the systems approaches to integrated development, and
- into the planning of integrated development, using the systems approach and systems analysis.

Empirical and conceptual foundations, basic features, historical and practical aspects are discussed together.

The phenomena denoted by the concept of 'development' are referred to not only by this term. Other related terms are also used, such as progress, advance, growth, modernization, evolution, transformation, etc. They have originated from different attitudes of researchers and practitioners, or from their different theoretical, ideological or political convictions. Superficially, the background of one concept may differ from those of others but on deeper examination, the different notions and their interpretations may complement rather than exclude each other. In this study the attitude of seeking and making explicit complementary views is very strongly preferred. The nature of phenomena denoted by 'development' and other concepts is so complex that it is necessary to think in terms of complementary and/or integrated concepts. This attitude and approach also determine the interpretation of the notion 'integrated development' accepted for this study.

Streeten (1979) gave a very substantial overview of how dominant development ideas emerged and how historical events influenced shifts in their usage. In his view, such ideas influenced development in different parts of the world, e.g. the concept of linear staged growth ; neocolonialism and dependence ; scarcity and independence ; harmony vs competition and bargaining ; the Third World as homogenous or heterogeneous. Some ideas reached hegemonical positions for a time, until new pretenders replaced them. Streeten also traced changes in another way by examining what "key concepts provided a focus for development thinking and policy making". He identified such issues as capital, entrepreneurship, skills and education, foreign trade, population, unemployment, rural underdevelopment, distressing political records and other obstacles. Each of these proved to be inadequate in itself, because when it became a ruling idea, many destructive or erosive forces were triggered off, which would not have been activated in the absence of such a ruling issue. For example, in the case of foreign trade, development did not occur as swiftly and as harmoniously as the doctrine of the big push would have predicted. Administrative, organizational and technical skills and appropriate institutions to direct them to the required areas were lacking. Concerning the issue of capital, Streeten in the same study remarks : "the importance of physical capital was downgraded and other missing components were added, such as entrepreneurship, skill, investment in 'human capital', innovation, know-how, institutions, and even birth control". It was also a mistake, when the goals of development "were defined narrowly in terms of GNP and its growth, and other goals such as greater equality, eradication of poverty, meeting basic human needs, conservation of natural resources, abating pollution, and the enhancement of the environment, as well as non-material goals, were neglected or not emphasized". Again, there arose the misbelief that only developing countries have developmental problems. "In contrast, development is now beginning to be viewed as a problem common to the whole world : it gives rise to problems that are shared by rich and by poor, with some common and some conflicting interests.

Streeten suggests less determined and more open conclusions than the condemned convictions above. His formulations might seem sophisticated at first, but they are in fact dialectical. "The solution of one problem creates a series of new ones... In a given situation attempts at piecemeal reform may be self-cancelling and the system will tend to reestablish the initial wealth and power distribution. Only deep structural change can enable reform to take root ; on the other hand, piecemeal reform may trigger pressures that lead to further reforms, whereas revolutionary change, as the many revolutions that have failed show, may not achieve its objective." The lesson is that "in many areas only a concerted, properly phased attack on several fronts yields the desired result and the application of some measures without certain others may make things worse".

Many conclusions emerge from the foregoing considerations. The two most important refer to and at the same time are derived from the triple contextual frame chosen above :

a) in developmental plans and planning work, the single usage of any ordering concept is inappropriate because it distorts the relevant representation of reality. Planners should find a collection of concepts (paradigms) which are sensitive to all relevant components and aspects of planned developmental phenomena. At the outset, planners have the important task of selecting and deciding which ordering concepts are most relevant in dealing with their object field ;

b) thinking and planning in terms of a number of concepts is not easy especially when not only compatible interpretation within a context is needed but also a conceptual arrangement which integrates the concepts into a really relevant picture. A conceptually clarified and well-founded master-scheme (ordering model) can serve as a tool to help reinterpret the component concepts in terms of the contextual frame, subsequently helping to integrate them. The basic syntax of the system models can be used as the core of such a master-scheme.

In this study, 'integrated development' refers to the co-existing spheres of natural, societal and artificial phenomena. Within this referential sphere, it is always some kind of organic unit - the societal entity together with its natural environment and human artefacts - which manifests development (or change, transformation, modernization, growth, etc.). The individual, family, school, university, settlement, industrial or agricultural production organization, state, alliance of states, ethnic community, etc., can equally be considered as organic units or societal entities, as some kind of 'whole' together with its parts. Moreover, we must also recognize such organic units in our natural environment, such as a tree, a forest, a lake, a river, a region, together with their relevant parts. The concept of system refers to the unity of interconnected parts in such societal entities. It is axiomatic that as an entity changes, develops or grows, its system also alters.

All these considerations can be viewed as a rather more evolved form of the contextual frame introduced above. Further description will be given in the first part of the study.

Part I analyses various theories concerning the three components of the contextual frame. Books, articles from different periodicals, conference and meeting papers, research reports, and others are the sources for this review. Most sources only partially cover the whole contextual frame. Some concentrate on different aspects of development ; others focus only on methodological features of the systems approach. For this reason, we review the three basic concepts - 'integrated development', 'planning', 'systems approach' - discriminately, although the essence of the concept of integration or of system does not permit discussion of basic concepts in isolation. After the review of integrated development, we therefore gradually combine its modalities with the system issues, and then both of them with planning issues. In this manner, at the end of Part I an integrated concept is gained compatible with the historical conclusions of Streeten and with the requirements of Unesco. In such an approach, the review of concepts has gone beyond simple acquaintance but also illustrates how rather diverging conceptualizations can be brought closer to each other and the pitfalls of simple but misleading paradigmatic approaches.

Part II reviews the state-of-the-art in the application of systems approach and methods. It was found that concrete cases could demonstrate the meaning and benefit of the use of the systems approach rather than abstract considerations about systems methods or methodologies. This choice is also nearer to IIASA activities. The bibliography lists the many studies undertaken by IIASA, some of which have been chosen to demonstrate the practical applications of systems analysis.

Part III outlines the conceptual core of the triple contextual frame. We have found that developmental phenomena, especially integrated developmental phenomena, can be studied more adequately and in more ordered form if we interpret development in terms of genesis, integrated development as polygenesis and the development pattern as genesis pattern. Considerations in Parts I and II can also be reinterpreted in terms of genesis, polygenesis and genesis patterns - elements which are the most important components of the conceptual core. It should be strongly emphasized that reality is not the same as the conceptual core. This core helps to orient planners among the very complex developmental phenomena. It contains the three basic concepts of the contextual frame but in a reinterpreted form.

Part IV is a short appraisal of the review. On the one hand, the judgment and evaluation of sources suggest some conclusions, and on the other, further research is proposed to augment results and to reveal undiscovered particularities of the referential frame.

This review concentrates on methodological issues within the boundaries of the contextual frame. The different philosophical, ideological, scientific or pragmatic aspects are not discussed, nor is consideration given to the kind of developments best or worst suited to the different developed or developing countries. There are already many far-reaching debates about these and similar questions.

Many reviews in recent years also acquaint readers with the state-of-the-art in this dynamic sphere, but we make it our duty to point only to those in which inadequate methods can be discovered. We do not give preference to hard mathematical methods, tools or

methodologies, but to those which first help recognize and understand the most relevant and very complex features of different
developmental phenomena and help deal with them conceptually.
Mathematical treatment comes only after such an understanding.
Nevertheless, 'hard' methods are not neglected. Though there is
definitely no agreement among systems analysts that systems analysis
should be restricted to modelling a system mathematically, yet a
large part of the community seems to have made a strong assumption
of this kind (Miser, Quade, 1986). We prefer, however, to use the
term of systems approach (Churchman, 1968) which allows each of the
three types of conceptualization, the third being a desirable combination of the hard and soft approaches, since "complex and multi-
faceted problems of today call for a broader integration of social,
natural and technical sciences. Forms of organization of science
that provide for an interdisciplinary study of pressing problems...
must be introduced on a greater scale" (Programme of the CPSU,
1986).

PART I - THEORETICAL OVERVIEW OF APPROACHES TO DEVELOPMENT

Studying the literature relating to the topics of 'development',
'systems approach', 'planning', and to the context mutually interpreted by these three basic concepts, some very instructive
discoveries are to be made. As the phenomenon of development is the
primary object of our review, and as the nature of development
carries the primary determinants compared to the other two, any
picture of the contextual framework depends mainly on what features
of this phenomenon are qualified as most relevant to this picture.
A more comprehensive overview is therefore needed of development
literature when we approach the conceptual foundation of the contextual frame. The other two can be treated more concisely than
development.

1.1 The nature of development

It is observed that the notion of 'development' can refer to a great
variety of different object spheres. Among these referential frameworks are animals, plants, humans, societal entities (family, group,
organization, ethnic community, etc.), economy, etc., each manifest-
ing themselves as organic units. The intuitively grasped image of
development depends on the nature of the organic unit which provides
the primary framework.
Deviations in interpretation of development seem, however, to
originate not only from the specific nature of the referential
frames but also from the different attitudes and perceptions of the

conceptualizers. At the same time, many analogies may be discovered when one compares the basic experiences behind verbal conceptualizations. Almost all of them speak explicitly about such manifestations as 'processes', 'sequences of changes', 'progressive changes', 'sequential changes during the lifetime of living organisms' and 'ordered formation of living beings'. Although parts of conceptualizations appear only in some samples and not in others, one can easily infer the undescribed manifestations and compare them with each other.

Many arguments lead to the conclusion that not only do the common features of development in the above examples render service to this study, but also that features showing the generalizable nature of developmental phenomena vary greatly. Common features may serve as a basis for consensus even if the accepted image of development seems to be a rather heuristic approach to more mature images. On the other hand, it is an obvious possibility to search for ways in which deviating conceptualizations - complementary to each other - can help to gain more complete images and interpretations of the nature of development. Both common and deviating conceptualizations can be exploited in our study as a departure to working out a contextual framework.

When the conceptualizations of different referential units are compared, vague differences can be perceived in their images. It is worth making these rather covert differences more overt. Some of them emphasize developmental changes or organismic units which already existed before developmental transformation started. Other conceptualizations focus on developmental changes in units which come into existence. These two kinds of conceptualization are not mutually exclusive but mutually complementary. If we operate within the frame of reproducing each kind of organismic unit - i.e. in the reproduction of plants, animals, human beings, families, populations, organizations, cultures, societies, etc. - we need the combined usage of the two conceptualizations. Insensitivity to either of the two developmental changes or their mixed manifestations may hinder our understanding of the complex nature of developmental phenomena. Other conceptualizations also appear in related literature, but here we can neglect them because the two kinds of development and their mixed occurrence are sufficient to our triple contextual framework mentioned above.

From the human point of view and from that of the chosen contextual framework, we may also consider two kinds of reproduction. The first is human societal reproduction together with artificial means and tools. The second is environmental reproduction, which implies all the organic (biosphere outside of mankind) and inorganic (air, water, etc.) components. Although this distinction is only a rearrangement of classificational images, it has many pragmatic benefits in planning practice. There is also no doubt that this polarized interpretation easily leads us to a confrontation between humankind and its natural environment. If we regard jointly, however, the terms of societal and environmental reproduction and those of their symbiotic interactions, such pitfalls may perhaps be avoided. The two kinds of developmental phenomena are also necessary in the images of societal and environmental reproduction.

Their ordering strength is not only indispensable when understanding the nature of reproduction but may facilitate our reflection upon harmony rather than confrontation between the two kinds of reproduction.

It is observable that certain basic concepts - not without a certain metaphysical charge - are applied as deepening and operationalizing terms in the conceptualizations and theories of development, for example structure, function, process, stages, sequence, life-time, transformation, transition, growth, progression, betterment, and so on. Each word denotes some basic experience in perceiving the features of developmental phenomena. Some conceptualizers seem to be sensitive only to process-like or sequence-like manifestations but insensitive to stage-like, progress-like or betterment-like manifestations in the development of an organic unit.

Plants, animals, humans and families are different kinds of organismic units, each having a special developmental character, both in the sense of transformation and of coming into existence. They and their population reproduce themselves and exist together on Earth. We may say that the specific developmental process of each unit is manifoldly conjoint to other units' development. For example, the development of plants and animals claim manifold adjustment from the rural worker in producing food, wood, etc., and determine the preconditions and constraints of the life of the human population on a territorial sphere. The development of an individual human being determines the life and development of a family. The strong impact of family development on the life and development of subsequent generations can hardly be debated. Healthy life of all kinds on Earth implies among other things undisturbed and mutually intertwined developmental processes of co-existing organismic units. Industrialization, which disturbs the manifold healthy developmental conjunctions in life on Earth has scarcely been considered. These observations must be taken into account when we clarify the connotations in the interpretation of 'integrated development'.

Finally a very existential feature of all development should be stressed. The stagewise sequential course of events is strictly constrained and ordered in time, not only in the changes of a unit's body and operation. We may say that every developmental process has its own duration (within permissible limits), and its own time. This belongs to the specific time-character of any living being. It may be called a natural vegatational time-character if we analogously extend the meaning of the notion 'vegetation'. In most cases the time-order in the development of an organismic unit cannot be accelerated or slowed down without endangering its existence. This means that the time-order - the individual vegetation time-character - of the development process manifoldly determines the duration of the conjunctions between the developmental events of co-existing organismic units.

We can observe that this individual time-character belongs not only to living creatures. The development of any artificial product also has its own time-character. Here the constraints are not as determined as in the case of living creatures. Acceleration and deceleration can possible occur within wide limits. Simple tools, large and complex products such as cars, planes, ships, computers or much larger and more complex systems such as nuclear power plants, automated factories there have their own individual time-character in their development and production processes, and progress in industrial possibilities can be indicated by shortening the time-scale in development and production. But when we consider the development of human abilities needed to develop, produce and use artificial products, the time-constraint - the individual time needed to develop a complex skill - becomes a very determining factor (Eckaus, 1984).

Concepts of macro-development

It seems that it is not only the conceptual vocabulary of a scholar's discipline that makes him sensitive or insensitive to one or other experience denoted by the terms mentioned above. There are other sensitizing-desensitizing factors depending on whether this basic concept is chosen, neglected or opposed by the scholar. For example, one may find among these factors certain ideological standpoints (capitalism, socialism, attitudes towards developing countries, etc.), apolitical commitments, traits of personality (conservative, radical, reformist). The following examples illustrate these aspects of conceptualization :

-   Transformation is understood as the unfolding or preservation of structures and processes which can yield and secure the basis for all people under just, equitable and therefore human conditions ; only this type of transformation deserves to be called development (Addo, Amin, 1985).
-   The evolutionist nature of dominant development theories and strategies, according to which development aims at a pre-determined goal, is fixed and irreversible, progressivist and cast within the confines of a nation-state, is to be criticized. Evolutionist tendencies in a number of historical and structural aspects of the modern Western world can be identified and all are related to corresponding ideologies and cultural projects. Such a mechanistic and impersonal conception of development lapses into total determinism, foreclosing any role for human action and freedom. The goal of development is precisely the full realization of the individual in every aspect of being. A radical humanist approach to development requires rejection of the determinist model of evolutionist development theories, and must restore to human beings their freedom to choose the future and act accordingly. The 'Green' approach to development has this aim in view (Addo, Amin, 1985).
-   Growth in GNP per capita is posited as the central problem of development, and everything follows from that : this is the basic standpoint of 'development economics', the specialized branch of modern economic theory (Aseniero, 1985).
-   If history is progressive movement, there remains the question of trajectory - movement from what, towards what ? Implicitly

or explicitly, the developmentalist conception of history re-
poses on a theory of stages through which the social unit that
is supposed to progress (primarily the nation-state) must
necessarily pass. We must here be aware of a crucial distinction. It is one thing to recognize distinct historical
systems and periodicities as a matter of historical fact and as
an analytical procedure, but quite another to hypothesize a
teleological scheme, typically dressed up in deterministic
language, the triumphalist hierarchical ordering of which
('backward-advanced', 'lower-higher') is of supposedly
universal validity and serves as an ideological justification
for the 'leaders'' dominance over the 'laggards', and pretends
to be a predetermined path (read : 'development strategy')
which 'latecomers' only need to follow. It is the latter sense
which characterizes the developmentalist theory of stages, even
if in some cases this is made to appear as purely conceptual
constructs (Aseniero, 1985).

This second set of examples shows less generalized, less abstract and less definition-like images about the nature of developmental phenomena than the first group. But at the same time these
latter examples more explicitly express the worldview, disciplinary
attitude, even ideological commitment of their conceptualizers than
the first group. Many other examples could be cited. Instead of
further quotations, it would be more useful to cite authors who have
endeavoured to find some order among the very different conceptualizations. Each of them expresses a critical attitude concerning all
past cases. While they characterize the main features of the different types of development, they do this in order to point to the
benefits of the new possibilities they suggest in contrast to redundant versions.
A very useful picture is offered by Friberg, Hettne (1985).
The title of their article, "The greening of the world - toward a
non-deterministic model of global processes", reveals their attitude. According to their political-historical approach, significant schools can be identified among the conceptualizations of
development. They depart from a strongly definite standpoint :
"Development is one of the oldest and most powerful of all Western
ideas. The central element of this perspective is the idea of
evolution, which implies that development is conceived primarily as
directional and cumulative, secondarily as predetermined and irreversible, thirdly as progressive, and fourthly as imminent with
reference to the nation state." From the Greek and Roman civiliz-
ations many historical events formed the European developmentalism
up to the modern idea of progress : "civilization has moved, is
moving, and will move in a desirable direction".
Friberg and Hettne then give a bird's eye view picture of
recent centuries. The pioneers of the natural sciences believed in
the possibility of influencing material bodies as well as human
beings and societies on the basis of the natural laws of mechanics
(nature and society being nothing more than a machine). Comte and
Saint-Simon represented this standpoint in a most articulate
fashion.

Spencer saw the development of society as a process of increasing
complexity, increasing differentiation and increasing division of
labour among the parts. Later new elements were emphasized :
economic growth, technological development, capacity to mobilize
energy and information, industrialization or socio-economic modernization. Behind all these trends one can perceive the evolutionist
way of thinking and its axioms concerning 'direction' (growth,
accumulation, expansion), 'determinism' (predetermined trends of
change), 'progress' (towards a better world), and 'immanence' of
development in every nation. The two authors discuss three most
recent movements among the evolutionists : 'modernization', the
'dependency school', and the 'world approach' in detail. Each
movement has its own identity, but at the same time, the second one
criticized the first, and the third criticized the second. A concise tabular citation of the basic ideas of the three schools will
provide a background to the elaboration of the contextual frame for
this study.

Table 1

Basic features of development in the view of three evolutionist schools

Modernization school	Dependency school	World-system school
Spontaneous inherent process (endogenism)	Obstacles to develop-ment are external (exogenism)	Need to transcend and synthetize endogenism and exogenism
Structural differ-entiation and func-tional specification	Central and peri-pheral regions in international division of labour	Core-state, semi-peripheral, peri-pheral positions exist
Staged development level along the development process	Peripherals are deprived from surplus, depend on centrals	Difficult to break dependency and initiate self-reliant develop-ment need to
Stimulated by com-petition, military threat	Periphery is under-developed and needs to strive for self-reliance	change position from peripheral to semi-peripheral
Traditional and modern sectors co-exist		
Modernization inherent in all societies in embyronic form	First remove obs-stacles, development will come	Strategies for development : seizing the chance; promotion by invitation; self-reliance

Friberg and Hettne, having reviewed and criticized the evolutionist movements, sketch a non-evolutionist alternative, the green movement. Greens look at development phenomena, which have a strong ontological status, without having strong epistemological knowledge about the nature of development. In their view, the most relevant features of development are the following : "Social change is neither a simple process of reproduction of the established system nor a momentary transition from one system to another. It should rather be regarded as a shift in the balance between the dominant order and counterorder, which is much affected by the autonomous choices of ordinary people. In the final analysis social orders themselves are human products. They should be seen as emerging out of the categories of thought and social projects invented by extraordinary creative groups and movements... All this suggests a conceptualization of social change, which avoids both the pitfalls of evolutionism-determinism, and the stumbling block of utopianism-voluntarism." The development concept of the Greens is based upon the hypothesis that the Green movement derives its strength from different sources : (a) from the traditionalists, who regard the non-modern features of cultures as indispensable for the future, (b) from marginalized people, who find no place in a soulless, modernized world, (c) from human-oriented rather than object- or means-oriented development. The traditionalists, especially, do not consider Europe to be the only cultural centre, believing the Middle East, China, India, etc., equivalent. The cultures of the latter offer interpenetration of each other's spheres. Were this really to occur, resulting developmental changes would be quite different to those which occur without such interaction. One of the most characteristic tendencies to be expected from this new development, and which can be characterized in the terms used by Durkheim and Parsons, is the proliferation of organizations with "organic solidarity" which emerge from the mass-culture of organizations with "mechanic solidarity" (Parsons, Peterson).

Friberg and Hettne's ideas cannot be accepted without any critique, but they nevertheless seem compatible with our approach. They will be evaluated after discussing other authors.

Another very comprehensive study is that of Alechina (1982). She reviews efforts made by various United Nations organizations (UNCTAD, UNEP, Unesco, etc.) to clarify the basic nature of development and its possible or desirable forms. Alechina refers to the Cocoyoc Declaration of 1974, which states that there should be development "not of things, but of man". She quotes Galtung's proposition for development : "Development is development of the people... It should not be conceived in terms of the production of goods and services, their distribution, the creation of institutions, structural transformation, cultural development or ecological balance. All these things may be indispensable 'social' means or conditions ; but development as such is that of man, of the members of society." This attitude is very new among the views of innumerable studies on development, and is connected with the similarly new concept of 'integrated development'. In her interpretation of Unesco's standpoint, cited by her, integration implies "the interaction of environmental, technical, economic and social

aspects of the development process", which "centred on man must be a
total, multirelational process, involving all aspects of the life of
a community, its relations with the outside world and its awareness
of itself". She argues against the conceptualization derived
chiefly from Rostow's theory of successive stages, Rostow's uni-
linear developmental stages from traditional to modern consisting of
(a) the traditional stage, (b) ideas and attitudes towards economic
development, (c) drastic change of production methods, (d) drive to
maturity, and (e) high economic growth (Rostow, 1960). The highest
stage corresponds to the present state of the United States of
America and several other industrialized countries. She argues that
countries in lower stages do not have to follow upwards through the
same stages. Instead of repeating this linear process, every
country has its own specific type of development, which is endogenous and should be based on its traditional values, on the
authenticity of its culture, and the creative attitudes of its
people. This country-specific development is necessarily interwoven
with many other local and global development processes.

Many important ideas are to be found in the article by Galtung,
et al. (1982), and each might also be useful for the contextual
frame of this study, either directly, or after some reinterpretation. Instead of applying all of them, however, it will be sufficient to quote an unmodified tabular summary of basic concepts.

Table 2

Aspects	Dominant strategies	Proposed strategies
Point of departure	The North is developed, the South is under-developed	Over- and under-developed areas and sectors in both North and South; globally the world is mal-developed
Level of analysis	States	Centres and peri-pheries Human beings
Roots of under-development	Poor, uneducated masses; gap between them and the sophisticated 'modern' societies	Domineering, exploit-ative forces from the rich centres creating growing inequalities within and among countries
Objective of development	Economic growth	Satisfaction of basic needs, material and non-material, above a minimal level, but not above a maximal level

Table 2 (continued)

Main priorities	Infrastructure, education, industry	Agriculture, industry, health, habitat, education
Role of material goods	Primacy of production	Primacy of distribution
Relation to nature	Exploitation and domination Anthropocentrism	Harmony and equilibrium
Relation of developing units to outside world	Associative Increasing integration into existing world economic system	Dissociative; selective de-linking; counting on one's own forces and using one's own resources
Concept of structures	Respect for, or limited reform of, existing national and international structures	Structural transformation to reduce internal and international inequalities Reduction of structural violence
Concept of processes	Fragmented and compartmentalized approach to restricted sectors of development	Totality of the process of development International based on systems analysis
Time perspective	Short- and middle-term planning Development decades	Solidarity with future generations, mainly in the use of resources and relation with environment
Applicability in space	Universal model, valid for all types of societies Uniformity	Respect for cultural diversity and hence for the diversity of development process

In this table, Galtung, *et al.* compare two fundamentally different conceptualizations of development. One of them is dominant, and has been practised in the last two centuries. The other is a proposed possibility, for which conditions have become ripe. The method of comparison of the two conceptualizations is interesting. Eleven analytical aspects common to both are chosen, in terms of which the differences between the two approaches can be characterized very significantly. The features in which the two developments differ seem to be applicable to our contextual frame.

The authors note that the two types of conceptualization (we prefer to use this notion instead of the word 'strategy') are not mutually exclusive in all respects. It is very likely that in a concrete case a mixture of the two types would be appropriate. It is also likely that the aspects in the left-hand column have only heuristical value, and it is doubtful whether in a more advanced conceptualization, or in practice, these aspects would be adequate to grasp the most relevant features of development. They have, however, a very great orienting strength. Finally it is not ir-relevant to mention that the authors' confessed ideological sources are such reformers as Fromm, Schumacher, Lauenberger-Schilling and Robertson. Fromm prefers being to having. Fundamentally different developmental forms can be generated within the frame which chooses 'being' to that which chooses 'having'. In Schumacher's conceptual-ization of development, antihuman economics is part of today's dominant development forms, containing within it a special 'equilibrium economics'. He considers that "the key to the future is not continuing expansion but balance, - balance within ourselves, balance between ourselves and other people, balance between people and nature". In the above table, the spirit of these conceptualiz-ations can easily be perceived.

Societal development goals

Among the different conceptualizations of development, there is a very significant group which makes developmental goals (objectives) explicit and from this point of view tries to understand the nature of developmental phenomena. Two comprehensive studies by Berling (1986) and edited by Laszlo (1977) were found to be useful sources for our review of the state-of-the-art. Both studies focus on the different versions of developmental goals.

Laszlo - under the banner of the Club of Rome - worked together with a number of contributors from many countries and institutions. The common leading idea behind their survey was the possibility of "change from self-centred and short-term goals to mankind-centred and long-term ones". The survey reviews the goals and objectives accepted in the mid 1970s by nations, regions, corporations and international organizations.

It is very remarkable that definite or quasi-definite organic units - nations, regions, etc. - are those which have goals, and the first classifying step refers to concrete states, countries, rather than to any general and abstract notions or categories. The des-cription of goals gives a broad panorama. From this picture the same goals can be perceived, but the majority deviate from each other very greatly. Within the national goals, some goal-types (as opposed to goals) can be identified :

a)   goals of official states,
b)   goals of religions,
c)   goals of ideologies,

d)   goals of political movements,
e)   goals of international organizations,
f)   goals of multinational corporations, and
g)   goals of cultural regions and subcultures.

    A collection of goals is listed in Table 3. The goals in this
list follow no particular order, and have been chosen as compatible
with our triple contextual frame.

Table 3

Goals for mankind

The list of goals has been collected from Laszlo's (1977) book
without any references to those choosing such goals. These collections illustrate only the very great variety of goal formulation.
The list contains group goals, the components of which occur con-
jointly with those of others.

1.   The individual - equality - democratic process - education -
     the arts and sciences - the democratic economy - economic
     growth - technological change - agriculture - living con-
     ditions - health and welfare - help to build an open and peace-
     ful world - disarmament - united nations.

2.   Peace and the protection of national interests - prosperity,
     full employment and economic stability - an orderly, just and
     free society - healthy populace - an aesthetic and healthy
     environment - a well-educated populace - a better world - good
     housing - livable cities - arts and culture. To all of these
     goals belong instrumental objectives such as : basic resources
     and energy - management and communication - science and tech-
     nology - transportation.

3.   Self-restraining - "small is beautiful" - conditions for human
     self-realization - more engaged in manual labour - close
     relationship with nature - simple lifestyle - practise mutual
     dependence among themselves - simpler smaller scale technol-
     ogies - rural communities - less environmentally damaging
     methods of generating energy - urban communes in international
     frame.

4.   Safeguarding the life and culture of man - peace and peaceful
     co-existence - effective production - build quickly and well -
     products of the highest quality - raising the standard of
     living of the people - stability of prices - increasing the
     income of the people - raising the material and cultural level
     of workers - increase industrial and agricultural production -
     improvement of trade and everyday services - developed foreign
     trade alliance with all progressive and peace-loving forces.

Table 3 (continued)

5.   Satisfaction of the needs for goods and services - improved human environment - applying the latest scientific advancement - greater efficiency and productivity - consolidated values and way of life.

6.   Values and aspirations in three interconnected spheres : basic needs related to material production - social needs related to social conditions - cultural conditions, higher consciousness and knowledge. Social and political stability - national independence - personal safety - social security - full employment.

7.   Stabilizing of commodity prices and full employment - security of life - lovable environment - harmonizing with and contributing to world economy development - economic security.

8.   Types of goals : political - economic - foreign policy - socio-economic - cultural - food production - foreign trade.

9.   Overcome the internal divisions between ethnic groups, between urban and traditional population, between central and peripheral regions. Preservation of cultural heritage.

10. Political and economic stability - increased welfare for broad mass of population - rapidly expanded production capacity - pace of economic and social progress.

Berting's article discusses the developmental goals of developed countries. His attitude rather differs from that of Laszlo. While Berting examines changing goals along historical time from the middle of the 19th century to the present day, Laszlo's picture can be regarded as an atlas of goals, distributed geographically among countries, cultures, etc.

Berting emphasizes that there is a shift in the attitude towards development, a change "from fate to choice", which implies the conviction that decisions with long-term consequences are made by human beings who take charge of their own fate. Berting identifies five different conceptualizations, each formulated at the end of the 19th century and during the first decade of the 20th century. He calls them Models 1-V. They represent not only considerations concerning the nature of societal development, but each of them also carries some worldview hypotheses. Except for Model IV, Berting qualifies the four others as representative of evolutionism, which in his interpretation means irreversible processes and a temporal sequence of forms : one form grows out of another ; culture advances from one stage to another. The five models are characterized as follows :

Model I. Industrialism and open society. Industrial convergence, increasing individual occupational and social mobility, growing equality of educational opportunities, fading differences between classes and life-styles are the goals of development according to this model.

Model II. Capitalist society as class society. This model is in contrast with the preceding one. Class struggle promotes the societal changes towards the goals of the socialist order.

Model III. Reformist perspective on societal change. Contrasting to the former two models, this model tries to avoid the inhuman and pathological consequences of industrial development with the help of professional organizations based on moral order and on organic solidarity (in Durkheim's sense). The goal of this development is better organizations and state, and cultured-educated people for the sake of this society.

Model IV. The development of rational society. In this view, trained lawyers bring formal and juridical rationalism into existence as well as a legal system functioning according to this rationality. The goal of this development is society and organizations with accurate, continuous, efficient and predictable bureacracies.

Model V. Elitist with social mobility and equilibrium of the social system. The basic idea is not the transformation of society, but an endless struggle between ruling political and economic elites, aspiring elites and masses, that is, between different interest groups. In the interpretation of this model, developmental goals are rather cyclical changes : rise and fall of elites.

Behind each model one may perceive persons who express that model most sharply. Following the sequence of the models, these are : Veblen, Marx, Durkheim, Weber and Pareto. Berting maintains that the five models of development not only influenced historical changes up to the 1960s but formed the minds of those "scientists and policy-makers who tried to understand the nature of societal changes occurring in the period 1920-1985". The manifestations of these models in reality led to recognition of obsolete goals, the obstacles inherent in each model, and suggest conclusions as to how the change from fate - strongly represented in the five models - to choice and social guidance would be desirable. Between the two world wars, many important political, social and economic changes occurred which strongly influenced images of possible development, both theoretically and practically. This is true of the Soviet revolution, of the 1929 depression, the emergence of fascist states, the gradual growth of the tertiary sector, and so on. The impact of these events and the different insights decreased belief in unplanned progress and weakened interest in processes of social change. In the United States of America, functionalism seemed to be a solution to many problems. "The society was conceived as a system that develops institutions with specific functions, enabling the system to adapt to changing environmental circumstances." There are values shared by the majority of American society, that are culturally defined and with more or less integrated goals. Development during the New Deal was based dominantly on functionalist ideology. In the Western European countries, a shift also started towards planned and controlled development, while the basic characteristics of capitalism did not alter. In Berting's view, Keynes, Mannheim and Burnham were the most significant representatives of the Western European style of development. The next period studied by Berting is between 1945 and 1985. He enumerates a long list of relevant events and changes within this time-span (20 in number) which influenced the conceptualization fo development. There is a very rich assortment of various types of theoretically found models which discuss the main features of the different versions in conceiving possible development. Berting goes further than we need in an orienting overview of goal-types of development. His concluding considerations offer some observations which will help to conceive the contextual frame of this study. The conclusions below are compatible with those of Berting, while at the same time deviating from them in some ways :

a)   Certain goals of development have proliferated, the sources of which are political reports, declarations, charters, etc. These documents are lists of goals, conditions, and restrictions rather than organically integrated goal-like images (plans). The goals formulated are the result of political debates among different interest groups, and the consensus is scarcely more than a collection of desirabilities without clarified interrelationships between goals, constraints and conditions.

b)   "It would be necessary to decrease the contradictions which exist within the modern industrial capitalist countries among such issues as rationality (as effectiveness and efficiency, related to economic growth and bureaucratic control), individual liberty (achievement, individual expressions, civil liberties), social justice (equality in the main areas of social life, not always restricted to national solidarity), protection of the environment and rights of collectivities to maintain or develop their way of life (e.g. ethnic or religious minorities, emancipation movements)."

c)   Although the concept of development denotes general phenomena, uniform schemes of development are unusable because the nature of every developing societal unit is unique and without replica, both in its being and its life history. Nevertheless, the notion of development refers to observable elemental as well as general phenomena, which manifest themselves in some concrete and unique combination in every societal organic unit. This means that it is reasonable to consider similar developmental goals of different units, although these goals can be realized according to specific combinations of different elemental orders and agents, which might also belong to different kinds of development processes.

On the development of the human individual

It is very surprising that the literature on integrated development reviewed for this study refers almost exclusively to 'macro' phenomena of societies and economies. Beyond the development, change, transformation, transition, etc., of society or the economy, analogous phenomena concerning the individual human being remain untouched. This observation is to say the least strange, because (i) the developmental phenomena of individuals organically belong and connect to macro developments, (ii) there are very rich research results and extensive literature about the different developmental features of human individuals, (iii) experience as well as the literature indicate that macro developments cannot come into existence without some parallel/synchronical development of individuals, (iv) any developmental plan for a country, region or organization will necessarily fail if it is not adjusted to the developmental features of individual human beings concerned by the plan. The developmental features of individuals are discussed in the literature mainly under the following themes :

a)   life-span development *,
b)   life-cycles of human beings*,
c)   life-events of human beings,
d)   ego-development, life stages of ego development (Ericson),
e)   stages of need hierarchy (Maslow),
f)   cognitive development and its stages* (Piaget),
g)   moral development and its stages* (Kochberg),
h)   human development*.

Issues marked * not only refer to developmental features of individuals, but are also the names of peculiar scientific schools. Knowledge of each of the features listed would be useful for the conceptualizations of the contextual framework. Instead of detailed discussion, it would be sufficient to restrict oneself to those elements which have occurred in national planning practice but not in the literature of integrated development. Although the developmental features discovered and studied by the different schools have not been made explicit, knowledge of them nevertheless has strong ontological status. These features must therefore not be neglected when developmental plans are being prepared for a society and its economy. Contrary to its weak epistemological status, this knowledge may guide the sensitivity and attention of planners and politicians when they identify developmental problems in macro frames. It was found especially as a first step that topics under 'life-span development', 'life-cycles', 'life-events', 'stages of need hierarchy' might offer aid to the contextual framework, but in a deeper study the others might also be important. As with previous issues, the review of these domaines is confined to only the moşt fundamental conceptualizations.
    The historical origin of the enquiry into life-span development is in the distant past, as can be learned from Reinert's (1979) profound histographical article. He reviews more than 2000 years' history and enumerates almost all prominent persons who tried to

understand developmental features of human beings. His suggestions can be paraphrased as follows : if theories and plans for societal or economic development take no account of differences in needs, aspirations, abilities, skills, efforts, life events, etc., of human beings, belonging to different and successive stages of their life-span, they are not only inhuman but antihuman as well. Carus' idea - age-oriented human sciences - is exactly what may be gleaned from Reinert's review. In a modified form, we might also say that any theory or plan of integrated development needs to be age-oriented, life-span-oriented. So the life-span developmental features of individuals should be explicitly expressed and represented in any images of integrated development of a society. It would be ideal to imagine pictures which represent all the individual differences, because of the unique nature of each individual. But at most there is a real possibility that planners and politicians think only in type-groups about certain individuals who have some characteristics in their life-span development in common. Although this labelling attitude may be dangerous, mis-orienting and might fail, it has been a practice for centuries to join micro- and macro-spheres of society or mankind.

These considerations can form part of the conclusions suggested by life-span development psychology. They are presented in rather abstract form, but planners who bear them in mind could evolve many implications from them.

The concept of 'life cycles in development' might be a prag-matic modulation of 'life-span development' from the planner's point of view. Pragmatic in the sense that it guides the attention towards shorter spans of life within the whole life-time, e.g. infancy, childhood, adolescence, youth, adulthood, mature adulthood and old age. Not only may individual life-cycles be important for planners, but family life-cycles as well, such as courtship, marriage, childbirth, rearing children, weaning parents from children, retirement and old age. Individual life-cycles are clearly defined through age. Family cycles are relative and less definite than individual cycles. In demography, one cycle marks a cohort within the population of a country, both in the case of individuals and of families. It is not irrelevant for national planners to be aware of population distribution according to the different individual or family life-cycles.

Another concept which can be borrowed from developmental psych-ology is 'life events of development'. This refers to phenomena which occur in different contexts of everyday life. Phenomena labelled as life events include experiences such as graduation, marriage, promotion, childbirth, failure, illness, divorce, death of a family member, etc.

Two very comprehensive articles proved to be good sources for our study, one by Hultsch and Plemons (1979) and the other by Reese and Smyer (1983). They point to many typologies constructed for life events from different points of view. An orienting table from Reese and Smyer (1983) seems very useful to our study. In it they identify fourteen contexts or areas of life space in which an event occurs, and arrange them into five superordinate sets (Table 4). This table was used initially to construct a very detailed taxonomy

Table 4

A sample of contexts of life events

Superordinate set	Context	Comments
Family	1. Family	Context is family of origin; parents, siblings, etc.
	2. Love and marriage	Context involves date or mate
	3. Parenting	Context refers to children, or having and rearing them
	4. Residence	Context refers to dwelling place
Self	5. Health	Context is own health and biological functions
	6. Self	Predominant reference of event is to the self
Social relations	7. Community	Context involves community relations and functions
	8. Friendships	Reference is to close friends, primary friendship, network
	9. Social relations	Context refers to psycho-social relations
Work	10. Finances	Includes all contexts related to money (including household economics)
	11. School	Context is schooling, education, training
	12. Work	Context is related to occupation and career
Miscellaneous	13. Law	Reference is to crime and legal matters; perpetration of crime; legal consequences (for victim of crime, context is classified elsewhere)
	14. Miscellaneous	Contexts that do not fit elsewhere in the list

for life events. Many considerations can be connected to life events. One may be interested in their effects, or in the affected person's perceptions of events. Others use the labels 'normative' and 'non-normative' to classify events. Reese and Smyer (1983) suggest qualifications such as 'desirability', 'prevalence', 'age relatedness', and 'cohort specificity' instead of a dichotomy. Are any benefits to be derived from the study of life events within life span development ? It is obvious that national or regional integrated development planners cannot deepen their images down to the specific life events of every individual. But it is to be expected that when planners consider different types of cohorts in different stages of life span development, the images they use to identify and solve problems will be much closer to reality. Precisely this possibility has induced us to discuss the topic of life events for our contextual framework.

From the point of view of the psychology of development, Maslow's (1962) hierarchy of needs also offers itself for our contextual framework. He proposes a gradient that parallels different levels of need-fulfilment. Through observation, he perceives that those who sufficiently fulfilled their basic physical and emotional needs cannot be motivated in the same way as those without such satisfaction. In Maslow's hypothesis, there are five successive stages of needs :

1. physiological needs,
2. need for safety,
3. need to belong and for love,
4. need for esteem,
5. need for self-actualization.

It is very seldom that someone who has not fulfilled his or her needs at a lower level aspires to higher grades. Maslow's stages are very peculiar expressions of the developmental changes of a human being. They are not dogmatic propositions. Nevertheless, together or separately these stages might serve as problem sensitizers for planners. It is obvious that the desired developmental goals in a population with needs predominantly at the first stage will differ from those of a population which strives to satisfy its needs predominantly at the fifth stage. Maslow's proposals may be a guide of higher heuristic value to integrated development planners.

It should be noticed that the different and acceptable conceptualizations of individual development seem incompatible with macro-images of a country's development or of the economy of a region. We are convinced, however, that the misbelief of incompatibility originates from exclusive usage and interpretation of each macro and micro approach. Recognizing that from each approach only imperfect images may be obtained, it is not impossible to find special ordered images in which these macro and micro images may complement each other, forming a more complete picture which may help planners to conceive plan-images closer to reality. Our contextual framework gives us to hope concerning the possibility of integrating the different approaches.

To continue the survey of the literature concerning individual development would take us beyond the limits of this study. For our contextual framework and from the methodological point of view, the examples discussed above are sufficient. Nevertheless, some ideas cannot be discarded without brief mention. Levinson (1986) conceptualized adult development from the component concepts of life course (concrete character of a life from beginning to end), life cycle (sequence of areas, each with its biopsychological character), and life structure (most important parts of life, sources, relationships with the environment, desires, etc.). Further, he provides an analytic basis for clarifying these component concepts and gives considerations for bringing together the developmental perspective (emphasizing the inherent maturationally built-in sequence) and the socialization perspective (focussing on the timing of life events determined by forces in the external world). Baltes (1979) points out that life span developmental psychology is capable of stretching the boundaries of the referential frame of any approaches to developmental psychology because of its primary concern with long-term processes, and there is a tendency to extend enquiries into the ontogenetic and biocultural changes, as well as into the historical alterations in development paths of successive generations. Hill and Mattessich (1979) discuss the importance and consequences of different perceptions of developmental phenomena in individuals as well as in families. They critically examine four different schools : the organismic, dialectic and mechanistic approaches, and the Chicago approach, which confines itself to adulthood and the benefits of mutually combining the 'development', the 'age stratif-ication' and the 'life course' approaches with each other. Among these attitudes, the organismic, the mechanistic and the dialectic schools are relevant to our contextual framework, and it is there-fore worth examining them briefly.

Mechanistic, organismic and dialectic approaches to development

Those who have compared the theories concerning the development of societal micro-organizations (individual, group, family) have re-cognized three kinds of attitudes - mechanistic, organismic and dialectic - in researchers' different approaches. Each of the three might also be taken as a commitment to one or another metaphysical *Einstellung*, or usage of metascheme. Recently, few scholars have interpreted these three approaches in such a way that the mechan-istic and organismic approaches are not mutually exclusive. They should, however, be brought together through dialectic syntheses since they can be treated as dialectical complements. Although it is debatable whether mechanistic and organismic views are dialectic complements, the benefits gained from their combined or integrated application can hardly be debated. Perhaps simply because of this doubt, others call the combination of mechanistic and organismic views 'relational', 'transactional', or 'dynamic interactional' approaches. The considerations below are taken from Hultsch and Plemons (1979), Overton and Reese (1973), and Hill and Mattessich (1979). Fortunately there are also certain non-pseudo dialectic interpretations.

In the mechanistic perspective, the basic metaphor is the machine and the theoretical construction is derived from this con-cept. The individual is treated as reactive to environmental im-pulses, to outer causes. Attention is focussed on events, from antecedents to outcomes. Developmental events are connected in chainlike sequences. Novelty or emergence are epiphenomena or re-ducible to qualitative changes. Age can be reduced to time, and time itself causes nothing. Processes and mechanisms underlie be-havioural changes at all ages, and therefore age itself as a focus of attention is relegated to a minor status.

In organismic perspective, the individual is a living human being and an active whole. Development is primarily a qualitative change, in which the component parts as well as their organizational structure change both qualitatively and quantitatively. The core of any conceptualization is the synthesis of organized complexities, and in the picture concerning it, the structure-function is preferred to an antecedent-consequent, and structural change to response change. Historical events are not causes, but rather integral components of organized complexity.

In the combined mechanistic-organismic perspective, the two kinds of picture might mutually amplify the comprehension gained through both of them. It is not the perceived features of development that seem erroneous in mechanistic or organismic approaches, but their one-sided exclusiveness. It is obvious that one can identify chainlike events and each elemental event can be antecedent and consequent. It is also empirical evidence that a living organism (organization) sometimes manifests itself actively and sometimes reactively. This and other evidence doubtless renders both approaches indispensable. Although their dialectic complementarity has not been proved, each contributes in its own way to carifying the nature of development.

For a dialectic approach to development, Hill and Mattesich (1979) offer observations and perceptions which are important although they place no emphasis on dialectics. A quotation from their article is worthwhile : "All people are alike in some respect due to the existence of certain biologically endowed personality determinants that are universal to the species ; some people are like some other people because of their membership in certain statuses (culture, ethnicity, gender, vocation) ; and in some ways, each person is unique because of his or her unique genetic composition and unique experiential encounters... the dialectic model is compatible with all three of these views of humankind : biologically universal, culturally variant, genetically unique."

These thoughts seem to us to have great heuristic strength in understanding the nature of societal development, namely from two points of view. First, the statements refer directly to societal micro-organizations and any societal macro development can hardly be imagined in which the three features - universal, variant, unique - of individual development would not be determinant in many ways. The second importance of these statements stems from the possibility of extending them by analogy. When the compared organic units are not human individuals or families but enterprises, greater regions, ethnic groups, countries, etc., one can also discover a universal, variant, unique manifestation among their developmental features. Consequently, any societal development can be interpreted in terms of these features, within an ever changing and contingent socio-historical context. In other words, the primary developmental phenomenon is in the first case the bio-phsycho-mental development of societal micro-organizations, and in the second the development of macro-organizations from different points of view, such as cultural, economic, technological, ecological, etc. Both cases imply three natural aspects of developmental phenomena :

a)   The body of the organization. In this specific appearance
     (human being, family, or habitat, enterprise, university,
     country, state, etc.), it manifests developmental transform-
     ations and changes.
b)   The stages of development, that are manifest as continuous and
     discontinuous successive changes in states, capabilities, oper-
     ations, etc., of the organizations.
c)   The sequence of stages, which is mostly predetermined and seems
     universal in the bio-sphere of human beings (embryogenesis,
     onthogenetic transformation of the body throughout life from
     birth to death). It can be found, in less determined but not
     undetermined form (variant and unique), in the psychomental and
     socio-historical spheres of man/woman. An analogous sequence
     of stages can be identified in the development of family organ-
     izations. Many experiments support the hypotheses that it is
     indispensable to think in sequence of developmental stages when
     we conceive (and intentionally transform) the nature of the
     development of societal macro-organizations ; although a more
     advanced statement than a hypothesis would remain unproven
     because of the lack of scientific enquiry into sequential
     changes, we may hypothesize the existence of sequential stages
     of great probability.

The dialectic interpretation of development quoted from Hill
and Mattessich, and our complementary comments represent very appropriate departures for dealing with the very old problem of dis-
criminating and integrating the universal-general, the variant, and
the unique features in the development of societal micro-organizations as well as macro-organizations.

As we have already mentioned, a counter-wave is now emerging
against Western-style development, and against those who spread it
hegemonically. In conceptualizations of this type of development,
certain stage-characters of transformations - 'industry first, then
other branches and social spheres' - are very strongly emphasized.
Since most of the troubles in developing countries are judged to be
a direct consequence of the 'industry first' strategy, there are
authors who identify and confuse the idea of 'stages in development'
with Western development. Unfortunately, not only do they confuse
them, but they also reject the concept of stages together with the
Western style in development. If we take into account the combined
general, variant and unique features in developmental stages, the
'industry first' stage cannot belong to general, but to unique or at
most to variant features, while stages themselves in development
belong to general features. A good example of a general feature is
Eckaus' proposal. He discriminates five stages with a determined
sequence in development, connected to investment : gestation,
maturation, learning by acting, maintenance, depreciation. (This
pragmatic conceptualization will again be referred to later in the
study.)

The concept of integrated development

In the relevant literature, the term integrated development has taken on increasing importance during the past few decades, and especially in the 1980s. Alechina (1982), who reviewed contributions to clarifying the development concept, stated that the developmental process is to be considered as the unity of all aspects - environmental, technological, economic, social, political and cultural - together with their dynamic interactions. This statement also conforms to Unesco's standpoint, which streses the need for new order in education, science, culture and communication. Stoehr (1981), in a leading article in a volume entitled *Changing perception of development problems*, stated that when considering developmental phenomena, it is necessary to perceive their natural, economic, social and political factors components as well as their interrelationships through self-sustaining organizations. Many other conceptualizations can be found, which do not differ substantially from each other. The essence of all of them is the complex integrated nature of developmental phenomena.

The term 'integrated development' also has many historical connotations, to which developing countries pay special attention. There was a long period in the history of these countries, most of which were colonized, when the economic aspect was dominant or exclusive in the conceptualization of their development. Many researchers into present-day and future development refer back to the colonial and neo-colonial era because the inertia of their one-sided views and trends has survived up to the present time. The impact of this inertia has diverse consequences and only a fragment of the latter have proved beneficial to the future. A variety of analytical means have been used to identify these impacts and their consequences. Stoehr's efforts have resulted in fruitful insights into the developmental features of these countries (Stoehr, 1981). He has observed that inadequate colonial and neo-colonial activity may cause not only distorted development, but may also disintegrate the developmental potential of a country or region.

Stoehr has identified two approaches to integrated development, and has called them (a) functional integration, and (b) territorial integration :

> "While the term 'integrated regional development' has often been used verbally, in practice, conventional regional policies signified large-scale 'functional' integration rather than regional and 'territorial' integration. Instead of improving the mutual interrlation of production factors and other (social, institutional, etc.) development potential within territorial units (territorial integration), they integrated each of these factors vertically into functional large-scale national or international markets (functional ingtegration). Thus instead of combining regionally available natural resources, labour, savings, technological and organizational capabilities with priority for the satisfaction of regional needs, each of these factors was integrated into the respective national (or international) labour market, capital market,

technology market geared by transregional organizational structures. These individual functional markets were inter- acting mainly at the national or international scales but hardly at the regional or local one. In commodity markets, national and international commodity circuits increasingly replaced regional and local circuits. Each of these functional markets operates according to its own dynamics and rules de- termined by national or international parameters, very often overruling specific local or regional requirements." (Stoehr, 1981)

Stoehr gives a demonstrative schematic representation of func- tional and territorial integration. He introduces factors which are to be integrated in these two ways :

- natural resources (n_i)
- human resources (h_i)
- capital (c_i)
- technology (t_i)
- economic interaction (e_i)
- social interaction
- political interaction (p_i)
- demand (d_i)

and $i = 1,2,...z$ marks smaller regions within a large-scale ter- ritory. In an arrangement with the two co-ordinates 'function' and 'territory', the above factors are organized in two ways :

a) in functional integration, $n_1,n_2...n_z$ are integrated into a larger unit, and similarly $h_1,h_2...h_z$, $c_1,c_2...c_z$, and so on ;
b) in territorial integration, $n_1,h_1,c_1,t_1,e_1,s_1,p_1,d_1$, are in- tegrated into a larger organization, and similarly $n_2,h_2,c_2,t_2,e_2,p_2,d_2$, and so on.

Stoehr remarks that the integration of all territorially avail- able factors may become the basis for more endogenously initiated, and even healthier development. This second type of integrated development makes it easier to avoid the disintegration of ter- ritorial development potential.

Stoehr's two types of conceptualization can be considered parallel to the two types of organization which occur in the sociol- ogical literature under different names. Durkheim and Parsons call the organization analogous to functional integration 'mechanic solidarity', and the organization analogous to territorial integra- tion 'organic solidarity'. Others think in terms of 'extensively' and 'intensively' integrated organizations. Peterson (1985), fol- lowing in Parsons' footsteps, recognizes that the development- oriented component of culture can be organized according to the distinction drawn by many European scholars between *Gemeinschaft* and *Gesellschaft*. One may say that the former integrate 'similar' components, and the latter 'dissimilar' components. Concrete exam- ples can be mentioned : corresponding to mechanistic integration – religious communities on the basis of the same beliefs ; trade unions for the same professions ; military troops for the same branch of service ; enterprises in which the same kind of professionals are sorted into the same department ; and corresponding to organic integration - the family ; smaller or larger settlements ; a string quartet ; a working team with members of quite different abilities and carrying out different tasks ; innovative industrial enterprises in which all the necessary types of professionals and experts work together in a relatively small organization and in easily alterable or interchangeable roles.

Organizations integrated mechanistically and organically differ from each other in their abilities and possibilities. Organically integrated organizations are obviously in greater need of ability and have a greater degree of freedom concerning their possibilities. It is also evident that developmental processes in the two kinds of organization differ fundamentally. If account is taken of the insights into the stages, sequences and timing of developmental processes discussed earlier, it also becomes clear that the two types of integration also differ from each other as far as these deeper developmental features are concerned. The concepts of mechanistic and organic integration are of course strong abstractions, and in reality only their combined versions are to be found.

The concept of integrated development implies goals and consequences as the end results of such activity. Developmental goals have already been discussed. How can we interpret goals for integrated development ? Alechina specifically considers goals to be environmental. If we take this idea a step further, goals might be embodied in many spheres, as for example :

Economy - GNP, investment, consumption, natural and financial
      sphere
Technology - Industry : machine, chemical, electrical, building,
                  electronic, nuclear, mining, printing, energy,
                  etc.
            - Agriculture : food, forestry, etc.
            - Biotechnology
            - Information technology
Natural resources - Air, water, minerals, vegetation
Human sphere - Reproduction, education, socialization, training,
      health care, culture, social work, quality of life
Environment - Local and global, surface, underground, air
Trade - domestic trade, foreign trade
Traffic, transport - Roads, railways, water and air transport
Science - Basic, applied research, R&D, etc.
State administrative organizations
Governmental organizations
Political organizations.

The list is evidently neither complete nor exhaustive, but each component is suitable for the interpretion and embodiment of goals. Integrated development in terms of goals can be conceived so that concrete (rather than abstract) complex goals are formed from the appropriate components of the different spheres listed.

The developmental process can also be interpreted from the point of view of integrated development. Concrete and various other types of processes - each terminating in a concrete part of the same concrete goal - are necessarily interwoven, not superficially but in order to fit in with the stages, sequences and timing of each other's component processes. This implies that the realization of any partial goal from start to finish cannot appear at a point in time, but along a series of states. The chief ordering requirement for each component process, and within them for their own stages, sequences and timing, stems from a self-evident requirement : that the intended complex end result should eventually be achieved. From this we may conclude that it is not sufficient to consider integrated development simply in terms of goals. Process is also inevitable and indispensable. In every developmental process, other concommitant specifying factors must also be made explicit, e.g. the concrete nature of the end result, its initial state, intermediate states, final state, the actors, their ordered and timed activities and ability to act to ensure the specified outcome and environmental conditions. Activities may also be self-reflective, i.e. the end result is embodied in the actor himself. If the concept of process implies certain modifying or transforming phenomena, then we must remember to change the concommitants mentioned above.

1.2. The systems approach to development

Contrary to the great variety and richness of the literature about development and integrated development, the systems approach to these topics appears rather poor. Only a very small fragment of the literature on development is devoted to the systems approach, and even so, interpretations and applications are very different.

Varieties of the systems approach

During the last two decades, the systems approach has assumed a stunning variety of aspects manifested under such expressions as systems analysis, systems engineering, systems methodology, systems philosophy, systems science, systems theory, systems thinking, etc. This review cannot deal with the voluminous literature accumulated in all these areas, and only the most important methodological aspects of systems analysis as a systems approach will be discussed here. (A good review of philosophy-related issues can be found in Mattesich (1978) and a more practical concept introduced by Checkland (1981).)

An 'approach' is one's special screening-selecting mental sensitivity to phenomena, and a way of tackling problems in relation to them. Obviously a particular approach may be relevant to more than one phenomenon and problem, and to more than one person applying it. A systems approach, however, although it conveys the idea of a method of attack - in enquiry, in cognition, in ordering and using knowledge - does not to most people readily convey many ideas about the content of the method. For example, the ideas conveyed by the word 'system' frequently refer only to methods using computers and computerized mathematical models. By now, both systems approach and systems analysis mean something more than computerized thinking, and at the same time mean sensitivity opened up to the recognition of new fields, instead of meaning fixed sensitivity.

The systems approach, in general, is based on the insight that if certain phenomena (entities, units, individuals) interact with each other in a special way, they can manifest themselves together as a unit with its own properties. When we consider such a composite unit, we can become sensitive to its 'system-nature' and look at it holistically. Enquiring deeper into the system-nature of a composite phenomenon such as a unit or an entity, we perceive its elements (members, components), the different kinds of interaction between the elements, the boundaries and the environment of the phenomenon. Furthermore, we perceive why these component-elements behave as a unit, what they do to maintain this unit or system-nature, how they eliminate the disturbances to their unit, how they change the system-nature of their unit to preserve it, how the different organic units of different magnitude and complexity co-operate, and so on. Many commonly used concepts (notions, categories) take on a special sense if we reinterpret them in terms of the system-nature of a phenomenon.

We may firstly interpret the 'organismic' nature of a composite unit in terms of system and as a first step we may obtain an operational interpretation through its system-nature. We may speak of the 'function' or 'purpose' of an organismic unit having a specific system. We may perceive that the system-nature of a unit has specific a hierarchical character from different points of view : hierarchy in the spatial arrangement of components within the phenomenon (whole-and-part relations), and hierarchy in the dynamic relations (linear-causal and mutual interactions) between the parts. Moreover, such hierarchical characters may be extended to the relation of the organismic unit and its environment. We could continue to give examples of reinterpretation of different concepts, but in the literature on integrated development, the basic ordering scheme of system-nature is not usually treated in greater depth. In this study, therefore, the systemic features described above will suffice. We do not take this interpretation as a theoretical conception, but as an image having strong ontological status, namely on the basis of empirical evidence.

The various knowledge which has grown out of this intuitive insight has been termed 'systems theory', 'systems research', 'general systems theory', 'systems analysis', 'systems technique', 'systems engineering', etc. Each combines its own particular methodological bases and practical methods. We may assert that the majority of those using these systems approaches behave analogously when faced with problems to be solved. They take a broad view, try to take all relevant aspects into account, and endeavour to identify all the problems that cannot be solved independently but only together in the context of their interactions.

The literature on the systems approach shows that the notion 'system' has different meanings in the minds of the various people applying it. Many experiments suggest that a clear and definite meaning (or definition) is not indispensable, and may even be impossible, and it seems reasonable to accept this point of view (Cavallo, 1979). We can, however, recognize systems approaches which seem compatible with the interpretations described above, and at the same time they are close enough to the triple contextual framework of this study. These approaches always focus on a referential unit, which exists in reality as an organismic entity with its specific system-nature, and which manifests developmental changes. Such changes may be of both kinds of development, namely : (a) development of an existing entity in the sense of its progressive alteration, and (b) development of an entity in the sense of its coming into being. In both cases, important insights are to be obtained into the nature of an entity's development, if the changes in its system during the developmental processes are observed.

By reason of man's limited capacity, he is not able to consider the totality of an organismic unit and its system, but only fragmentarily, although the unit exists in its totality. Looking at a region, one can grasp the transport-aspect in its system-nature, as well as the settlemental aspect, and the economic aspect, etc. Each of us perceives this region as a black box from a different viewpoint and are only intuitively aware of its totality. That is why Ashby (1955) suggested that : "we, the system theorists, have in fact been studying not a Black Box, but a larger system composed of two parts, the Black Box and the Investigator, each acting on the other". In other words, we must be aware of our selective - rational and value-laden - perceptions, of our 'cool' and 'hot' cognition, because they are largely responsible for what we consider relevant in an organismic unit and its environment. When we identify a problem situation in a region or in a society, we are deeply involved in this situation objectively as well as subjectively.

We have mentioned that among users of the systems approach there is no consensus about the interpretation of the system-nature of an organismic unit. Here we have proposed one version, which has been tested in planning practice, has heuristic value, is supportable and which helps to avoid many confusions (e.g. mistaking the system of abstract notions for the particular-peculiar systemic features of a concrete organismic unit).

A recent development in the systems approach places special emphasis on the organic unity (integrity) of the objective and subjective parts (elements) of a system and system-image. On the one hand, there is a certain type of integration in systems studies (this unity is called integrity by Gvishiani (1984)), and on the other, the recognition of the fact that the role of subjective perception and attitudes in systems analysis has softened its conceptual basis compared to earlier conceptualizations. This is referred to by Majore (1986) as the three stages of systems analysis : operations research (in the 1940s), systems analysis (in the 1950s) and policy analysis (in the 1960s and 1970s) (Table 5).

Table 5

Distinguishing features and characteristic problems at three stages of systems analysis

	Operations research (1940s)	Systems analysis (1950s)	Policy analysis (1960s-1970s)
Disciplinary aims	Discovery of empirical regularities in operations; operational design; prediction and testing	Resource allocation; analysis of conflicting systems; system design; systems engineering	Problem formulation; analysis of distributional consequences and institutional constraints; design of decision-making procedures
Evaluation criteria	Technical efficiency; cost minimization; output maximization	Economic (allocative) efficiency	Political and administrative feasibility; consensus on policy
Characteristic features and methods	Unitary decision-making; system, policy, and goals given; statistical inference; differential equations; search theory; queuing and inventory models; control theory	Group decision-making; policy and goals often not given; operations embedded in larger sociotechnical systems; microeconomics; constrained optimization; decision and game theory; simulation; econometrics	Public policy-making; ill-defined goals; institutional framework given; public finance and political economy; organization theory; data analysis and large-scale social experimentation

Table 5 (continued)

Typical applications	Tactical operations; logistics; production scheduling; waiting lines; inventory control; programming	Choice among weapon systems; strategic studies; resource allocation in a national health system; development of water resources	Policy planning; reform of existing national systems of health, education, or social security; pollution control; programme evaluation; programme implementation

Source : Miser, Quade (eds.) (1986), *Handbook of Systems Analysis*. North Holland, Amsterdam, p. 50.

At this point, two clarifications are necessary in order to avoid misunderstandings. Firstly, the terminological distinctions between operations research, systems analysis and policy analysis, while fairly common in English-speaking countries, are by no means universally accepted or used. In many countries a single label such as 'operations research' applies to all three stages or forms of analysis distinguished above. In such cases, 'operations research' assumes exactly the same meaning as 'systems analysis'.

Secondly, it is important to realize that a classification such as the one suggested in Table 5 is only a cross-section of the entire process of disciplinary evolution. To obtain a complete evolutionary representation, one would have to combine a cross-sectional description with a longitudinal study. Such cross-sectional and longitudinal study of operations research, for example, would show not only the successive changes in the pool of concepts and techniques available at different points in time, but also a continuous evolution in aims, methods and evaluative criteria.

This shift in emphasis is the result of a common concern that systems analysis and its sister disciplines such as operations research, have too often failed to achieve successful implementation because of incomplete and often incorrect methodology. Analysts have been making assumptions, sometimes subconsciously, that do not stand serious examination. An example of such an assumption is that the 'hard' part of a problem, which can only be expressed in mathematical terms, could be usefully isolated from the human and organizational elements, which could thus be eliminated from the analysis. Another false assumption is that implementation is an activity entirely separate from the analysis itself (Tomlinson, Kiss, 1984).

The omission of social, political and institutional consider-ations - health and environmental effects of different modes of, let us say, energy production, safety problems, the risk of nuclear proliferation, issues of scale and of the political implications of alternative energy paths - did not appear too serious in the early stages of the policy debate. But, as opinions have become polarized and public appreciation of the more remote implications of policy choices has increased, the need to deal explicitly with the broader social and political issues has been generally accepted by the modelling community. (Cf. "Lessons from global modelling and model-lers", Meadows, 1982). After years of rather fruitless debate, even the most technically-minded analysts have been forced to realize that technology and economics can only play a limited role in the ongoing energy controversy, and that energy policy belongs in-herently to the interdisciplinary field. "It involves economics, law, politics, engineering, resource geology, biomedical impacts, and environmental risk assessment - along with the methodologies that are already familiar to the operations researcher : optimiz-ation algorithms, simulations, decision analysis and econometric estimation" (Manne, et al., 1979).

The changing paradigm outlined above is clearly reflected in the Handbook on Systems Analysis (Miser, Quade, 1986). It definitely states that

> "systems analysis cannot conform to an accepted, predetermined outline, it must respond to the conditions in the problem context and exploit such opportunities for assistance to decision-makers as it may offer. Similarly, the disciplines involved, the methods used, the forms of communication adopted, and the schedule for the work must all respond sympathetically to the needs of the context and the officials with roles to play in it. Good systems analysis can be short and concise or long and arduous ; it can employ no more than clear thinking, or very complicated mathematics...
>
> While it is possible to conceive of a large-scale system problem that lies in the hands of a single decision- or policy-maker, the case of multiple responsibilities and interests is so much more usual as to be virtually characteristic. Thus, the findings of a systems analysis must, a fortiori, be aimed at, and be communicated to, a varied community. This provides systems analysis with another important role : unifying the knowledge base, logical framework, and overall perceptions of this community."

It is an important aspect of the expanded subjective factor, that systems analysis concerns people who usually enter its objects as important elements and whose individual and collective behaviour eventually determines many essential features of the system's be-haviour. If the problem situation depends on the behaviour of various people, then it necessarily depends on the way these people perceive it. Therefore systems analysis lays special emphasis on the adjustment of the external view of the problem situation (on the part of the researcher and 'customer') and the internal view (on the part of the system's active element) (Gvishiani, 1984).

Among those authors who have successfully applied the system view or system thinking to developmental phenomena, Dopfer's (1979) contribution is important. He observes that "the empirical evidence challenges increasingly not only the validity of single hypotheses, but of the entire set of premises on which these hypotheses are based". Major developmental outcomes - such as increasing socio-economic differentials (asset, income, productivity, etc., differentials), imbalance in ecological development, persistent population pressure and increasing mass poverty - are difficult to predict and to explain within the existing "paradigm". Only a "reassessment of the basic sets of premises and assumptions" can help in the formulation of an acceptable and working theory. Dopfer bases his conception on the classical political economy, but his empirical observation that "in the past a range of sophisticated policy instruments produced unsatisfactory results... The failure can be due only to the inappropriate frame of theoretical reference upon which the application of these instruments is based... The present situation (in Asia, as in other developing countries) impresses upon us the need to rethink some of the major theoretical positions rather than to formulate 'policies' or improve planning techniques on the basis of the existing theories". In his search for a new theoretical basis for the treatment of developmental phenomena, he is aware of the fact that any approach which includes only the economically relevant part of reality must necessarily misstate the nature of the problem. Dopfer suggests that a holistic and interdisciplinary approach is needed instead of a single paradigmatic approach. Systems analysis promises proper methodology : phenomena are viewed in their complexity. "The generalized concept of system allow us to expound *a priori* some basic characteristics of phenomena which are composed according to the characteristics of a system." For studies of developmental phenomena, Dopfer points to the importance of dealing with three different frames of phenomena : the macro-micro frame, the macro frame, and the micro frame. His conceptualizations are arranged around two main developmental aspects : population dynamics in a finite world ; and the theoretical and empirical outline of major socio-economic processes. The concept of system proved very useful in orienting Dopfer's considerations, even if the conceptual picture of the general systems-nature is simple.

Hill and Mattessich (1979) study family development and life-span development together and consider the 'systemness' of the family through specific qualities, such as relatively closed, boundary maintaining, equilibrium seeking, adaptive, and differentiated from other forms of family rendered residual by the framework, such as the family as a domestic institution, the extended family, kindred and household. The structure (or body) of the family may be composed of such criteria as position, role, role cluster, which may belong exclusively, changeably but asymmetrically, and interchangeably or symmetrically to the adult and non-adult members. These components change continuously or discontinuously over the life-history of the family, and changes - life-span development - are ordered by sequential regularities such as role sequences, careers of family positions, intercontingencies of careers, and all alterations and development in family members along the life-cycle of the family, strongly determined by the concommitants of different ages. In their article, each of these concepts occur, but the authors make no attempt to re-arrange them.

Buckley (1967) discusses the meaning of the applications of the systems-concept from the sociological point of view, focussing mainly on societal organizations. Two terms in his discussion seem more especially fruitful for the contextual frame of our review : morphostasis and morphogenesis. Both refer to basic processes within an organization, and between them and their environment. Morphostasis refers to those processes in complex organization-environment exchange which tend to preserve or maintain the form, state and system of an organization. Morphogenesis refers to those processes which tend to elaborate or change the form, state and systems of an organization. Homeostatic processes in organization, or ritual in socio-cultural entities, manifest morphostasis ; evolution in the biological sense, enriching and maturing capabilities in societal entities exemplify morphogenesis. Buckley evolves and discusses the two concepts in a more detailed context, which suggests that both are useful and compatible in a complementary manner to our ordering pictures.

Sztompka (1974), a Polish sociologist, raises certain important questions : What is the form of the process of change ? What is it that changes in the process ? What is the object of transformations ? He answers these questions through the systems approach, and introduces four types of change : directive, non-directive, total and partial. Directive change is a series of interlinked transformations of a certain object towards a standard state. Non-directive change is the singular, accidental, cyclical transformation of the object. Total change concerns the total object and its system, i.e. change in all its elements, interrelations, states, etc. Partial change concerns the alteration only of certain elements, relations and states, the object retaining its basic identity. Real objects usually combine all four aspects. Development means the process of total and directive change.

Aganbegyan (1981) is not sufficiently explicit in describing the constituents of his picture of the system-nature. Nevertheless, his discussion informs us that the systems approach is widely used in the integrated approach to regional development. "The complexity of the subject, in which so many different elements are interrelated both historically and functionally, has required such a comprehensive approach. Scientific methods of systems analysis now widely in use have strengthened the integrated approach and have greatly increased its applicability to the study of complex socio-economic and natural systems."

Zaslavskaya (1981) is one of the members of the Siberian group which investigated the application of the systems approach to the study of social problems in the large rural region of West Siberia. The main characteristic of his approach is that he focusses on the subject under study as a functioning and developing whole. The subject of his study are specific societal entities : cities, regions, rural communities and production teams. His conceptual basis was a simple system-picture combined with a methodical sequence of operation in order to obtain an adequate system-picture about rural studies. First he broke the subject down into its component elements and investigated each element in detail to discover its functions within the whole, its internal structure, pattern and development trends. In a second stage, the links between structural elements or subsystems were clarified. The systems approach was very fruitful when the subject was studied not only by itself, but in its relation to and interaction with its milieu. For the Siberian countryside, this milieu was Soviet society as a whole, the development level and trends of which vitally affect the condition of the countryside. The researcher's conclusions may be quoted : "the systems approach to the study of social entities opens up possibilities for the formulation and solution of entirely novel research problems".

Among those who apply the systems approach in their enquiries, a very active group is the community of World Systems Analysis. The leading personality within this group is I. Wallerstein (1982) who, together with Hopkins and other associates, declares : "If there is one thing which distinguishes a world-system perspective from any other, it is its insistence that the unit of analysis is a **world-**system, defined in terms of **economic** processes and links, and not any units defined in terms of juridical, political, cultural, geological, or other criteria." The world-system is a whole, a spatio-temporal whole. "It is a spatial world within its expanding geopolitical boundaries, but it is also comprehensive and singular in time, forming a temporal world as well over the course of its deepening synchronization, chronologically ordered growth, and cyclically modulated rythms of expansion and contraction." Considering such images, the task of social scientists is to explain why some societies started earlier than others, why some have proceeded much further than others, why and at what cost some develop faster than others, and why those currently lagging behind (developing countries) are lagging and what they must do in order to develop (Hopkins, Wallerstein, *et al.*, 1982). Another member of this group, Bach (1982), discusses "what is meant by the whole and its parts and how they vary over perspectives". He examines the question from three points of view : modernization, interstate dependence and world-system perspective. In other words, the spectator's attitude determines what he identifies as a whole, a unit and its parts. Although the efficient use of the systems-concept is not the strong point of the school of world-system analysis, its results may nevertheless cause us to reconsider many older conceptualizations which have rather local contextual frameworks.

Finally, we return to Stoehr's conceptualizations concerning integrated development. He conceives two types of integration : functional and territorial, and observes that both may serve as a guiding agent for developmental transformations and for emerging-solving societal organizations. We have stated that they correspond to two types of organization, labelled mechanistic and organismic, and asserted that their developments differ fundamentally. It is also obvious that their systems are completely different. Stoehr's proposals are so valid that they also have great ordering strength in their original conceptualization. It is easy to perceive, however, that they can be reinterpreted in the language of the systems approach ; first intuitively, and later in a more artic-ulated form, after some elaboration.

The use of picture-image concepts in the systems approach

Through the systems approach, we can consider the development of an organic unit in very specific pictures and in a special way. The following pictures can be treated as ordering schemes for consider-ing system-nature :

a)   Pictures represent overtly and explicitly the systemic-organic nature of the phenomenon studied, which is a relatively well identifiable unit, having boundaries, a lifetime and an en-vironment.
b)   During developmental transformation, the peculiar systemic nature of that unit also alters in some sense, continuously and/or discontinuously. The interactions between the unit and its environment also alter. The pictures must be suitable to represent all of these.
c)   Thinking in terms of pictures, the 'integrated development' of a unit can also be interpreted first of all as a series of developmental alterations in the system of the unit as a whole, in its parts (number, property or quality), in the interactions between parts, and between the outer environment and the unit's parts. Interactions may alter in their nature, tendencies, course, and in their arrangement in space and time.
d)   The pictures may overtly represent the 'process-character' of integrated development, namely the developmental alternations in the system of a unit, which can be described in terms of ordered changes with sequential stages and timing, where stages are not interchangeable, and timing strongly belongs to the specific nature of the kind of unit, and the intertwined-interwoven processes within the unit are fitted to each other according to their stages, sequences and timing. Such process-character of developmental alternation can be described in more articulated ways, for example :
     (i)   through the synchronous-diachronous relations of events in the alternation (event network in time dimension) ;
     (ii) through the parallel-serial order of changes in the states of the units as a whole, in the states of their parts and the interaction of the environment with the whole unit and its parts.

With the help of the pictures described, we may be able to penetrate much deeper into the system-nature of a developing organic unit. Such a unit may be a human being, a family, enterprise, settlement, town, ethnic group, society, country, state, group of states, etc. Obviously each kind of unit has a special system-nature, and within it the phenomena of integrated development occur in a unique form. Nevertheless, the pictures conceptualized above are valid for each of them. Moreover, these pictures of the systems approach do not lose their validity even if the composition of a unit is very complex ; that is, if the unit is a greater region with towns, villages, etc. (within which individuals, families, enterprises, farms, etc., exist), these components or parts are embedded into a natural environment of great variety, and in the development of this region each component, small or large, takes part. The systems approach is also able to deal with such hierarchical arrangements, in the sense that the larger contains the smaller, and the system-picture interprets this fact in such a way that in the system of the whole, an organic unit contains partial systems, or - in deeper representations - it contains some elements.

A 'development path' is a widespread and widely used metaphor in itself, as well as in the context of integrated development. In this metaphor, a very important, intuitively grasped experience has an individual verbal representation. When we consider development only in terms of metaphors, a development path proves a useful guide in focussing our attention. 'Path of West-imitating development', 'path of slowdown growth', 'path of extensive development', 'path of intensive development', path of development through 'revolution' or 'reform' or 'incremental' changes, and so on. The metaphorical meaning of all such expressions implies a certain process-character of development along a path, which is initially self-evident. Difficulties begin to emerge, however, when one tries to translate these metaphors into the concrete phenomena or organic units already mentioned. In this case it is not easy to avoid the pitfalls offered by specialized theoretically-based disciplines such as economics, sociology, etc., because they suggest well-sounding but very one-sided interpretations. It seems possible that if one were able to interpret a developing unit and its developmental path in terms of ordering pictures of the systems approach described above, one would rid oneself of the prison of metaphors as well as having a better chance of avoiding disciplinary pitfalls. With system-pictures, the path of development can be identified according to the conceptualization in (d) above. The pictures described render explicit the process-character of integrated development in the system of a unit. This is the conceptualization which may help to resolve the difficulties encountered when one wishes to understand the developmental paths of an organic unit, especially in terms of the systems approach.

It is easy to see that by using systems thinking and its pictures we can approach reality much closer than by using a large list of classified aspects (cultural, educational, rural, regional, economic, etc.). Their names and states are juxtaposed and one has to think in these juxtaposed terms when considering integrated development. We emphasize that these nominal lists might be very useful in certain cases. They can also be built into system-pictures, in which they gain their conceptual status and contextual positions in an organic sense. A list cannot by itself, however, be a substitute for system-pictures.

So far we have intentionally avoided using the words 'model' or 'plan'. The pictures conceptualized above, however, can also be considered in more advanced and formalized versions. In this study we use the words 'model' or 'plan' only to denote these more advanced versions of pictures.

It is crucial that the plan-images (types of basic plan) adequately represent the relevant reality. Inadequate images are obstacles to the evocation of the benefits of planned work and planned integrated development.

Interpreting the plan-images according to the components of the problem-situation - images of initial state, final state, strategy, etc. - presupposes that the images of each component are adequate separately. The adequacy of such images in national planning practice can be examined from two different points of view :

i)   how complete are the images of the components ?
ii) what kinds of ordering schemes make planners sensitive to relevant reality and arrange the content of plan-images ?

One important answer to the first question is that the lack or inadequacy of the images of any component limits the usefulness of the others. This is based on empirical observation.

The second issue is too complex to be settled as simply as the first. A certain amount of detailed examination is necessary within two different frameworks. Ordering scheme (a) may be considered in relation to the triple contextual framework, and (b) is important from a methodological point of view. The methodological frame strongly relates to highly formalized images and models, and will be discussed later. The relations of different ordering schemes to our contextual frame suggest some considerations, which can be touched upon here. The lack of profound critical research on the ordering schemes of the conceptualizers of new integrated development planning only allows an intuitive approach. The essence and the conclusions of this approach can therefore be briefly discussed.

The concept of integrated development in terms of system emphasizes that we must think in terms of organic societal units which have their own developmental nature. Further, we must think in terms of schemes which render overt the alteration in system-nature of a societal unit during developmental change, as well as the sequentially staged process-character of development, and the different but interrelated processes and their dynamics. What is to be found, from this point of view, in national plan-images ?

It is worth listing the most frequently used ordering schemes which are responsible for what their users judge to be relevant features in the object sphere of planned work. Among others, two highly elaborate and brilliant sources have helped us in screening out the schemes (Meadows, Richardson, Bruckmann (1982), and Meadows, Robinson (1985)). The main source, however, is experience.

(a) **Nominal schemes** - In verbal plan-images, classified lists of notions (categories) label certain common features (types of attribution) of societal entities. Usually the carriers of such labels are countable. Verbal statements can be made about

labelled features in terms of integrated development. The
ordering strength of these schemes corresponds to that of
formal logic.

b)   **Statistical schemes** - Highly sophisticated classificational
arrangements of notions (categories) which label the carriers
of 'genuslike' or 'specieslike' attributes. The carriers are
countable, and are those which are represented in different
kinds of statistics (demographic, economic, cultural, technological, health, etc.). The ordering strength of statistical
schemes corresponds to that of formal logic. Their inherent
possibilities in representations and inferences are rather
restricted. Constraints may be loosened by different techniques, e.g. time-series, cross-typologies, correlation techniques and stochastical methods. Statistical schemes may be
useful when the distribution of certain attributes (educational, health time-series, etc.) indicates changes in the
frame of integrated development. For example, the number of
educated, healthier people increases, the income of certain
societal strata increases, and in the progressive changes these
aspects may mutually influence each other.

c)   **System dynamics schemes** - Its basic elements - variables - are
analogous to the classifiable indicators of statistics. But
system dynamics goes further. It makes us sensitive, for
example, to the directed (channelled) flow of carriers of
certain labels, to the sources from which such carriers emerge
(production), to the sinks into which such carriers disappear
(consumers), and to the inventories where the flowing labelled
carriers assemble. These flowing carriers may be population,
goods, cash, pollution, information, materials, energy, income,
expenditure, etc. A mathematically formalized and computerized
technique has been built upon such elements. The ordering
schemes of this technique are very suitable to the study of
problem-situations in which the most relevant features are
manifested by flows, stocks, material, information and people,
and certain economic indicators (prices, etc.) are also joined
to them. Such phenomena may also be relevant in integrated
development, but the ordering scheme itself is hardly more
sensitive to integrated development than to pure statistical
schemes. Their possibilities in the representation of objects
and in inferences are much more than in the case of pure
statistical schemes. For example, system dynamics can represent causal relations in their definite dynamic aspects.
        The 'flow' is a phenomenon which may be stationary, may
change in time, and the character of change may oscillate
increasingly (unstable) or decreasingly (stable), or may be
transient in other ways.

d)   **Econometric schemes** - The basic ordering scheme of econometrics
is the same as that for statistics, and it uses the concept
flow and stock which may change in time in the same way as for
system dynamics. The carriers of different labels are those

(variables) which have relevance to the national or smaller economies, such as goods, services, resources, production, consumption, capital, investment, depreciation, import and export, money and prices. All these may be arranged in static and dynamic interpretation. Highly elaborate mathematical formalization and technique is based upon these elements, suitable for the study of the interrelations of the economic variables mentioned, when exogenous and endogenous variables can also be distinguished among them. The possibilities in the representations and inferences are more articulated than in the case of system dynamics, but causal relations or inferences can be gained at most indirectly. Econometric schemes are in essence rather insensitive to relevance in integrated development, similarly to system dynamics.

e)   **Schemes of input-output analysis.** - Input-output analysis is also mainly based on statistical ordering schemes. In this analysis such phenomena are relevant as intersectoral flows of money, resources, goods, services, energy, pollution, etc., or, briefly, flows of materials between suppliers and consumers. From the point of view of statistical classification, these abstract labels (categories) may be disaggregated into highly sophisticated depth. The images gained through such economic relevance are static : pictures of balance and of shifts from balanced states. One might say that they are snapshots. But snapshots for subsequent years (like time series in statistics) may extend the use of these ordering schemes on the time scale. A highly formalized mathematical technique adds static images which may also be combined with other dynamic methods. Its possibilities for representation and inference are very much articulated within its limits, which are the same as those for statistically based ordering schemes, especially in their relationship to the organic features of integrated development.

f)   **Schemes for optimization.** - This technique has a basic ordering scheme with elements such as objective activities for its realization, and constraints and boundaries within which an objective may be implemented. In the case of a given objective, options for activities are available, and one may choose that which ensures greatest success, the measure of which is expressed by goal function. The representational sensitivity of this ordering scheme differs from the foregoing. In a sense, this scheme describes the 'worker-object' interaction together with inner and outer constraints. A complementary mathematical technique may be added to this scheme to help to select a desirable combination of activities and constraints. The duration of such conditions, however, is usually short and as it is replaced by a new situation, so a new optimum must be found, and so on. This is one of the basic weaknesses of this scheme, stemming from its static character. Integrated development is rather far removed from phenomena which can be adequately represented through snapshot images.

The possibilities in inference are also determined by these issues.

g) **Composite schemes.** - Each of the schemes discussed above can be combined. Such cross-fertilization may modify the possibilities of representation of details and inferences, but do not bring us any closer to the essential nature of integrated development of organic societal entities.

h) **Programme-oriented schemes.** - Most of these represent their object-sphere in terms of concepts which are close to conceptualized features of integrated development. Firstly, one may find in these schemes conceptual elements such as an end result of the programme (from its starting phase, through intermediate states, to its final state), activities and their parallel-serial connections, resources, timing, actors with responsibilities and duties in the framework of division of labour, the arrangement of actors in the organizational framework, etc. It is easy to perceive that these elements are compatible with the conceptual core of this study in many ways. But while these programme-schemes make us sensitive mainly to the 'worker' and his 'abilities', 'activities' and 'resources', the developmental nature of the object is not represented, or at most the parallel-serial altering states of the developing object are nominally marked. These management techniques were conceptualized for general use. Their object-sphere may be development in the industrial, rural, territorial, health care, etc., areas. Schemes, therefore, which order the representation of the object can only be very abstract and generalized - usually nominal markers (labels) - of that object. Here we should refer to the core-concept of our study. In this core-concept, 'worker' and 'object' taken together make up a special, temporary, organic unit, with its own system. The developing component must not be absent from the representation of this composite unit - neither in the asymmetric nor in the 'self-reflective' case. The ordering schemes or programme managements neglect exactly this component. Nevertheless, these kinds or ordering scheme are very close to the scheme necessary for plan-images of integrated development.

A very promising conceptualization of a scheme for 'industrial complication' has been proposed by Giarini (1986). It deals with two key problems in the sphere of industrial production, namely vulnerability and uncertainty. Here we confine ourselves simply to his basic ordering scheme which is very close to our core-concept. Moreover, it also suggests practical complementarities. Giarini describes the modern industrial production sphere as very complex, and in the arrangement of its system-nature, three major kinds of complication (system-builder) manifest themselves together with other factors :

-   Vertical complication concerns the multiplication of steps through which raw materials are transformed into finished products. The range of steps is perceivable by two ordering approaches. Firstly, one kind of raw material can be processed for many kinds of end product, and a directed treelike graph may map the path of intermediates. Secondly, many kinds of raw materials need to be processed into one kind of end product. This may also be mapped by a directed treelike graph, the difference being that the starting points are at the ends of the branches.

- Horizontal complication concerns all service activities (transport, warehousing, finance, etc.) which accompany and support the production activity itself.
- The vertical and horizontal complications are accompanied by increasing multiplication of the steps involved in production and distribution, and with highly differentiated specialization. These tendencies increase the necessity of new kinds of organizations with new abilities connected to production, distribution, co-ordination, management, economy, etc., not only in stationary operation, but also in contingencies and development. In reality, the vertical and horizontal complications are embodied not in a unique, giant organization, but in an organic assembly of many smaller organizations. Such complex organizations are vulnerable, and have to work under uncertain conditions. Beyond Giarini's ideas, a third complication (system-builder) may also be identified, that of organizational complication.

The three kinds of complication are compatible with our core-concept, and suggest possible conceptual enrichment for it. Their threefold ordering scheme has appeared here only in intuitive form. It nevertheless demonstrates quite clearly that in terms of this scheme we can make these three complications explicit in any integrated development. One could say that the input-output analysis also speaks of such relations in its intersectoral flows. But the profound difference is that while the input-output ordering scheme maps reality according to 'genus-species' properties, Giarini's modified scheme works according to a 'whole-parts' scheme. It offers evolving possibilities for plan images in representations and inferences. Moreover, the threefold complications can be extended as an ordering scheme to spheres in which the end result is the human individual, or any societal entity.

We have given examples of ordering schemes which are in use (the last one being only conceptualized) among national planners, and which are compatible enough - at least conceptually - with the contextual frame of this study. It is obvious that the examples only cover the latter contextual frame fragmentarily, but no better possibilities were to be found in the literature available.

Some remarks are called for concerning statistically-based images. It is easy to see that statistical-classificational schemes directly destroy the organismic-systemic nature of images representing societal entities. So far nobody has found any manipulations by which organismic features can be restored to statistically ordered representations. This type of ordering scheme is directly suitable only for cases in which a great number of elements must be counted

and separated according to common labels. There are many national
planning problems for which statistical images are indispensable
(e.g. accounting and distribution of resources, products, services
in supply and demand situations). But in those cases, when the
organismic nature of plan-objects is very complex, the fact of
thinking only on the basis of statistical images may even be harm-
fully disorientating. Integrated development is just one of such
cases. Nevertheless, statistical schemes are indispensable when
planners apply a contextual frame similar to that of this study. A
very important criterion must, however, be satisfied : a preliminary
organismic-systemic image must be elaborated which will order data
collection. It may also be that the category structure of normal
statistics implies data needed by system-planners. But in most
cases when a preliminary ordering scheme does not adjust data collection to the organismic-systemic nature of the plan-object,
planners are compelled to consider only those topics on which they
have collected data.

Conclusions

A short review of the systems approach to development has perhaps
demonstrated the great importance of this approach in dealing with
developmental phenomena, if we have ordering pictures concerning the
systems-nature of an organic unit through which we can interpret its
systems. System-pictures help us follow alterations along a
developmental path in greater detail. This is a difficult task,
because developmental processes are intertwined and interwoven. The
authors cited support these conclusions, though none of the conceptualizations was as articulated - from the methodological point
of view - as the proposed ordering pictures. The latter are open to
further enrichment and reconsideration.

1.3. Planning integrated development through the systems approach

Basic concepts of development planning and their enrichment

The conceptualization concerning plan and planning for our contextual frame is based on empirical evidence. When a human being
acts on an object in order to change it, he is able to imagine
(a) the initial, intermediate and final states of the object ;
(b) his actions adjusted to each stage of alteration ; (c) the
abilities he will have to activate ; (d) the resources he needs in
order to render his abilities efficient. These are general experiences. The product may be large and complex, or small and
simple. The actor may be a unique individual, or be many thousands
of people, or the population of a nation, with shared abilities and
activities, and so on. Moreover, the product may be an inanimate
object or a living plant, animal, human being, or a societal group,

organization, institution, or a population with a high level of
culture. The experiences described are invariable in principle.

Images of the object, its alteration and final state may be
called the product-plan. Images of activities, their sequence,
order and timing are action-plans. Images of abilities, and of the
resources indispensable to activating those abilities and subsequently adjusting them to the action-plan and the product plan,
are plans for allocation ; the economic plan can be conceived from
these and other images. It contains images of the effective (successful) and efficient (economic) activities of abilities, adjusted
to action-plan and product-plan, and may be called an image of
strategy. Finally, images of the relevant environment (natural,
socio-economic, cultural and artificial) are also needed.

In these concise and very abstract conceptualizations, the
'process character' of planned work is represented by two phases :
(a) the intellectual preparatory phase, within which plans are
worked out in the mind ; (b) the implementation phase, during which
the results of planned work are embodied in a planned way. This
widely used interpretation needs extension. The use of the finished
results, or life together with results realized may be planned or
unplanned. Plans may be elaborated after results have been
realized. But it is preferable to anticipate this phase - that of
living with results - during the intellectual preparatory or
planning phase. It is therefore preferable to conceptualize the
work planned in three phases, and to adjust each kind of plan to
these phases. These considerations suggest a corrected interpretation of the planned work of human beings, the basic concepts of
which are as follow :

Three phases of planned work   Types of basic plan

1.   Planning phase   1. Product plan
2.   Implementation phase   2. Action plan
3.   Phase of living with results   3. Allocation plan
                                            4. Economic plan, containing
                                               a strategic plan
                                            5. Images of the environment

Based upon these preliminary steps, the sense and the essence
of the ability to carry out planned work may be considered to be
twofold :

a)   Greater chance of success and less risk in relation to the
     product and in using the product (i.e. the person has carried
     his action plan through as foreseen, and lives with the results
     as he had imagined them).
b)   Abilities and resources used with greater efficiency, greater
     economy of action during the implementation and utilization
     phases (i.e. the person may avoid trial and error action, and
     have greater probability of adjusting to the nature of the
     product and to environmental constraints).

In both groups of proposals, the probabilistic element should be emphasized.

It has been found that these basic conceptualizations concerning the sense and the essence of human ability for planned work are very useful when trying to understand the possibilities and pitfalls of planning culture. They are not exclusive and closed, but open to any enrichment, whether theoretical, interdisciplinary or pragmatic. In order to bring these conceptualizations closer to the triple contextual frame, some pragmatic enrichments are discussed below.

Relationships and interactions between human actors and their environment may be very different, and may change along a continuum :

a)   On the one hand, the actor has the knowledge and the ability to enable him intentionally to influence a certain sphere, with desired outcomes.
b)   In his relations with other spheres, the actor's knowledge and abilities are only sufficient to enable him to forecast events without being able intentionally to influence them.
c)   At the other end of the continuum, the situation is quite different : the actor does not possess the knowledge or the ability to influence or predict events in certain spheres, and he can, at the most, expect the unexpected and act by trial and error.

These categories are obviously simplified. When object-spheres are human or societal phenomena, the actors face mixed types seen from many points of view. For example, in the division of labour some actors are able to plan and influence a few parts of the object-sphere. Others can do nothing more than make predictions concerning other parts. The remainder are 'able' to expect the unexpected. There are many other modulating factors which increase the variety of the relationships between the actors and their environment. Nevertheless, the three categories can be considered to have great heuristic value and may even preserve their ordering strength in relation to very complex object-spheres. The sequence of categories also indicates how the possibility to plan breaks down along the described continuum.

Another possible enrichment is suggested by an observation. A product can be planned and implemented in co-operation with nature. In the case of living objects or human beings, this co-operation is always necessary, whether we are aware of it or not. In education, co-operation is necessary with the nature of the body and personality of a human being ; in socialization, co-operation with the nature of a subculture ; with the family included, traditionally inherited roles and abilities, etc. In socio-cultural progress or development, co-operation is needed with the nature of a local ethnic culture. Symbolically it might be said that there exists between man and nature a very articulated division of labour and sharing of abilities. When such co-operation criteria are neglected, the intentions and consequences of developmental activities surely fail.

These considerations focus on and highlight those experiences in which rationalities are dominantly expressed. Beliefs, values and incentives (interests, compulsions) also affect the human being, however, during his planned and unplanned work. These impacts may determine what the actors intend to produce and how they intend to produce it, with what resources, in what environmental circumstances, within which co-operative framework, etc. These non-rational, or not simply rational factors may also be considered as enriching possibilities. Furthermore, other factors accompany these non-rational factors, such as attitude in perception and selection among relevant and non-relevant issues ; existence or absence of competence ; aspirations ; features such as conservatism, progressivism, radicalism, reformism ; the ability for short-term or long-term vision, or both (Kiss, Mayon-White, 1985, 1986).

All these factors, as well as many others which have not been mentioned, may be interpreted as being compatible with the core-conceptualization of planning and may be combined with each other. They are concisely qualified as examples of 'plural rationalities and interests' among planners. Bager (1985) has identified an interesting variety of plural rationalities and interests, as follows :
- 'means vs. human beings' ;
- branch or sectoral ;
- 'cosmetic' ;
- using one or another method in planning ;
- using different over-simplified schemes for plans and planning procedures, for the sake of political decision-makers ;
- prestige of experts ;
- priority seeking rationalities and interests of top decision-makers along the planning procedure ;
- comprehensive (state, society) vs. fractional (branch, country) ;
- specialist vs. layman ;
- competing for a share in limited resources ;
- diverging efforts of corporations to lose one or another economic regulator ;
- of those representing the different parts, strata, communities, etc., of the population in the different stages of planning ;

We may add to Bager's observations the rationalities and interests of the members of state administration, who have the power of decision and which may profoundly deviate from the rationalities and interests of the population at large, who cannot choose but bear the consequences of the decisions of the experts. This case leads us directly on to the question of democracy, and to the people's participation in planning and decision-making.

Plan-varieties emerge from the different rationalities and interests. Thinking in terms of varieties requires a special effort throughout the phases of planning in order to reach an acceptable consensus of opposing parties as well, of course, as finding an acceptable version among the possible plans.

Planned development through the systems approach :
a core-concept

How are these conceptualizations to be connected with the systems
approach and with integrated developmental planning ? As a first
step, ordering pictures can be combined with the preliminary pictures of basic conceptualizations about planning. Concisely, we may
propose the following :

a)   The systems-nature of the work object must be identified, as
     well as its parts, the interrelations between parts, its basic
     processes and main operational features, before any work can be
     carried out on it. If the actor works on the object, he some-
     how changes its state, so the product plan should represent
     these alterations and make explicit how the system of the
     object (whole, parts, etc.) is altered. If the object is a
     societal entity, the worker considers what originally happens
     within its body, and tries to co-operate with and adjust him-
     self to the nature of the object. The work may cause progres-
     sive, retrogressive, modifying, enlarging, etc., change in the
     object and its system. Developmental work results in progres-
     sive alteration.
b)   The worker identifies and then represents in the plans the
     abilities necessary in himself and his own system. He then
     clarifies his action on the object and his activated abilities
     manifesting themselves in action. He must ajust these abil-
     ities and actions to the order and sequence of the changing
     states of the object and identify necessary resources, and the
     means-tools for his abilities and activities. These are the
     worker's plans concerning his own work within the duration of
     the work plan. In other words, these are the action plans.
c)   The two entities in the developmental plan are the worker and
     his object. It is reasonable to interpret them within the
     duration of working time - during the planning and implement-
     ation phase - as a special unit. This unit has its own
     specific system-nature, in which the worker's system and the
     object's system are part-systems. Naturally the systems of the
     worker's tools and means are also part-systems within this
     temporally generated referential unit. The plans must repre-
     sent this larger referential unit, its system and part-systems,
     as well as the relevant environment of the unit in terms of its
     systems-nature. In the phase of living with the result, the
     term 'user' replaces the term 'worker'. The user together with
     the transformed object becomes a new entity which has its own
     specific system.
d)   It is important to note that in societal spheres the worker and
     his object may be (i) two different entities, and in this case
     their relationship is asymmetric, or (ii) one and the same,
     in which case their relationship is self-reflective. We may
     therefore speak firstly of planned development work on the
     other entity and the worker's outer result, and in the latter
     case of self-development work and the worker's inner result.
     In the third phase an in asymmetric relation, the worker is

replaced by the user, and in the self-reflective case the worker himself becomes a more developed worker. For example, the results of schools and universities are outer results, and the process of their implementation is characteristically developmental. But the modernization of these institutions needs work with inner results, and the realization process is also of a developmental nature. Inner results may for example imply enriched ability through teachers, learning (individual and social learning), the structural and functional reorganization of institutions through changing members, the creation of new responsibilities and liquidating those which are obsolete. In the third phase, the worker acts in a more developed fashion, because his inner results have enriched him. This example can be generalized. The plans for the two kinds of developmental processes must represent the synchronous-diachronous relations of changes in object and worker, in terms of their own and of their integrated systems. In a majority of complex, large societal units, developmental results need to be combined with inner and outer results.

These brief interpretations of how the three conceptual components of the contextual frame can be integrated renders nothing more than a conceptual core, which may orient our intuitive considerations concerning the systems approach to integrated development planning. We do not intend to use this conceptual core as a 'super-meta-conceptualization' or as a 'superrational construct'. Its methodological idea is very simple and pragmatic.

In the case of very complex phenomena which demand a poly-conceptual (polyparadigmatic) approach in order to understand their nature and be able to work on its development, a beneficial first step might be to prepare a core concept. This is a specific image of the phenomenon to be investigated which brings together the most relevant ordering concepts (paradigms) in such a way that they interpret each other. A contextual frame should help this mutual and specifying reinterpretation as well as finding places and relationships of component concepts in the core concept.

For the purposes of this study, •the integrated development and the system nature of organic societal entities are ordering concepts, which together might evoke the benefits of planned development, as opposed to impoverished or trial and error development. In the case of societal entities, the planned version must not mean totally planned change (which would in any case be illusive). At most it might mean that on the one hand a worker consciously reckons with the natural developmental features of the object, includes them in his plans, and, on the other hand, adjusts his planned artificial interventions and expected results to a natural order, sequence and timing of the object's natural developmental alterations. Draft plans for which an adequate polyconceptual core concept renders an ordered basis might have greater ordering strength than plans built on monoconceptual bases and in great detail. Hazy interpretations of component concepts in the core concept are acceptable as a first step, because they represent simple but profound orientations. Moreover, hazy interpretations

may be enriched and strengthened when they are brought closer to
concrete representations. For example, we may include in the core
concept considerations concerning the nature of development and the
practical use of the systems approach.

Complex development programmes

In the past, many complex programmes were implemented without making
their system-nature explicit. Empirical evidence suggests that by
using the ordering schemes of the systems approach, more benefit is
to be gained from such programmes. The most important system
features of complex programmes can be briefly summarized. At the
start of the programme, the following elements must be clarified :

a)   What are the boundaries of the referential frame or unit of the
     programme, and what belongs to the relevant socio-economic and
     natural environment ? In other words, what would an acceptable
     referential frame be, within which the complex problem situ-
     ation can be adequately treated ? This referential frame
     should interpret the economizing unit of the programme in space
     and time.
b)   What is the system-nature of the referential frame and its
     environment ? Within the referential frame, the members should
     be identified, as well as the static structure of the frame,
     its operational and developmental features (functions and co-
     operation of members), the above members being labelled
     'worker', 'object', and those 'living with the results' of the
     programme.
c)   The real system-nature of the referential frame changes con-
     tinuously during the programme, and this change requires
     special types of transformation, organization and management.
d)   Special evaluation should be fitted into every phase of the
     programme (i.e. into planning, implementation and utilization
     phases). Those who contribute to evaluation are organic com-
     ponents of the referential frame. Their work must be adjusted
     to the nature of the frame and its system as a whole, to the
     nature of 'workers', 'objects', activities, results, resources,
     forms of economy, etc.

     It can be imagined that a complex programme may be successful
even if its inherent system-nature remains covert. Experience
shows, however, that thinking in terms of the systems approach
substantially improves the programme framework. Problems can be
more clearly identified within themselves and in their interrelationships. Preferences and sequences in problem solving can be
recognized on the basis of organic relationships. The contributors
can co-operate with each other in a highly organized way. Those who
live with the developmental results can prepare themselves to
receive the results more consciously and adequately. The very
complex economic requirements can be more appropriately satisfied.
Briefly, the culture of planning, organization, realization,

management and economy can be much more developed than it would be without a consistent application of the systems approach.

Conclusions

We have endeavoured to review the conceptualizations concerning planning, which seem useful from the point of view of the contextual frame of this study. In the above section, we have gradually evolved certain possibilities which can enrich the core concept of our conceptual frame. It is impossible to deal here with many other possibilities, although they would also have been important. Some examples of undiscussed issues are mentioned below :

a) adaptivity - dealing with the unexpected and risk - in three-phased planned work ;
b) adaptivity within planning, continuous planning ;
c) adaptivity in the third phase of planned work ;
d) developmental macro-plans for states, mezo-plans for regions, micro-plans for small organic economic units such as enterprises, settlements, institutions and families ;
e) transmission between the three different scales - macro, mezo, micro - of developmental plans ; direct and indirect administrative control of planned work ;
f) continuous and discontinuous changes in societal development ;
g) critical branchpoints in socio-economic developmental paths ;
h) types of developmental style, such as reform, radical change, revolution, incremental change ;
i) progression, conservatism, retrogression, as tendencies of alterations in development ;
j) developmental goals with two kinds of strategies : 'conquering nature' vs. 'living with nature' ;
k) developments in dominantly competitive vs. co-operative societal media ;
l) the need for reinterpretation of the - sometimes complacent - disciplines and their theories and methods, and the need for interdisciplinary studies, in the spirit of integrated development.

We can do no more than list these issues. All are capable of enriching our core concept and helping bring the conceptualization discussed closer to reality. It would be necessary to carry out many theoretical tasks and much empirical examination in order to discuss them in terms of our contextual framework.

In the core concept of our conceptual frame, we have brought together the three basic concepts of our study. This core can be enriched not only by conceptualizations of planning, but by that of the two others. The core concept demonstrates how the three basic concepts interpret each other in the context built up from them. We have also tried to avoid any mono-paradigmatic or monodisciplinarian statements about the planning ability of human beings and their planned work. This explains why we have chosen the intuitively grasped core image of a worker who is able to plan his actions and results, and implement his plans, rather than the notions or paradigm of 'planning'. This image has proved very fruitful and suggests that we should return to this intuitive core when we lose our train of thought and our understanding in the complexity of integrated development, in our co-operation with nature, and among the highly proliferated concepts, disciplinary aspects, diverging interests and value changes. This intuitive core image has been reinterpreted in terms of integrated development and of the systems approach, as has occurred in the advanced and evolved core concept. Building upon this core concept and the different considerations concerning the components of our triple contextual frame, we conceptualize a more advanced interpretation for that frame. Similarly to the intuitive core image and to the core concept, in this third step we use a similar, very concise form. New conceptual elements will nevertheless also appear in this clearer image of the contextual frame.

The following part concentrates on the methods and intellectual tools of the systems approach and move the focus of the study onto the worker, within the worker-object unit.

PART II - THE STATE-OF-THE-ART OF THE SYSTEMS APPROACH APPLIED TO INTEGRATED DEVELOPMENT

Part II discusses the very practical use of the systems approach and of systems analysis. Section 2.1 acquaints us with the experience of the International Institute for the Application of Systems Analysis (IIASA), Laxenburg, Austria, by reviewing different case studies. Section 2.2 sketches a research programme for studying the West Siberian countryside ; the research team used the systems approach and systems analytic methods. Finally, Section 2.3 gives an historical overview of some of the main practical features and techniques of systems approaches.

2.1   IIASA studies on rural/urban/regional development

a)   The TVA case study

Before outlining this study, it is worth mentioning that the Tennessee Valley Authority (TVA) project is considered as one of the forerunner activities of programme budgeting on which the introduction of the whole PPBS (Planning, Programming, Budgeting System) was based in the mid-1960s (Chartrand, 1971). The experience of the TVA were studied by IIASA as a "successful programme of regional development from an international perspective, with a multidisciplinary team of scientists skilled in the use of systems analysis". A report in two thick volumes was published in 1976, and another in 1979 (Knop, 1976 ; Knop, 1979). We note that TVA is a very good example of three-phased planned work.

The first report asserted that "TVA was an ideal subject for systems analysis". It has been operating for nearly 40 years, and as such it was more accessible for study than a new development, which is usually in a state of flux. TVA is a dynamic organization, and maintains a basic philosophy of improving the living standards of the people of the region through a programme of integrated regional development. This task is an unfinished, continuous one. The importance of the component functions has been changing over time, and today the most important single function is the power supply. The economy of TVA is embedded in the national economy in a very peculiar way. An economic simulation model was made, through which it was possible to study the impact of both national and regional forces on the regional economy, and the impact of policies on regional conditions. The model was built up from two submodels : a model of population-labour, and a model of employment. This model was formulated to run for the TVA region as a whole and for nine sub-regions within it, for the period 1960-2020. Many other studies were carried out on different kinds of economic features and components (plant location and sub-regions). Besides the economy of the region, its organization is also peculiar and unique : it is a corporate agency of the Federal Government, with some of the autonomy and flexibility of a private corporation. This organization was also discussed in the reports. Different groups of papers focussed on the systems of electric energy supply and integrated water control, on the forestry and mineral resources, and on the regional-national agricultural and fertilizer development. Five schemes were chosen from different papers of the report to illustrate the use of systems analysis. Figure 1 shows the land management decision course. Another (Figure 2) illustrates the ordering and conceptual scheme of a model which simulates the impact of predicted or proposed land-use change on the natural resources of the region. Two schemes refer to the systems of farms for the years 1930 and 1964, illustrating the shifts in relevance (Figures 3 and 4).

The second report about TVA studies (Knop, 1979) "covers four major aspects of the TVA program : the systems approach to regional industrial development programs ; the managerial structure of the TVA, including specific management case studies on several key departments ; the applications of models and computer techniques to management ; the integration of environmental factors into the TVA management and planning processes, including a case study dealing with the environmental decision-making process in the siting of a nuclear power plant". The introduction of this IIASA report made definitely explicit the purpose of such IIASA studies :

1.   to identify and systematically characterize the approaches, the methods, instruments, decision-making procedures and organizational forms of regional industrial complexes ;

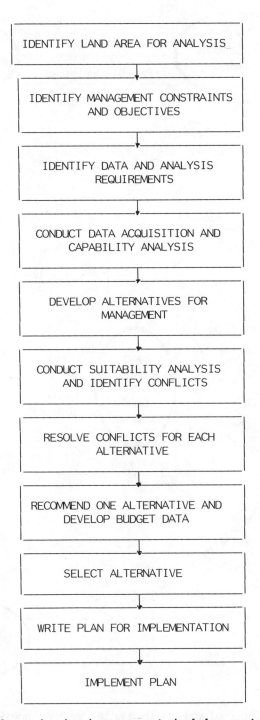

Figure 1 – Land management decision system

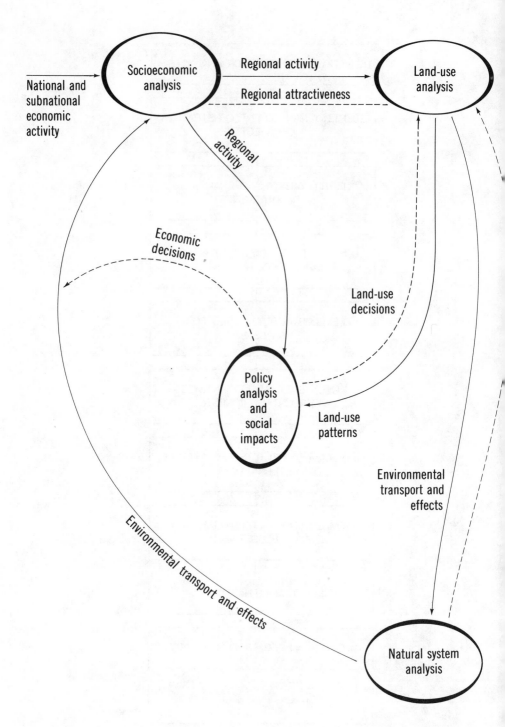

Figure 2 – The regional environmental systems analysis process

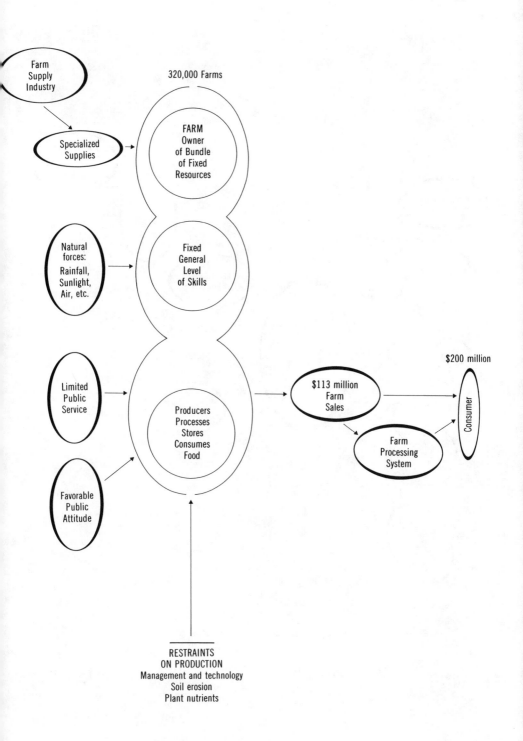

Figure 3 — Farm system 1930

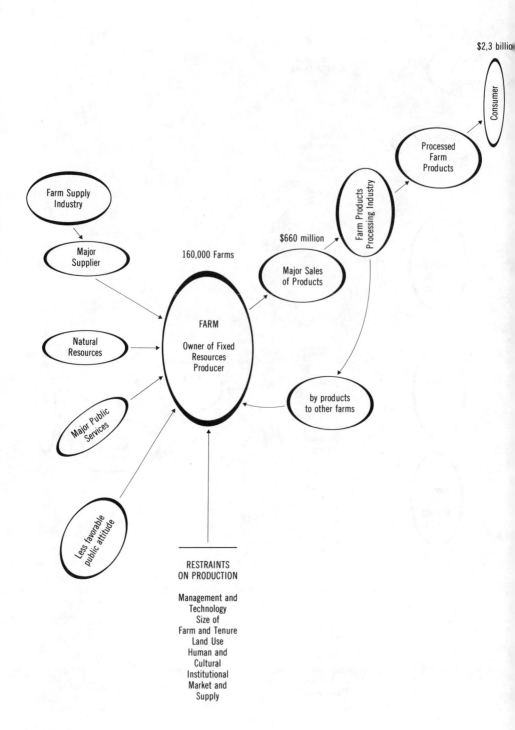

Figure 4 – Farm system 1964

2. to generalize and formalize the most advanced part of the methodology ;
3. to make these methodologies available for solving similar problems in other parts of the world ;
4. to compare approaches, methodological solutions and organizational forms under different social and political conditions.

This same introduction summarizes the strengths and weaknesses of studies in order to suggest conclusions for subsequent work. The study's main strengths are as follows : basic information was gathered by advance questionnaire ; an interdisciplinary and international (East-West) group ran the study ; direct interactions were realized with TVA managerial staff and with many people living in the area who are directly affected by TVA activities ; co-operation and frankness of TVA staff ; many managerial units were visited and interviewed. The weaknesses stem from the following : a lack of IIASA experience at that time in field studies of this kind ; the last-minute formation of work-groups containing a high proportion of visiting scientists ; the lack of contact with the social and political environment of the TVA (governmental and local authorities) which could not be included in the study programme.

In the second report, a highly elaborate chapter describes the historical changes in the managerial characteristics of the TVA from the beginning up to the 1970s, when "the TVA can no longer play the key role in the management of regional economic development". Today many factors beyond TVA control influence the development of this region, such as state taxation policy, credit policy of banks, and location of industrial enterprises ; many profitable branches are not part of TVA ; TVA relations with banks are weak. In the future, the major influences on the development of this region will come from private companies and state authorities. These new situations present new requirements for complex regional planning and management, as well as for TVA's projected achievements. These new conceptualizations are based on a systems approach to regional management complexity. This means first of all that the system of management must reflect the systemic characteristics of the organization managed, and is itself an integral part of it. The goals, structure and functions are the basic determinants in socio-economic organization. The main functions in the organizational sphere of regions are social services (health care, education, information) ; circulation and distribution of goods and finance ; protection, conservation and development of the natural environment and available natural resources ; and all these functions are located in enterprises, plants, factories, etc. The principal managerial functions in the interactions with the region are : (a) to analyse the economic and social conditions, demographic, climatic and natural resource characteristics at the beginning of development ; (b) to determine the objectives of regional development derived from national, regional, social and political interests ; (c) decision-making for the different regional areas of development ; (d) to manage the implementation based on information and incentives, directed towards all groups and individuals involved, as well as demonstration, training, etc.

A long chapter discusses the management relationship to planning and brings together the organizational structure, planning methods and implementation means. The organization chart in Figure 5, and Table 6 illustrate elements of the planning characteristics of the TVA. Among the components, the specific nature of the following should be stressed : situation assessment ; programme planning and budget ; feed-back control ; and evaluations. The effectiveness of planning depends on whether the planning and decision processes are intertwined adequately.

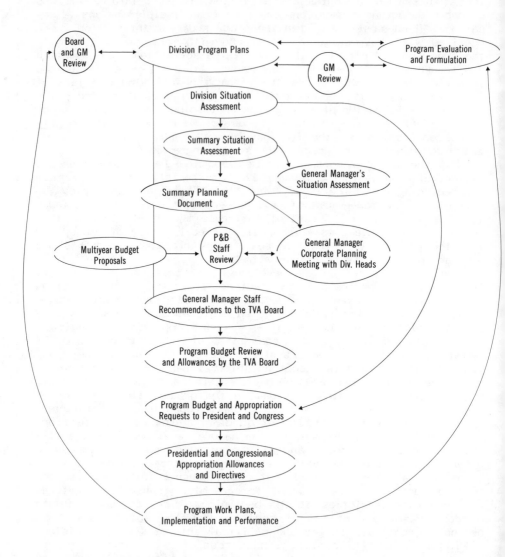

Figure 5 - Organization chart of the TVA planning system

Table 6

Responsibility in the planning process

Level of responsibility	Task	Identification of needs, opportunities, etc.	Project formulation	Activity formulation	Description & justification statements	Activity statements
General Manager	Recommend & concur	—	—	—	—	—
Director	Select & approve	Approve Identify	Approve Select	Review Concur	Approve	Review Concur
Branch Chief	Recommend & select	Identify	Select	Approve	Approve	Review Concur
Section Supervisor	Recommend	Identify	Recommend	Recommend Concur	Approve	Prepare input or concur
Project Supervisor	Recommend	Identify	Recommend	Select	Prepare Submit	Prepare input or approve
Resource Specialists	Recommend	Identify	Recommend	Recommend	Information input	Prepare input information
Consultants	Information input	Information input	Recommend	Recommend	Information input	Information input

Good planning should ensure the availability of a plan, or set of plans, for the organization as a whole (where the plan is defined as requiring statements of desired goals, the ways in which they are to be achieved and the resources required). In addition, a good plan should contain information on the assumptions made in the scenarios and the means of determining contingency plans. As far as medium- and short-term planning are concerned, the TVA system can be said to meet most of these requirements, every division and section within a division having its medium-term plan. Although no formal system of management-by-objectives is used, the staff know their objectives. No strategic plans for the whole TVA are available. However, in view of what has already been said about strategic planning at national and state levels, it is difficult to see what form such plans could take.

Good planning procedures should ensure that the plans in (a) above are effective. The procedure adopted by the TVA encouraged the search for alternative actions, and demanded that an assessment should be made of the consequences of the various alternatives. Basically, these are good planning procedures. They can be criticized, however, on the grounds that the evaluation procedures are qualitative. Thus, although some aspects of possible future courses of action are studied in detail, such as, for example, those relating to possible energy consumption and the use of fertilizers, there is no systematic exploration, nor are the studies undertaken made generally available to the various operating divisions. The whole planning process would be strengthened if there were an overall assessment of trends for the main variables in the TVA region, regularly updated and used as a planning basic for all divisions and offices.

A good planning system should be an essential element in the rationalization and unification of the various operations within an organization. This is particularly important in the case of the TVA because of the unevenly balanced dependence of many of its activities on power operation. It would be very easy for the Authority to operate as a subsidiary of the Office of Power, whereas in practice it operates with Power as an important but essentially secondary part of the organization.

On the whole, the planning procedures seem to have gone some way towards developing improved co-ordination and have revealed a number of weaknesses in the present organizational structure, one of which is the shortage of planning staff, operational research workers and systems analysts at Head Office. To obtain maximum value from the present procedure, it would be desirable to have a small team of analytically trained problem-solvers in the Office of Planning and the Budget at headquarters, linked with similarly skilled personnel in the operating divisions.

Effective planning should lead to efficient decision making. The relationship between the latter and the planning process is not easy to identify. This is partly due to the many ways in which decisions are made. Those concerning the allocation of resources are linked very closely to the planning and budgeting processes. Moreover, the processes by which budgets are agreed upon lead to a consideration of general policy, which forms the inevitable background to further discussion. Certain major decisions, however, such as the building of a new nuclear plant, do not seem to be as influenced by the planning system. On the other hand, the system does not hinder the decision-making process, which is perhaps more than can be said for many logically designed systems.

In conclusion, the planning procedures recently introduced have undoubtedly been beneficial. They are flexible and conducive to good planning, but weak in their lack of use of modern forecasting and analytical techniques, and in the absence of a team at Head Office capable of undertaking studies, developing general methods of analysis and co-ordinating the overall decision-making process. It is an inverted medium-term planning system and would by many standards be considered inadequate for strategic planning.

The second report relates to operational management activities adjusted to the TVA objectives, such as navigation, flood control, power production, reforestation, development of marginal lands, agricultural and industrial development, and the development of other regional resources such as manpower and recreation facilities. Some of these are also connected to separate but co-ordinated pro- grammes. Each major activity has its own operational management. A special indirect mechanism guides those activities for which the TVA does not have direct authority, such as agriculture, forestry, wildlife, fisheries, recreation, human resources, business and industry. Beyond direct demonstration, consultation and persuasion indirectly influence the work. The authority has created regulatory laws for activities within the framework of the indirect management mechanism. These features are strongly related in order to avoid overcentralization of management.

The third chapter of the second report describes the instrumental and informational basis of the TVA planning and decision-making process. This area includes highly computerized activities in different fields, such as statistics and the mathematical modelling of different planning tasks. At the outset, these computerized facilities were rather isolated both conceptually and operationally, because of the similar nature of the planning activities they served. There is now a tendency to strengthen co- operation between them and to use computerized facilities for decision-making processes.

An important chapter discusses the integration of environmental factors into TVA planning and management. In its approach, environ- mental management includes not only the control of those projects producing an environmental impact, but also the provision of recre- ation and education facilities and the preservation of the environ- ment. The IIASA study endeavoured to reveal how these aspects could be integrated, and to what extent they were comprehensive, in- tegrated and effective.

The comprehensive aspect may be related to such processes as :

- determination of environmental goals and the objects of en- vironmental management ;
- environmental research, planning and monitoring ;
- environmental communication (internal and external) ;
- environmental impact assessment capabilities.

Integration implies that all of these are joined together with normal management, and environmental management is an organic part of decision-making, at the same time having an independent status. Some environmental activities have been running since the beginning of TVA's activities, but new activities have continuously emerged. Table 7 shows a brief history of such activities. It is also worth illustrating the role of TVA in three areas of environmental management activities (Table 8) and the scheme of TVA environmental policy setting (Figure 6). The last part of chapter 3 of the second report deals with choosing a location for a nuclear power station, and its environmental consequences.

Table 7

	1933–1950	1950–1967	1967 to the present
Air quality		xx	xxx
Energy conservation			xx
Environmental education		xx	xx
Health programmes	x	x	x
Natural and scenic resources	x	xx	xx
New town planning		x	x
Radiological research			x
Resource recovery	xxx	xx	xx
Solid waste management			xx
Water quality	x	xx	xx
Strip mine reclamation	x	xx	xx
Vector and weed control	xx	x	x
Wildlife and waterfowl resources	xx	xx	xx

xxx - Intensive programme
xx - Active programme
x   - Programme

Table 8

Roles of TVA offices and divisions in
three areas of environmental management activities

Activity / Office	Solid waste management	Air quality management	Water quality management
Environmental planning	-Planning/co-ordination, internal TVA -Interagency technical advice/assistance -Interface with regulatory and other agencies -Field advisory and inspection -Research/ demonstration projects -Liaison with educational groups in Solid Waste Management -General source for planning, etc.	-Internal TVA planning/co-ordination -General planning and review assistance for Offices -Monitoring and data analysis -Complaint investigations -Assessments of emissions on agriculture and forests -Research for emission control -Recommendation for air quality control requirements -Plan evaluation and review for compliance	-Planning and co-ordination, internal -Water quality surveillance -Pollution complaint investigations -Field investigations -Downstream water use impact assessment -Collaboration with internal TVA Offices on water impoundments and pollution impacts -Technical assistance in local groups -Technical assistance in planning and operation of waste disposal facilities -Research on municipal and industrial waste -Interface with state and federal agencies

(continued)

Table 8 (continued)

Office of Engineering Design and Construction	-Technical studies on solid waste separation and use in construction -Design and construction of solid waste disposal facilities	-Design, cost estimates, and specifications -Construction services	-Research on engineering improvements for water quality control
Agriculture and Chemical Development	-Research on disposal and applications of composting -Assistance/ advice on strip mined land to FF&WD -Research on animal and agricultural waste, fertilizer, and crop residues -Research on solid waste from fertilizer plants	-Chemical engineering research on atmospheric waste emission -Control for National Fertilizer Development Center	-Research on agricultural and chemical waste on water resources -Methods for control and use of waste -Provide facilities for waste disposal
Power	-Research and liaison with organizations working on use of solid waste from power generation	-Research on waste control -Liaison with other electric utility organizations	-Research on waste impacts -Oxygen depletion research in reservoirs

(continued)

Table 8 (continued)

Water Control Planning	-Hydraulic, hydrological & geological data -Sample collection assistance for DEP -Research on surface and ground water pollution -Site selection for solid waste disposal facilities	-By request : total responsibility for atmospheric and meteorological monotiring systems -Liaison with National Weather Service for data and forecasts - service to other offices	-Engineering research for improvement of water control -Water quality monitoring and investigations -Research in water quality, geology and hydrology -Collection of samples for surveys with DEP
Navigational Development and Regional Studies	-Assists in planning, including economic aspects	-Studies of economics, waterfront industries and water commerce -Advice for industrial and urban development -General economic advice -Public relations on TVA air quality policy -Information on zoning and planning approaches	-Water quality measurement procedures for abatement requirements of pollution agencies, joint with DEP -Demographic and economic projections for long-range regional pollution control
Reservoir Properties	-Programmes with regard to reservoirs and reservations -Promotional campaigns, demonstrations with DEP	-Public relations of TVA air quality objectives in dealing with land right purchases -Deed compliance with air quality provisions	-Pollution control provisions for deeds and permits involving reservoir lands -Studies of recreational use of water resources with DEP (continued)

Table 8 (continued)

Reservoir Properties (continued)			-Secures compliance with control provisions in deeds for land rights
Forestry, Fisheries, and Wildlife Development (FF&WD)	-Research on impacts in operation of forests and harvesting of forest products -Demonstrations of disposal on strip-mined lands -Advice/assistance to OACD and DEP in forest studies	-Studies of airborne emissions on forests -Biological and forest air quality investigations, including economic impacts	-Impact on wildlife, aquatic life and fisheries - research -Stream water quality investigations with DEP
Law		-Prepares provisions incorporating air quality control requirements for land conveyances	
Property and Supply		-Incorporates air quality control provisions in land conveyances	-Incorporates antipollution provisions in land conveyances
Tributary Area Development			-Reviews plans/ approves water quality studies in tributary area development -Co-ordination of water quality technical advisors with tributary area development

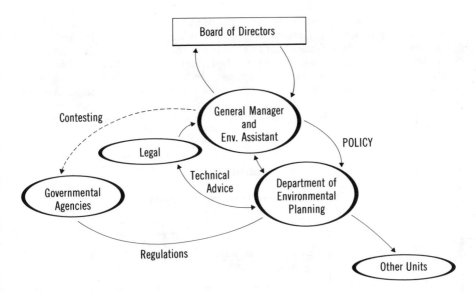

Figure 6 - TVA environmental policy setting system

b)   The Bratsk-Ilimsk case study

The second study of the experiences of large-scale regional development refers to the Bratsk-Ilimst Territorial Production Complex
(BITPC) in the Soviet Union (Knop, Straszak, 1978).   The final
report of this study was based on a variety of local studies.   Different working groups were constituted for different areas of study,
such as :

-    BITPC goals, variants and strategies ;
-    planning and organization ;
-    models for regional development and planning ;
-    automated management systems ;
-    integration of environmental factors in BITPC development ;
-    energy supply systems ;
-    water resource development.

     Each group was made up of Soviet scientists and IIASA staff
members.
     The BITPC pre-decision period dates back to 1930.   In 1952, the
basic decision was made to build the Anagara-Yenesei Cascade and the
Irkutsk Hydro-electric Power System.   The criteria behind these
decisions were of an economic, technological, social, military and
environmental nature and these aspects were important in selecting
the various aspects of the study.   Sectoral territorial input-output
relations, the proportions of production sectors and services,
population and manpower structure, financial relations, etc., and
their interdependence were the basic factors studied.

BITPC necessitated special organizational and managerial arrangements and as such represented an example of how to solve the problems of sectoral-territorial interface in the Soviet economy. Many tasks had to be synchronized between such activities as planning, industrial development, social infrastructure and competing industries. The planning work was strongly embedded in the national, and regional-territorial planning systems.

Table 9 shows the organizational characteristics of all these factors.

Table 9

Organizational response chart

Management Challenge	System Responding/ Functions	Process
1. Defining specialization	National - Policy and planning functions	Preplanning stages State long-term and five-year plans
2. Defining complex community development (a) infrastructure (b) competing industries and others	Local (Oblast) - Policy and planning functions	Local preplanning Drawing up of town plans Local five-year plans
3. Synchronization of construction (a) between sectoral objects (b) between sectoral and territorial objects	National - Control and co-ordination and Local - Control and co-ordination	Annual plans for Bratskgesstroi from Ministry of Power Operative plans Operational decisions of Bratskgesstroi Direction of Housing

The report discusses the models for regional development planning, which are economic in nature, with special reference to territorial and regional problems. A large model-system was created from the various component models. Figure 7 illustrates the system of models for perspective planning, and Figure 8 gives an overview

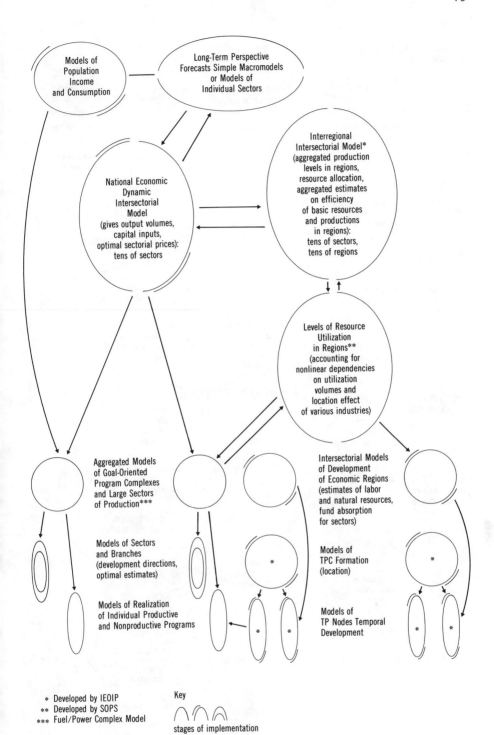

* Developed by IEOIP
** Developed by SOPS
*** Fuel/Power Complex Model

Key

stages of implementation

Figure 7 – System of models for perspective planning

80

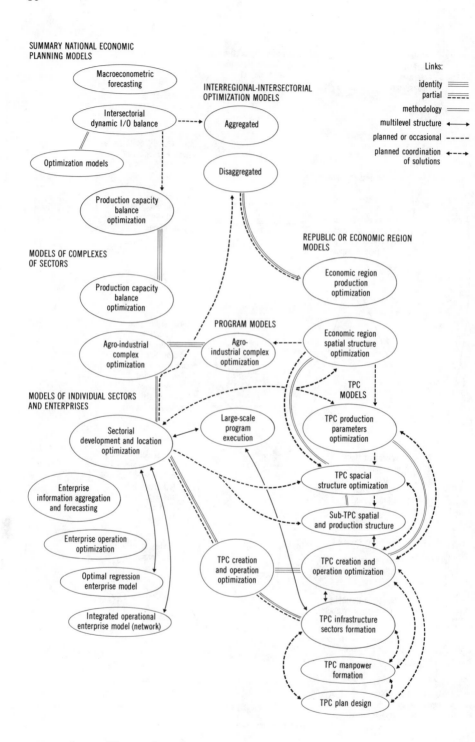

Figure 8 – An overview of the model system

of the model systems. National, sectoral and regional frameworks were integrated within the framework of concrete programmes.

The integration of environmental factors in the development of territorial production complexes has received widespread attention in recent years, because this type of production complex generates new problems which have not been anticipated in economic development programmes. These problems need both short- and long-term treatment. A separate chapter in the report discusses efforts to deal with environmental problems. Theoretical and practical studies were needed to clarify the problems of integration. Many questions remained unanswered but it should be noted that the importance of environmental research increased during the IIASA studies. This new trend and conceptualization are discussed in the chapter on integration of environmental factors.

c)   Regional development modelling

Regional modelling, its theoretical bases and practical uses are reviewed in Albegov, Anderson and Snickars (1982). Table 10 below gives an historical picture of modelling. The above-mentioned authors provide a very comprehensive source on current trends in regional development modelling and a good overview can be gained of the shifts in approach to modelling and the differences in modelling market and planned economies. Table 11 provides four case studies on regional development modelling with their basic features. The purpose of IIASA's research was to "create integrated systems for regional and sectoral development and to apply them to the regions under study... The types of problems analysed include investments in sectors of production, use of energy and other primary resources, interregional location, population, transportation policies, planning of new and existing towns, and the construction of industrial and agricultural production complexes". IIASA's intention was to provide "policy-makers with better tools to enable them to cope with the essentially dynamic, uncertain and interdependent factors regulating long-term economic and technological growth and structural change at a regional level".

In their introduction, Albegov, Anderson and Snickars (1982) assert that applied regional systems analysis considers long-term problems of policy-makers, and that economic analysis has a central place in studies. The users of this type of systems analysis consider that "economic, ecological, technological and demographic components should be related to each other, in an essentially dynamic and spatial analysis. This implies that a large number of variables have to be linked, which requires large-scale model-building and hence a very sensitive tradeoff between realism, simplicity, and ease of parameter estimation". Albegov et al. mention the unsolved problems of regional development modelling, one of which is related to problem clarification and the interaction between policy-makers and modellers in problem formulation. The other problem is "that systems-analytic approaches employing mathematical models must necessarily be complemented by 'software'

Table 10

Classification of regional development modelling research

Spatial scope	Type of model	
	Explanatory and predictive	Planning and policy

Interregional or multiregional	Input/output
	Spatial general
	  equilibrium
	Central place
	Migration
		Multiregional planning
		Economic growth
		Transport and/or
		  investment cost-
		  minimization

Regional	Input/output Basic/non-basic Growth pole	Mathematical program- ming Spatial competition
Intraregional	Urban land equilibrium Transportation Spatial interaction Lowry-inspired	Transportation/land use optimization Cost-benefit Accessibility

approaches to the problems defined by the humanities and some social and behavioural sciences". A third problem is related to uncertainties. "Development scenarios should be judged not only in terms of their benefits, costs, accessibility, environmental impact and other easily quantifiable consequences, but also with respect to their inherent adaptability, flexibility and resilience in the face of unforeseen changes in behaviour and technology."

Table 11
Summary comparison of four regional development case studies

Region	Main economic character-istics	Main develop-ment problems	Main collab-orators	Main methods and models
Notec, Central Poland	Agricultural region	Shortage of water, out-migration	Central- and regional-level planners, water-resource experts	Simplified system of regional models, linked to elaborate agriculture and water-supply models
Silistra, Northern Bulgaria	Agricultural region	Slow growth in the basic agriculture sector	Central-level planners, various research institutes in Sofia	Linked models of agriculture, water-supply industry, etc., and breakdown models
South-western Skåne, Southern Sweden	Specializes in agri-culture, the food indus-try, and the chemical industry	Rather slow growth, spe-cialization in protected industries, land-use conflicts	Regional Planning Office of South-western Skåne (SSK), University of Lund (water problems), Swedish Council for Building Research	Hierarchical system with emphasis on multi-objective land-use models
Tuscany, Central Italy	Specializes in the textile and leather in-dustry, and tourism	Vulnerable position in the world economy, ex-posed to competition	Regional economic planners in Florence, research workers at the National Research Council, Rome	Inter-national and inter-regional trade models of main industrial sectors, and labour-market models

d)   Policy analysis of development

Policy analysis is a recently evolved stage of systems analysis.
Miser and Quade (1986) and Johnston and Clark (1982) describe the
basic concepts and methods of policy analysis applied to rural
development.   They observe "that the rural poor have often failed to
benefit - indeed have sometimes even suffered - from the development
effort", and recognize the need better to understand what was going
on in development.   Their answer to this need is their overview of
key issues, the wide constraints, the feasible opportunities and the
main priorities of development debates, seeking complementarities
among them.   They then attempt to rethink the "development mess" in
terms of policy analysis based on debates about rural development.
Policy analysis attempts to turn messes into problems.   To render
this transformation easier, the authors propose a "three-pronged
approach" which simultaneously emphasizes programmes for production,
consumption and organization and which ensures adaptive strategies
for policy-makers.   Figure   9 concisely communicates the conceptualizations based on the three components, resulting in rural
well-being measured in terms of "per capita consumption of goods and
services".

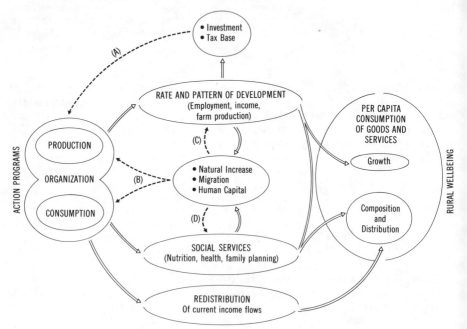

Figure 9 - The determinants of rural well-being

Note : Heavy solid arrows denote direct effects ; light solid
arrows, indirect effects ; and dotted arrows, major feedback.

2.2 Systems analysis applied to the countryside

Zaslavskaya's (1981) paper acquaints us with the experiences of a
research team which applied the systems approach to the study of a
large societal and territorial community and a large rural region
within the West Siberian countryside. This area needed to be
treated as a whole in its nature, operation and development.
At the time of the research project, the West Siberian countryside
was already a region of highly accelerated development, with great
inmigration, and proliferating workplaces in industry, construction
and transport. The main source of labour was drawn from the sur-
rounding rural areas, which caused depletion of trained rural
labour. The research team studied the factors explaining this
migration and methods for its control. Detailed studies included :

-    the quantitative parameters of rural migration ;
-    the demographic and social composition of cross flows ;
-    laws governing migration ;
-    economic, social and demographic factors affecting migration ;
-    local and societal interests in controlling migration.

It was discovered that almost all social and economic developmental factors, such as societal reproduction, education, living
conditions, leisure and the like, were responsible for the extraordinary migration from rural regions. A traditional approach
proved insufficient for the study of this particular migratory
phenomenon and a systems approach became necessary.
The system-nature of the countryside was conceived with a
socio-economic character, manifested in the vital activity of the
rural population. Its components were therefore "quite naturally
specified as spheres of this activity aimed at performing relatively
independent functions" in the process of social reproduction.
Specific goals, methods and results were ascribed to each function.
The research team identified seven types of component within
the countryside, and each type had a specific part-system within the
whole. These were as follows :

1.   social production ;
2.   personal subsidiary plots ;
3.   the sphere of demographic reproduction (the family) ;
4.   the sphere of education and further training ;
5.   reproduction and protection of the environment ;
6.   the sphere of material consumption and daily life ;
7.   the sphere of intellectual consumption and leisure.

The output of each component-type contributes to the operation
of the others. Thus, for example, the income generated in material
production becomes the main source of development of non-productive
(sic!) spheres of the countryside, and so on. Within the countryside, these component-types therefore support one another and create
the conditions both for the functioning of other components and for
the fulfilment of the countryside's external tasks set by society as

a whole. Not only could the countryside be compartmentalized into the component-types mentioned above, but other societal-territorial entities such as cities and regions could be divided into the above components.

The body-components described and their interrelationships with the countryside determine the patterns which govern the operation and development of the entities studied. The following separate themes were studied :

a)   patterns and prospects for socio-economic development of social production in the countryside ;
b)   patterns and prospects for the modernization of subsidiary personal plots ;
c)   patterns and prospects for demographic development in the countryside.

In the description of the countryside's component-types a general formalized ordering scheme was applied. A component-type can be interpreted in terms of the blocks of formal organizations and of people's activities with respect to their social roles.

In the component-types for "social production", the agricultural, industrial, construction and transport organizations together represented the first block, and their personnel the second. Each block was subdivided into functional elements :

-   the agent (i.e. actor, worker) ;
-   the object (i.e. expected result) ;
-   the means ;
-   the methods ;
-   the results of activity.

These functional elements were characteristic both of the activities of organizations and of people. After analysing each component-type in terms of these functional elements, and making explicit their system-nature, "contradictions and disproportions of development could be studied" which might disturb not only the system of component-types but that of the countryside and of society as a whole.

All these formalizations, as ordering schemes, can be taken as the model language of systems technique. It helps not only to analyse the operational and developmental features and to identify problems, but, more important, to synthetize the fragmentary images of analysis.

In the framework of this research project, the "patterns governing the development of the main countryside element and their prospect" were studied, not separately, but in the context of mutual interaction between elements, and between the countryside and society.

Zaslavskaya describes the special types of data collected for this research through the systems approach. Very relevant and interrelated data were required, representing sociological and statistical aspects of the nature of the countryside. The statistical data did not, however, adequately reflect certain processes of rural societal development and special information was therefore collected for the research work.

A particular problem which emerged at the outset was the decision concerning the boundaries of the countryside and its system. Two criteria were applied in searching for the answer : (a) the fact that the population was mainly employed in agriculture ; and (b) the territorial community (locality) in question was part of a rural area. Definition of boundaries adjusting to (a) was used by economists, and to (b) by ethnographers and sociologists. The totality of the various rural communities to be studied depended on the accepted definition. The researchers were aware of the distorting impact of any overemphasized criterion. They therefore endeavoured to find pragmatic points of view for identifying the system-boundaries : "the social entity defined by sectoral criterion is losing its integrity with time, being, in effet, absorbed into a broader system, i.e. the rural locality which is more constant and may therefore justifiably be identified with the concept of the countryside as a relatively autonomous system".

2.3 Developmental programmes through a systems approach

Referring to the previous section, we should underline that systems analysis is one possible systems approach. Even within systems analysis there are different interpretations. Although the words 'systems' and 'analysis' are clearly defined and when separate have about the same meaning in all languages, when they are joined together in the form of 'systems analysis' uniformity disappears. Many scientists interpret systems analysis as the analysis of systems - an attempt to describe and explain the system-nature of complex organismic units, that is, as the act or process of studying a unit (system, such as a business, manufacturing plant, telephone network, or physiological function) in order to define its purposes and discover how it works. For others, it means general systems theory or systems science. A few scientists even define systems analysis as systematic analysis. It is hard to think of any analysis being other than systematic.

In certain other fields, such as business, computers or psychology, systems analysis has even more specialized meanings. Most commonly, however, for most of the policy research community systems analysis is interpreted as a guide to decision-making.

The concept of Soft Systems Methodology, introduced by Checkland (1981) is another approach to systems analysis. A whole series of other approaches could be listed, especially among those which were dominant in the 1970s. From among these, we shall give a brief description of the so-called Rand-type systems analysis, or more precisely the most widely used systems technology, the Planning-Programming-Budgeting System (PPBS).

This 'technology' is a good example of project management in various American development programmes in the 1960s, internationally introduced in the 1970s (Chartrand, 1971). In the Soviet Union, the 'object-programme-method' emerged as an analogous systems technology for project management. In the mid-1960s, the United

States Congress became aware of interlocking social and community problems and the imperative need for effective policies and programmes. The potential of systems technology for solving these non-defense, non-space public problems was examined and later introduced. It was a nation-wide activity to launch a programme on systems technologies, and two kinds of concept received attention : the PPBS and specific problem-oriented system development activities (Full Opportunity, Small Business, Technology Transfer, Pollution, etc.).

In this context, systems technology refers to the application of scientific tools and techniques to the analysis and design of decision-making, information-handling or product-preparation functions. The merging of traditional problem-solving procedures with the flexibility and exactitude of innovative man-machine techniques is featured.

The systems approach, in that context :

-    is a body of highly developed capabilities for the solution of complex problems ;
-    looks at problems through their interrelationships in contrast to the more traditional view, which only sees large problems through their separate parts ;
-    discards the trial and error method, and does not solely rely on the inductive method (i.e. gathering all the facts and then analysing them), since the very data chosen can limit the view of the problem and thus restrict the number of possible solutions ; and
-    uses the inductive approach to gather and analyse information while giving paramount importance to the deductive process.

It is important to point out once again that systems analysis is only one element of the systems approach.

The PPBS system features four distinctive characteristics :

1.   it focusses on identifying the fundamental objectives of the Government and relates all activities to these, regardless of organizational placement ;
2.   future implications are explicitly identified ;
3.   all pertinent costs are considered ; and
4.   systematic analysis of alternatives is carried out. This is the crux of PPBS. It involves (a) identification of government objectives, (b) explicit systematic identification of alternative methods of carrying out the objectives, (c) estimation of the total cost implications of each alternative, and (d) estimation of the expected results of each alternative.

While there were cases of procedural and attitudinal impediments to change, the diverse components gradually integrated the systems approach into many facets of their operations. Attention was given at the highest levels to ways in which the decision-making function could be refined and upgraded, and the intricacies of the evolving man-machine system were examined continuously.

After PPBS had been in operation for a sufficient period of time to assess its strengths and shortcomings, the decision was made to place PPBS in operation in all major executive agencies and establishments. This approach penetrated the whole field of management, including development programme management, and is still also dominant in international development agencies.

The tools and methods applied in systems analysis depend on the level of the given problem. Global level systems analysis needs different instruments to those used at the local level. The list of tools overlaps, of course, in part but there are also specificities characterizing their use at given levels, and depending on whether they are used in a top-downwards or bottom-upwards approach.

An example of techniques used in regional analysis, for instance, is listed below (Chatterji, 1981) :

1. Location theory and comparative cost analysis
2. Regional demography
3. Regional and urban historical analysis
4. Economic and related urban growth theories
5. Regional and interregional social accounting and intergovernmental transfers
6. Regional and interregional input-output models
7. Interregional programming and other optimization techniques
8. Industrial and urban complex analysis
9. Interregional multiplier and business cycle analysis
10. Central place theories and application of classification techniques, such as factor analysis and discriminant analysis to analyse regional problems
11. Spatial regularity models
12. Regional systems and simulation
13. Regional econometric modelling
14. Interregional general equilibrium theory with political, social, economic and ecological variables
15. Spatial organization theory and graph theory applied to regional problems
16. Nearest-neighbour approach. Point distribution, pattern recognition and application of mathematics of topology to point distribution, remote sensing and other abstract models
17. Regional allocation of resources within a fixed time horizon
18. Survey methods in regional planning, problems of implementation
19. Transportation studies and diffusion models
20. Housing and rent studies
21. General areas of management of public systems, such as hospitals, educational administration, and the like
22. Regional and interregional energy modelling
23. Entropy and its application
24. Fuzzy systems and their application
25. Catastrophe theory and its relevance to regional decline
26. Statistical ecology
27. Application of mathematical biology to regional growth
28. Application of conflict management to regional systems
29. Regional grouping of nations
30. Multinational corporations and regional growth.

Conclusions

The examples from applications of systems analysis and the systems approach were selected to illustrate the main results and the basic strengths and weaknesses of these results, and to suggest some possible further progress. One might wonder how they derive from the triple contextual framework and to what degree the images of integrated development through the systems approach are adequate for three-phased planned work. Important conclusions are to be found in the answers to these queries.

1.   The method of applying the systems approach and its ordering schemes to integrated development cannot be fixed, but is ever-changing together with the natural and historical alterations of the developing phenomena, and with the understanding of these phenomena. In selecting the approach, the relevant, rational and value judg-ments, interests, ideas in vogue, ideologies, etc., play a de-terminant role which should be borne in mind. (See Kiss, Mayon-White (1985) on cultural and professional filtering mechanisms and the problem of perception.) In the TVA and Bratsk-Ilimsk examples, one can easily perceive that initially only a very small proportion of the total object-sphere was qualified as relevant for planning work. In time, an increasing number of components, differentiated aspects and interrelationships were recognized as non-negligeable in planned work, especially in planning, policy-making and decision-making. Earlier, planners considered mainly natural resources, industrial and agricultural production, manpower, transport and basic economic aspects. Gradually societal and environmental com-ponents and aspects have also appeared, perhaps with greater relevance than before. During its 40 years' history, the TVA has undergone complete metamorphosis. At the outset, the functions of the region were manifold and equally ranked. Today the most im-portant function is the power supply. The farm system has also changed because of a shift in relevance. It is also important to note that TVA is of decreasing importance in the management of development in this region ; many outside factors influence the region's alteration, such as taxation, relationship with banks, etc. The system of management must be transformed to cope with these alterations. All these changes would be difficult to manage without the use of systems techniques and systems analysis.
    The case of Bratsk-Ilimsk is similar. As the regions and the rational and value-judgments changed, systems techniques have also had to be modified.

2.   Settlements, especially the urban regions, were considered by urbanists and planners in various ways, which often gave deeper insight into the nature of complex human settlements, towns and urban regions. Experience in urban development has, however, shown that the life and dominance of such pan-ideas are very short in the mental sphere, but long in their concrete consequences. The order-ing schemes of the systems approach combined with integrated development are by no means foolproof, but the very attractive pitfalls of one-sidedness can be recognized and avoided. No unique,

revolutionary new idea in vogue can help solve settlement problems, but rather an ever deepening understanding of the organic, historical and inherited nature and unevolved potentials of settlements. Albegov *et al.* (1982) try to transform these experiences into considerations of how to build adequate models for regional development, not only for planners, but for policy-makers. They suggest some improvements, such as co-operation between policy-makers and modellers ; complementing hard mathematical models with human-societal representations ; and applying the flexible applicability of models and methods to uncertainties and unforeseen changes.

3.   Systems analysis offers common ordering schemes for planners, modellers, policy- and decision-makers, who have different tasks and positions in the division of labour within the planning framework. Although there is a common conceptual basis, in practice political decision-makers do not necessarily think in the same very detailed ordering scheme which a modeller uses. Johnston and Clark (1982) explain why they have raised a three-pronged construct from among the ordering schemes : the production-consumption-organization triad. If at the outset of policy making this triad orders the considerations concerning the mapping of the 'developmental mess' into ordered plan-images with policy implications, the detailed considerations will be more consistent. It is not rare that in images of the developmental mess, 'organization' fades almost entirely from view, and 'consumption' is given increased importance. Such cases are to be found in centrally planned economies. Although we consider the three-pronged construct to be necessary, it is not sufficient.

4.   The two case studies on the TVA and the West-Siberian countryside seem to be most compatible with the contextual frame proposed in the Introduction. Both describe the developing object-sphere conceptually in terms of systems-nature. Although the modellers use ordering schemes and models which have a statistical basis, the system-images have primacy over them. One might also say that the statistical models take their meaning from the conceptual models in terms of the systems approach, and not inversely. We are convinced that these combinations can be more consciously and consistently used. The two studies have only very fragmentarily exploited their possibilities.

5.   Both case studies and the systems approach apply a certain image of systems features. Components may be recognized within each image which are important to integrated development. Although the outlines of these components are not as sharp as we have tried to make them, certain component-images may be identified as follows :

i)   an image of the object-sphere which develops. Its members are population, the natural and artificial environment, organizations, institutions, etc., distintinguishing the initial, intermediate and final state of each ;

ii)   an image of the worker-sphere, which transforms the developing
      object-sphere through planned-spontaneous implementing work.
      The relation of the worker-sphere to the object-sphere may be
      asymmetric and/or self-reflective.
         The members of the worker-sphere may be individuals,
      organizations, institutions, certain members of the population,
      sub-cultures, etc. ;
iii) images of both types of development : development or pro-
      gressive transformation of existing objects, and development or
      'coming into existence' of objects ;
iv)   images of those members of society who live together with
      implemented results of development, and who may be called the
      user-sphere, if it is prepared to receive the results of
      development ;
v)   images of administrative organizations which are responsible
      for the planned and co-ordinated operation and development of
      each of the three spheres (object-, worker- and user-spheres) ;
vi)   images of process or planned developmental work which ex-
      plicitly represent at least the following :
      -    the changes in objects or the unfolding of both types of
           developmental results ;
      -    the workers, their abilities and activities, and control-
           ling laws and rules by which they are governed ;
      -    resources and their distribution and allocation ;
      -    the controllable, the uncontrollable but predictable, the
           unexpected-spontaneous phenomena among those mentioned
           above, and the uncertainties and risks ;
      -    the three basic phases of planned work : the preliminary
           and planning work, implementation work, the phase of
           living with results, and specific decision points along
           the three phases.
      These elements of planned work are usually represented not
      as a list, but organically ordered in space, time and syn-
      chronous-diachronous order. It is also to be noted that these
      co-ordinated elements are also interpreted in terms of problem-
      situations. This image of the problem-situation has proved
      more suitable than the traditional plan-image in making ex-
      plicit the differences in rational and value-laden judgments
      about problem-situations, and in treating them as variations
      for developmental goals and strategies. When these variations
      are conceived, the chance of finding acceptable variations
      (through societal participation) will be much greater than in
      other ways ;
vii) images which co-ordinate the foregoing component-images to some
      extent, even if these images are not very homogenously and
      consistently applied for each component and for every inter-
      relationship.

     These component-images can also be found in the practical tools
of the systems approach and systems analysis. They have been found
helpful in understanding how practical systems approaches satisfy
the requirements of our triple contextual frame. Without more
thorough examination, we may state the following :

a) It would have been desirable, had these component-images of systemic features occurred in the case studies and in the practical systems approach and systems analysis not only separately but in co-ordinated form. The examples discussed in Part II satisfy these two expectations rather inconsistently. Some focus on the object sphere (human settlement study, regional development modelling). Others mainly emphasize the aspect of planned developmental work (PPBS, programme-management techniques). Numerous branches of the techniques of systems analysis mainly grasp the aspects of problem-situation and problem-solving, and within these, more especially decision-situations, and try to represent the object sphere by representations which are more suitable to political decisions. The cases of the TVA and the Siberian countryside can be qualified as the most advanced regarding the satisfaction of the application of component-images separately and together.

b) It would be desirable for the two kinds of development, mentioned in component-image iii), to be conceptually and practically discriminated, and if they occurred in less confused form. Although most cases of integrated development involve both, we must be aware of their quite different nature which must not be mistaken. We may conclude that it would be very helpful if development planners had planning tools and methods to suit the two kinds of development.

c) The conceptualization and representation of the system-nature or organic character of an object sphere is not satisfactory. It would be necessary to understand integrated developmental features through the systems approach as well, and then apply this knowledge to practical plan-images composed of at least component-images i)-vii).

d) We have observed that the three phases of planned work are emphasized very differently in developmental literature, especially the themes of Part II. The planning phase is most strongly stressed. The implementation is referred to on occasion superficially, but is usually neglected. The third phase is also generally neglected, except in the case of the TVA and Bratsk-Ilimsk studies. We must recognize the importance of three-phased planned work, and elaborate techniques which are compatible with the requirements of the three phases. Continuous planning using this type of reflexion, but only fragmentarily.

We should like to close our study with some ideas on more advanced conceptualization of our contextual frame. Part III proposes a possible ordering scheme.

PART III - AN ORDERING SCHEME FOR THE CONTEXTUAL FRAME

For planned work, we use the symbol of the 'worker-object' unit. It is the object which changes during the process of integrated development and the nature of which also very strongly determines its developmental nature. The worker can only adjust himself to this nature. This statement is invariant to both the asymmetric and self-reflective relations between worker and object. In Part I, the object was the focus of study. Part II concentrated mainly on the worker, in the sense that it is he who must understand the nature of the object-sphere in order to plan its changes and transform it, or to contribute to its natural changes with progressive outcome. Concrete examples have demonstrated the activity of the worker in the preliminary phase and during planning, and the use of the systems approach and systems analysis in this work. Part III suggests an ordering scheme for the worker-object unit which preserves the ordering strengths of the contextual frame and explicitly represents integrated development, but in a reinterpreted form. Before discussing the ordering theme, we may quote Perroux' thoughts on the matter :

> "The point is that development has to do with man as subject and agent, and with human societies and their aims and obviously evolving objectives... a series of new developments could be expected, conditioned by successive variations in human values and the way they have historically translated into deeds and actions..." (Perroux, 1981)

New development sets out to be global, integrated and endogenous. For this new development, the "foundations of economic thought" must be reconsidered with emphasis "on the relationship between people and groups of people, not on the relationship between people and wealth..."

We may think in roughly quantifiable features such as growth, development, advance and progress. Growth means the increase in the size of a unit, usually a country, changes in the proportions and in the relationships between parts within a whole.

"Development presupposes dealings between people in the form of exchanges of goods and services and of information and symbols." In the economic context, it can be grasped in three frames : (a) in the linking up of the parts of a whole : branches, industries, regions, enterprises, material, infrastructures, communication are connected by networks of flows ; (b) in the interactions of the parts, and actions - in the language of systems analysis - need to be regulated ; (c) in evolutionary structures, all forms of human resources promise some chance of gaining in effectiveness and quality. These three frames may also indicate anti-developmental changes, as in the case of developing countries : defects in the linking up of the parts of the whole ; distorted interaction between stronger and weaker sections ; and wastage of human resources. Any development policy consists in (a) promoting the dynamic factors in development, just as in human life ; demographic trends and quality of a population ; capacity for invention and innovation, to renovate institutions from family to production organizations, from property laws to market controls and distribution ; (b) providing the material facilities and information services. There are dangers in 'growth without development', and in 'development without growth'.

Advance and progress consist in such phenomena as increase and improvement of real income, greater security and freedom, conditions for education and training, and general extension of benefits.

These examples are very voluntarily selected. They can represent no more than conceptual keys for a précis. Without their contextual background, the most they can render are intuitive insights. However, the quotations might bear witness to what we have perceived as relevant among Perroux' thoughts.

In Perroux' interpretation, the systems features are less overt, the desirable features of future development he enumerates are richer, the policy-charge is stronger than in our study. Nevertheless, we have discovered convergences and compatibilities between his and our conceptualizations.

A referential frame in studying integrated development

Any society is able to reproduce not only its members such as human beings but its different kinds of societal entities such as family, kinship, educational institutions, different settlements, and is able to reproduce its culture, ethnicity, etc. All these reproductions are existentially important for the survival of any society throughout the generations.

It may be observed that many considerations concerning planning discuss the reproduction of society only in statistically interpreted aspects. These aspects are only quantitative, and in a very narrow sense. Those national plans which are confined only to such countable aspects of societal reproduction, and are insensitive to other qualitative and very complex reproducible results and entities after their implementation, surely damage the societal reproduction ability. The planned results of any integrated development should contain the complex qualitative results of societal reproduction and not only those which are quantifiable. In other words, societal reproduction primarily determines the results that should emerge from integrated development.

Societal reproduction depends on the reproduction ability of the natural environment. If the reproduction of the environment is disturbed, it will sooner or later be dangerous to the reproduction of the different societal entities. Any integrated development should therefore be fitted to the primary determinants of the reproduction of the natural environment.

If we consciously connect the idea of integrated development with the reproduction of society and the natural environment, the systems approach becomes indispensable. Sensitivity to organic features cannot be absent from planners' images delivered by the systems approach.

The results of the reproduction of society and of the natural environment appear as successive generations in both spheres. Certain definite events or life-phases can be identified during the life of any societal entity and of entities of the natural environment - birth, growth, maturity, old age, death, to mention only the most important life events. This series of events has a sequential character. Early events cannot be replaced by subsequent events. From the point of view of reproduction, different generations live in different phases of their life-span development. Planners of integrated development must be sensitive to these differentiations in life-span events and to the entities, the nature and alterations of which are strongly interrelated with the phases of their life-span. We may say that in any life-span, the states and manifestations of entities (both in society and the environment) represent prime determinants to which planned integrated development must be adjusted. Here we must reckon with the manner in which societal entities interact with environmental entities.

Based on the above considerations, we propose that the two interacting spheres of societal and environmental reproduction should serve as the most comprehensive framework for any planning of integrated development.

Many observations support this rational proposal, which holds a strong value-change. In an intuitive approach, a great number of societal and environmental problems can be explained by the fact that this proposed referential frame has been rather neglected in planned integrated development. There are national plans which cover at best one generation, mainly based on countable relations (population, labour, etc.). But health care plans, cultural plans, agricultural plans, environmental plans which cover several generations, especially combined with aspects of social discount for the same time-span are hardly ever seen. Mankind is just beginning to realize the harmful consequences of neglecting the framework of twofold reproduction. In future, planners may perhaps learn to think in terms of several societal and environmental generations, and within the twofold reproduction framework. Conservative, retrogressive and progressive tendencies in both types of reproduction are equally possible.

Integrated development in terms of polygenesis

In socio-economic planning practice, the term development is used in roughly two senses. One refers to existing entities which alter themselves to become other entities. The other refers to entities which come into being, or bring others into existence.

In the first case, the alterations are progressive and come about mainly by adaptation, gaining in effectiveness and quality (Perroux, 1981). The duration of development in time may cover the life-span of only one, or of several generations. Long-lived institutions, culture, ethnicity, production organizations, settlements, towns, regions, etc., usually develop in this way.

In the second case, progression is relative. Entities which have recently come into being may have greater carriers than older ones. Products of R&D, investments in industrial, agricultural, new branches and organizations of technology, etc., develop in this way.

In reality, mainly in very complex entities, both variations are mixed. The mixed form is one type among integrated development. They must not, however, be confused. Problem-situations in some cases are very different. Planning tasks also differ, especially if we think in the frame of three-phased planned work. Co-operation with nature also requires very different interactions in the case of one and other kind of development.

All this suggests that conceptualizations of development should be reconsidered, because it would seem that the use of this term is charged with misleading connotations. Other terms can be found which promise to be more favourable because they have scientific connotations which emphasize their reference to organismic phenomena. Such is the concept of genesis. (See also Buckley (1967) ; Novak (1982) ; Waddington (1969).) Genesis in common language refers to something which comes into being.

In the sphere of societal entities, many particular genesis-like processes can be perceived (range of events, series of sequential states, ordered synchronous-diachronous alterations in the body and its system). We have chosen some very important examples. Each genesis orders some type or work - the work of a human being or of nature - and the outcome is a living or inanimate but organismic entity. The process and the range of events along a genesis are ordered by different 'agents', to which the term genesis refers.

1. **Ergono-genesis** - The prime determinant is the sequence of alteration in the worker's object from its initial state to its final state, the order of the worker's activated abilities, the sequence of actions on the object, and interactions with the relevant environment (natural, socio-economic). This kind of genesis can be identified in innumerable cases of human work, such as manufacture and mechanized work, natural resource mining and industrial processing work, industrial and agricultural work, chemotechnical and biotechnical work, educational and social work, material and spiritual (information processing) work, energy transformation work, managerial and governmental work, health maintenance and curative work, scientific and everyday-life information processing work, etc.

2. **Epistemo-techno-genesis** - State-sequence in unfolding the worker's ability. It begins from the lack of knowledge about the end result and technology of how to realize it, and finishes at the ability and skill (in ancient Greek : τεκηνε) to produce the end result in a special way. Each ability can produce a special result : scientific discovery and intuitive insights, from which inventions are realized. This kind of genesis may be manifested on the basis of everyday life experience, or in the frame of scientific innovation (R&D and production use).

3. **Idea-genesis** - A sequential range of events with three phases, corresponding to three-phased planned work. Plans may be traditions inherited through several generations (images about means, tools, families, communities and the way of living together in them). But

plans may also be new intellectual constructs. When work starts on intuition of a planlike image, many trial and error steps are necessary.

4.   **Anthropo-genesis** - A sequential range of events from pregnancy (embryo-genesis), through the birth of a human being, and along the whole process of his life-span development, his whole onthogenesis - education, socialization, cultural evolution, proliferating everyday-life experience, etc. - up to the end of life.

5.   **Organo-genesis** or **socio-genesis** - A sequential range of events beginning with separate individuals. The mature organization is unfolded and built up from these individuals who have mature abilities to live and work together, within the organization and its relevant environment. Finally that organization reaches the end of its existence. Mechanistic and organismic organizations have different socio-geneses.

6.   **Genesis of exchange** - Sequence of events in the exchange process between producer and user in the frame of the division of labour and distribution of goods. The trade-chain between producer and user may be very long, with many mediating stages. Two flows (goods and money), opposite to each other, belong to the essential nature of exchange, and to the range of events of this genesis. The latter is not connected only to material goods. Psychology has observed the exchange of emotional gestures.

7.   **Genesis of economizing** - A peculiarly ordered sequential range of events in the distribution and allocation of resources, and in the acceptance and use of benefits. Costs and benefits take on pecuniary form in only a very tiny fragment of economizing situations. In the sphere of different societal entities, they can best be interpreted only by intuition and represented by non-numerical value-charged images. We expect the economizing concept to be extended to untouched areas and longer time-spans than are usual today.

8.   **Genesis health or recovery** - Ordered events in the life process to remain healthy or to strengthen the ability to remain healthy. Another range of events in the life process in becoming ill, followed by the process of health care from diagnosis and cure to rehabilitation.

9.   **Genesis of peace** - Peculiar range of events, states of unfolding capabilities and activities to maintain peace ; or in accepting and ending hostility.

10.   **Genesis of societal and environmental reproduction** - The concept of this twofold genesis is based upon the intuitive hypothesis that if we made the genesis-like features in the images of reproduction explicit, then we should understand their nature better. We suppose that the proposed comprehensive referential

framework for integrated development can be interpreted in terms of the nine types of genesis discussed above.

The ten kinds of genesis proposed are only those which appear in considerations about integrated development. All kinds of development may be interpreted in terms of these geneses. For example, the statement that integrated development means "integrating the educational, scientific, technological, social, economic developmental processes" can be mapped into genesis-interpretation in the following way :

a)   First one identifies the imagined goals of development, and the nature of the spheres to which they belong. The main stages of their realization and the order in which the stages of different processes are connected to the stages of other processes are then clarified in terms of ergono-genesis.
b)   In cases where the final result of a development is in human individuals (or other societal entities, organizations, etc.), the ergono-genesis must be combined with anthropo-genesis and socio-genesis.
c)   The economic relations and processes can be introduced by images in terms of the genesis of economizing.
d)   When preliminary scientific and other research is needed for any genesis in one of its stages, the ordering scheme of epistemo-techno-genesis will be adequate.
e)   When making explicit the concommitants of the division of labour, the processes and stages of the genesis of exchange must be combined with other genesis-images discussed above.
f)   All these images can be taken as elements of the plan-images necessary in idea-genesis which can also be unfolded.
g)   All these images in terms of genesis - polygenesis - can be interpreted in terms of the genesis of soceital and environmental reproduction and in the frame of adequate time-span perspectives of the generations involved.

It is easy to see that all the elements discussed in the foregoing sections concerning the planning of integrated development through the systems approach can be interpreted in terms of polygenesis.
The situation of integrated development in various countries is usually characterized by different development patterns. This kind of problem-situation can also be described in terms of polygenesis, i.e. by genesis-patterns.
Here we may refer to Hilgard's (19..) results. He has observed that man is capable of thinking, processing information, drawing conclusions and planning according to different cognitive structures, and the use of these structures becomes automatic after training, while the cognitive-emotive control system separates competing structures and manages competition between them. Interests, values, preferences are responsible for the type of cognitive structure chosen - paradigms, ordering schemes, theories and techniques - rather than rational considerations. The usual schemes of integrated development have their own ordering strength. The

polygenesis schemes proposed are also useful, but their ordering and heuristic strength seems higher than that of usual schemes.

The contextual framework in genesis interpretation

At this point we may summarize the kind of contextual framework that is desirable in enquiries into the domains of this study. So far, three basic concepts have represented the contextual framework. The introduction of the empirical composite-concept of polygenesis is our major contribution to studies on integrated development and its planning through the systems approach. This contribution is at the same time part of the review of the state-of-the-art. Our proposed conception is as follows :

1. It would be desirable for the reproduction of society and the natural environment to be the most comprehensive referential framework in any study and plan of integrated development, and for the time-span to be extended to a greater number of generations. This means that twofold reproduction would be the referential framework for the contextual frame.

2. The images and plan-images of integrated development and development patterns should be reinterpreted in terms of polygenesis and genesis-patterns. The concept of planning was conceived separately as idea-genesis, and the referential framework has also been linked to genesis-interpretation.

3. Descriptions about the contextual frame with its referential framework give an account of how we interpreted the subject of our study.

PART IV - CONCLUSIONS AND RECOMMENDATIONS

In our interpretation, integrated development means that national, regional and local planners are highly aware of the organismic nature of societal and environmental entities. Integrated development can only be applied to those which preserve their organismic nature rather than destroying it. All efforts to replace obsolete plan-images - which render planners unaware of organic development - with more adequate plan-images are justified. The review of the state-of-the-art of conceptualization and practical application shows that many valuable results have been obtained by replacing obsolete images and methods. This process has, however, only just begun.

We therefore recommend that more advanced studies on concrete development phenomena be carried out. Theoretical foundations should make organismic developmental features more overt and at the same time help reveal features which have so far remained covert. Practical and concrete cases are indispensable because complex phenomena such as developing regions and countries can only be dealt with in a way similar to the practical method of action research. It would also be fruitful to study and compare concrete national and regional plans on the same theoretical basis.

5.1 Conclusions

It will already be apparent that the major conclusions emerging from this study concern the need for frameworks within wider perceptions and a more useful view of development. The summary of the state-of-the-art with respect to integrated development revealed several reasons for the lack of effective action or change in response to earlier studies of integrated development. This conclusion does not deny the value of these studies in drawing attention to the inter-relationship between these problems. However, only the more recent studies in the systems analysis mould have had a policy orientation. The Unesco *Second Medium-Term Plan* has a similar constructive orientation towards action.

Another conclusion concerns the distinction between those policy measures and actions which are designed to deal with the crises which emerge from world problems (e.g. famine from failure in food production) and those measures which are directed at creating conditions to prevent crises developing from the chronic states called world problems. The first category of disasters and crises are the indirect concern of Unesco, though other members of the United Nations family have a major and direct role in this area. Unesco does have an important and continuing role in the second category, especially in the field of education. The importance of this less visible activity should be emphasized. It is frequently overlooked by most people and ignored by the media, yet this study suggests that education has a fundamental role to play in increasing and broadening perceptions of developmental problems. This is coupled to the recognition that education is at present primarily directed at the next generation and not the present. In the present study striking evidence of this pattern of forward planning was revealed in the plans which are now being implemented in a number of developing countries. Such plans which form a central part of a country's economic and social policy are clearly a model which deserves close examination, despite some reservations about the use of these measures as a control instrument in economic planning.

Two other general conclusions emerged from this study. These have implications for development planning. The first of them concerns participation, and the second the use of Northern technology by the nations of the South. Neither is a new argument, but both bear reinforcement. The projects reported from different parts of the world refer to the explicit use of methodologies in designing strageties for community development by a nongovernmental agency. The projects involve the use of participative techniques to design and implement change on a local scale and start with training and education. Similar projects were reported by FAO and are being deployed under other programmes of the United Nations. It seems that if these practices were more widely adopted, then some of the worst features of inequalities might be removed in some areas.

The second conclusion concerning development planning is directed at the difficulty of achieving technology transfer (from North to South) without causing dualism and exacerbating inequalities in the importing nation. No prescription can be attempted here beyond a general conclusion that individual governments have a responsibility to recognize the risks associated with technology transfer and to devise policies for economic development which either minimize such risks or avoid them by alternative strategies. A great deal of useful work is already being done in this area but it is suggested that greater co-operation and integration might be encouraged.

The final major conclusion concerns two aspects of economic growth. The first is a rejection of economic growth as an adequate goal for human society. The second is placed in the context of development (in the economies of both North and South). It is argued that an alternative set of goals embodied in the concept of man as end result of development would be more desirable (Hajnal, Kiss, 1985).

All of the above conclusions and the following recommendations depend on a single general observation about the importance of process. In one sense many of the recommendations have been made by others on other occasions and in other places. As anyone could remark, 'the world is full of recommendations'. Similar conclusions were formulated in our earlier study on "World Problems and their Perceptions" (Kiss, Mayon-White, 1985). They reappear simply because efforts to put them into practice fail. The need to pay special attention to process and methodology is justified solely in terms of these earlier failures. Agreement still exists on the desirability of the activities proposed. The conditions to which these activities are directed deteriorate and do not improve. There are no perceptions which dismiss these conditions as unimportant and irrelevant. There is a growing agreement about their importance instead and the need to find new strategies for intervention. Attention to process and participation is one such strategy which emerges as most important from this study. Achieving it will involve quite different ways of working and new forms of consultation. In other circumstances it has been found that similar strategies are more expensive in terms of human resources and money, but in the long term yield greater benefits simply because their objectives are achieved.

5.2 Recommendations

The recommendations which follow from the conclusions are summarized below and each is then considered in more detail.

1. Increase the involvement of representatives from the countries of the Southern hemisphere.

2. Review the possibilities for sponsoring meetings of individuals and institutions engaged in studies of world problems.

3. Increase cross linkages between Unesco and other bodies in the United Nations structure in order to strengthen their activities, and to reduce the risk of duplication.

4. Initiate an education process on world problems and their perception.

5. Prepare and integrate teaching material for schools in all cultures on the perception and understanding of world problems.

6. Publish a summary of work in the area of report.

7. Review a range of methodologies appropriate for use in Unesco's Major Programme VIII.

8. Initiate a study of the role of the media in forming perceptions of integrated development problems (not detailed).

9. Review the policy goals of governments in relation to integrated development (not detailed).

10. Divert resources in Unesco's activities to support local integrated initiatives (not detailed).

5.2.1   Increase the involvement of representatives from the countries of the Southern hemisphere in order to develop (a) better understanding of the problems of interdependence and (b) alternative and pluralistic perceptions of development problems. Preference should be given to those institutions and individuals working in policy and action-oriented programmes which suggests that non-governmental organizations as well as government institutions should be considered.
    It is widely agreed that some features of development problems have special importance for the countries of the South and it is here that there exists a real need for improved exchanges of views in order to encourage better understanding of interdependence. Unesco's long experience with initiatives of this kind will be of considerable value here.

5.2.2   Review the possibilities for sponsoring meetings of individuals and institutions engaged in studies of development problems with a view to promoting better exchanges between the community of computer modellers and those individuals and groups working on different interpretations of development.

During the 1970s, IIASA sponsored a series of meetings on global modelling. At that time several groups in different parts of the world were engaged in constructing and running computer models which were of varying complexity, had different degrees of disaggregation, and were based on different simulation methods. The meetings enabled the various teams to exchange ideas and to learn more about the assumptions underlying the different models. For those actually engaged in modelling the experience was invaluable as is reflected in "Groping in the Dark" (Meadows, *et al.*, *op. cit.*). At the present time there are no regular meetings of this kind and some argue that the need still exists. However in the much changed climate of opinion in the 1980s, the authors do not consider it appropriate to consider an extension of such meetings. Instead it is proposed that a new arrangement be considered to promote exchanges between those groups and teams working on different perceptions and interpretations of development problems. There is a need to bring together developmentalists, economists, policy scientists, cosial anthropologists and others in order to promote a better understanding of the epiphenomenon of these problems.

Unesco would be an appropriate body to host such meetings, and locations outside Europe might be appropriate. Any such formal conferences would not need to take place more frequently than every two years.

5.2.3   Increase cross linkages between Unesco and other bodies in the United Nations structure in order to strengthen the value of their activities, to reduce the risk of duplication and to promote the effective deployment of resources to address carefully targeted problems and issues.

One of the difficult characteristics of world problems is that at a certain level everything is, or appears to be, connected to everything else. This then suggests that a response of an integrated nature is required. Experience reinforces the lesson that this is difficult to achieve in practice.

There is a range of liaison arrangements between the organizations of the United Nations family, and many projects rely on a high degree of co-ordination for their execution. It is proposed here that the structure and operation of these linkages might be examined in the light of Unesco's Major Programme VIII. The difficulty of ensuring that projects have the intended desirable efforts in the countries to which they are directed is considerable, and the examination should be directed at ways of improving systems for managing joint projects.

In carrying through this proposal, it is suggested that particular projects which are being executed in a collaborative manner might be examined to determine where risks of duplication exist, to determine how these are minimized. Because of the interconnected nature of development problems outlined above, it is thought likely that effective action on the whole web of problems, even at local levels, would be beyond the scope of individual agencies.

In carrying out this recommendation it is not anticipated that UN agencies would be involved directly at the local level. Instead it is expected that a framework for such meetings would be devised by Unesco and other agencies, in conjunction with the Member State concerned.

5.2.4   Initiate an education process on integrated development and its perception for a range of specific target groups which might include decision-makers in governments and corporations, and specialists in a range of technical disciplines.

Education is one of the most important of Unesco's activities and it is hoped that steps will be taken to ensure that this aspect of integrated development problems is channelled through the existing Unesco education programmes.   In this context the term is used to refer to education in all parts of the tertiary sector with special emphasis on those activities which fall under the heading of continuing education.   The following recommendation in this series deals with the needs of future generations in the primary and secondary sectors of education as a separate issue.   In the formal sectors of tertiary education this recommendation refers to the need to adapt the provision of courses to provide interdisciplinary studies on integrated development problems and their perceptions.   A range of issue topics is already explored in many institutions such as aspects of policy studies, development theory, applied systems, analysis, international law, etc.   Designing special integrative courses requires a somewhat different approach and it is here that the identification of the 'target group' becomes important.   Post-experience learning materials need to be tailored to fit their expected audiences.   Traditionally it has been assumed that adequate information is available through the press, television, radio and popular books, etc., to give people in these groups balanced perceptions of issues.   However, in the context of development problems the view has emerged that specially designed educational materials, such as distance learning courses in addition to materials for use in conventional settings, would be of considerable benefit.

Unesco could play a special role in this respect by producing pilot materials and by encouraging Member States to adopt similar practices.   In carrying through a recommendation of this kind it is expected that any project would involve collaboration with those institutions which already prepare and disseminate materials of this kind.

5.2.5   Prepare and integrate teaching materials for primary and secondary schools in all cultures on the perception and understanding of development problems, to meet the requirements of the different age groups of children involved.

In many countries, especially those with large conurbations, the problems of multicultural education are well recognized.   It is believed that in such settings the challenges of pluralism are accepted and in many cases well prepared educational materials designed to give children broader perceptions of multi-cultural and world problems already exist.   It is thought that such materials could provide a model which Unesco should develop through its existing education and liaison programmes. The proposed materials would specifically address the questions of perception and world problems in the manner outlined in the body of this report.

5.2.6   Publish a summary of work in the area of this report for circulation to the target groups identified above.

This specific suggestion refers to the present report and our former report (Kiss, Mayon-White, 1985), and is intended to emphasize the importance of perception as a process which sheds some light on the manner in which development problems are understood and tackled. The main target group for this report would be the other members of the UN family and Member States, and the exercise would need to be carried out in a manner designed to generate involvement and co-operation along the lines discussed earlier. This is thus not intended to be an independent activity, but one carried out in conjunction with some of the other recommendations.

5.2.7   Extend the review of systems methodologies with potential applications to Unesco's Major Programme VIII.

The need to develop a methodological framework for work in Major Programme VIII, and more especially subprogramme VIII.1.2, has been identified by Unesco. In this report, a number of tentative suggestions for the use of systems methodologies have been made. In carrying these ideas forward, it is recommended that a specific study be commissioned to review the existing methodologies which are appropriate to the Unesco project. Such a study sets itself the task of identifying, testing and developing an appropriate framework for use by Unesco. A study of this kind would require some direct involvement by Unesco in its testing and development phases.

SELECT BIBLIOGRAPHY

Aganbegyan, A.G., 1981. "Towards an integrated approach to research into development prospects of Siberia's productive forces", in A.G. Aganbegyan (ed.), *Planning and Projecting the Siberian Experience*, Mouton, The Hague.

Albegov, M., A.E. Anderson, and F. Snickars (eds.), 1982. *Regional Development Modeling : Theory and Practice*, IIASA, North Holland, Amsterdam.

Alechina, I., 1982. "The contribution of the United Nations system to formulating development concepts", in : *Different Theories and Practices of Development*, Unesco, Paris.

Aseniero, G. "Reflection of developmentalism : from development to transformation", in H. Addo, *et al., Development as Social Transformation*, Hodder & Stoughton, London.

Bach, R.L., 1982. "On the holism of a world system perspective", in T.K. Hopkins, and I. Wallerstein (eds.), *World System Analysis. Theory and Methodology*, Sage Publ., Beverly Hills.

Baltes, P.B., 1979. "Life-span Developmental Psychology : Some Converging Observations on History and Theory", in : *Life-span Development and Behavior*, Vol. 2, Academic Press, New York.

Banathy, B.H., 1986. "A systems view of development", paper presented to a Meeting of Experts on "Goals of Development", Unesco, Paris/Budapest, Hungary, 13-17 October 1986.

Berting, J., 1986. "Goals of development in developed countries", paper presented to a Meeting of Experts on "Goals of Development", Unesco, Paris/Budapest, Hungary, 13-17 October 1986.

Blair, H.W., 1986. "Approaches to integrated social development planning and implementation at the local level, *Regional Development Dialogue*, Vol. 7, No. 1, p. 31.

Breheny, M.J., and A.J. Hooper, 1985. *Rationality in Planning. Critical Essays on the Role of Rationality in Urban and Regional Planning*, Pion Ltd., London.

Buckley, W., 1967. *Sociology and Modern Systems Theory*, Prentice Hall, Englewood Cliffs, N.J.

Chartrand, R.L., 1971. *Systems Technology Applied to Social and Community Problems*, Spartan, New York.

Chatterji, M., 1984. "Techniques for analysis of urban-regional and resource management in developing countries", in M. Chatterji, *et al.* (eds.), *Spatial, Environmental and Resource Policy in the Developing Countries*, Gower, Aldershot.

Churchman, C.W., 1968. *The Systems Approach*, Dell, New York.

Checkland, P., 1981. *Systems Thinking, Systems Practice*, Wiley, Chichester.

Checkland, P., 1985. "The approach to plural rationality through soft systems methodology", in M. Grauer, M. Thomson and A.P. Wierzbicki (eds.), *Plural Rationality and Interactive Decision Processes*, Springer, Berlin.

Eckaus, R.S., 1984. "Some temporal aspects of development", *World Bank Stall Working Papers*, No. 626, The World Bank, Washington, D.C.

Encyclopaedia Britannica, 1974. "Macropaedia", Vol. 5 (a, b, c).

Friberg, M. and B. Hettne, 1985. "The greening of the world - Towards a non-deterministic model of global processes", in H. Addo, *et al. Development as Social Transformation*, Hodder & Stoughton, London.

Galtung, J., 19.. *Goals, Processes and Indicators of Development. A Project Description*, United Nations University, p. 1.

Galtung, J., R. Preiswerk, and M. Wemegah, 1982. "Development centred on human beings : Some West European perspectives", in : *Different Theories and Practices of Development*, Unesco, Paris.

Galtung, J., 1983. "Development of society and development of the person", paper presented to a Meeting of Experts on "Philosophical Investigation of the Fundamental Problems of Endogenous Development", Gabon.

Galtung, J., 1984. "On the dialectic between crisis and crisis perception", *International Journal of Comparative Sociology*, XXV, 1-2.

Ganapathy, R.S., 1986. "Methodologies for development planning : a critical review with special reference to social and cultural factors"; in : *Socio-economic Studies*, Vol. 12, Unesco, Paris.

Gelman, R., 1982. "Complexity in development and developmental studies", in W.A. Collins (ed.), *The Concept of Development*, Laurence Erlbaum, Hillsdale, N.J.

Giarini, O., 1985. "The consequences of complexity in economics", *United Nations University Newsletter*, Vol. 8, No. 3, May 1985.

Grabe, S., 1983. "Evaluation manual", *Socio-economic Studies*, Vol. 6, Unesco, Paris.

Gvishiani, J.M., 1984. "Materialist dialectics as a philosophical basis for systems research", in J.M. Gvishiani (ed.), *Systems Research - Methodological Problems*, Pergamon, Oxford.

Hajnal, A., 1981. *Knowledge, method and culture in the systems research movement. Notes on the Cavallo Report*, National Planning Office, Institute of Economic Planning, Budapest.

Hajnal, A., 1985. "Genesis patterns of societal entities. An approach to the study of discontinuities in social changes", paper presented at the IIASA Task Force Meeting on "Discontinuities in Social Changes", Budapest, 10-14 June 1985.

Hajnal, A., 1985. *Health Care in National Economic Planning*, National Planning Office, Institute of Economic Planning, Budapest (in Hungarian).

Hajnal, A., and I. Kiss, 1985. *Altering Approaches to World Problems : Emphasis and Trends*. Background considerations to the Unesco-IIASA study, prepared for the Task Force Meeting on "World Problems and their Perceptions", Unesco-IIASA Project, Budapest, Hungary, 25 February-1 March 1985.

Hilgard, E.R., 19.. *Neodissociation theory of multiple control systems*.

Hill, R., and P. Mattessich, 1979. "Family Development Theory and Life-Span Development" in : *Life-Span Development and Behavior*, Vol. 2, Academic Press, New York.

Hopkins, T.K., I. Wallerstein and associates, 1982. "Patterns of development of the modern world-system", in T.K. Hopkins, and I. Wallerstein (eds.), *World-system Analysis. Theory and Methodology*, Sage Publ., Beverly Hills.

Hultsch, D.F., and J.K. Plemons, 1979. "Life-events and life-span development", in : *Life-span development and behavior, op. cit.*, Vol. 2.

Johnston, B.F., and W.C. Clark, 1982. *Redesigning Rural Development. A Strategic Perspective*, The Johns Hopkins University Press, Baltimore.

Johansson, B. (ed.), 1986. *Dynamics in Metropolitan Processes and Policies*, RR-86-8, IIASA, Laxenburg, Austria.

Johansson, B. (ed.), 1986. *Spatial Dynamics and Metropolitan Change*, RR-86-9, IIASA, Laxenburg, Austria.

Kawashima, T., and P. Korcell, 1982. *Human Settlement Systems : Spatial Patterns and Trends*, CP-82-S1, IIASA, Laxenburg, Austria.

Knop, H. (ed.), 1976. "The Tennessee Valley Authority Experience." Proceedings of the First Conference on Case Studies of Large-scale Planning Projects, 28 October-1 November, 1974.

Knop, H., and A. Straszak (eds.), 1978. *The Bratsk-Ilimsk Territorial Production Complex : A Field Study Report*, RR-78-2, IIASA, Laxenburg, Austria.

Knop, H (ed.), 1979. *The Tennessee Valley Authority*, RR-79-2, IIASA, Laxenburg, Austria.

Kochetkov, A., and A. Straszak, 1986. *Concepts and Tools for Strategic Regional Socio-economic Change Policy. Study Report*, Systems Research Institute, Polish Academy of Sciences/IIASA, Warsaw/Laxenburg.

Majone, G., 1986. "Systems analysis : A genetic approach", in H.J. Miser and E.S. Quade (eds.), *Handbook of Systems Analysis*, North Holland, Amsterdam.

Majone, G., and E.S. Quade (eds.), 1980. *Pitfalls of Analysis*, IIASA/Wiley, Laxenburg/Chichester.

Malaska, P., 1985. *Organic Growth and Renewal. An Outline for Post-industrial Development*, Tulevaisuuden Tutkimuksen Seuran Julkaisd Sallskapets foer Framtidsstuddier Publication. Turkv. Abo.

Manne, A.S., *et al.*, 1979. "Energy policy modeling : a survey", *Operations Research*, Vol. 27, p. 1.

Markley, O.W., and W.W. Harman, 1982. *Changing Images of Man*, Pergamon, Oxford.

Maslow, A., 1962. *Toward a Psychology of Being*, Van Nostrand, New York.

Mattessich, R., 1978. *Instrumental reasoning and systems methodology*, Reidel, Dordrecht.

Meadows, D.H., J. Richardson, and G. Bruckmann, 1982. *Groping in the dark*, Wiley, New York.

Meadows, D.H., and J.M. Robinson, 1985. *The Electronic Oracle*, Wiley, New York.

Miser, H.J., and E.S. Quade (eds.), 1986. *Handbook of Systems Analysis. Overview of Uses, Procedures, Applications and Practice*, North Holland, Amsterdam.

110

Munn, R.E., and V. Fedorov (eds.), 1986. *An Assessment of Environmental Impacts of Industrial Development - with special reference to the Doon Valley, India.* Vol. I : *The Environmental Assessment.* Vol II : *Software and Data.* Vol.III : *Reports by Collaborators.* SR-86-1, IIASA, Laxenburg, Austria.

Newell, A., J.C. Shaw, and H.A. Simon, 1960. "Report on a general problem-solving program for a computer. Information processing", Proc. Int. Conf. Inf. Process., Paris.

Newell, A., and H.A. Simon, 1972. *Human Problem Solving*, Prentice Hall, Englewood Cliffs, N.J.

Nieuwenhuijze, C.A.O., 1982. *Development Begins at Home. Problems and Prospects of the Sociology of Dvelopment*, Pergamon, Oxford.

Parsons, T., 1977. *Social Systems and the Evolution of Action Theory*, The Free Press, New York.

Peterson, R.A., 1985. "The culture of socio-economic development : tasks for research", in E. Laszlo, and I. Vitanyi (eds.), *European Culture and World Development*, Corvina, Budapest.

Perroux, F., 1981. *A New Concept of Development*, Croomhelm, London and Unesco, Paris.

Quade, E.S., and H.J. Miser, 1986. "The context, the nature and the use of systems analysis", in Miser & Quade (eds.), *Handbook... op. cit.*

Reese, H.W., and M.A. Smyer, 1983. *The Dimensionalization of Life Events. Life-span Development Psychology. Non-normative Life Events*, Academic Press, New York.

Reinert, G., 1979. "Prolegomena to a history of life-span developmental psychology", in : *Life-span Development and Behavior*, Vol. 2, *op. cit.*

Rondinelli, D.A., 1983. *Development Projects as Policy Experiments. An Adaptive Approach to Development Administration*, Methuen, London.

Rossi, P.H., H.E. Freeman, and S.R. Wright, 1979. *Evaluation. A Systematic Approach*, Sage, Beverly Hills.

Rostow, W.W., 1960. *The Stages of Economic Growth*, Cambridge University Press, London.

Ruttan, V.W., 1975. "Integrated rural development programs : a sceptical perspective", *International Development Review*, No. 4, p. 9.

Shniper, R.I., 1981. "Fundamental aspects of the formation of an integrated regional economic development concept", in A.G. Aganbegyan (ed.), *Planning and Projecting the Siberian Experience*, Mouton Publ., The Hague.

Simon, H.A., 1961. "The control of the mind by reality : human cognition and problem solving", in S.M. Faber, and R.H.L. Wilson (eds.), *Control of the Mind*, McGraw Hill, New York.

Sinaceur, M.A., 1981. "Foreword : development - to what end ?", in F. Perroux, *A New Concept of Development*, Croomhelm, London, and Unesco, Paris.

Solomon, E.S., 1986. "Preface", *Socio-economic Studies*, Vol. 12, Unesco, Paris.

Stoer, W., 1971. "Towards 'another' regional development ? - In search of a strategy of truly 'integrated' regional development", in R.P. Misra, and M. Honjo (eds.), *Changing Perception of Development Problems*, United Nations Centre for Regional Development, Regional Development Series, Vol. 1, Maruzen Asia, Singapore.

Straszak, A., and J.W. Owsinski (eds.), 1985. *Strategic Regional Policy*, Polish Academy of Sciences, Systems Research Institute, Warsaw.

Streeten, P., and R. Jolly, 1981. *Recent Issues in World Development*, Pergamon, Oxford.

Strombach, W., 1983. "Wholeness, Gestalt, System : on the meaning of these concepts in the German language", *International Journal of General Systems*, Vol. 9.

Schwarz, B., K.C. Bowen, I. Kiss, and E.S. Quade, 1986. "Guidance for decision", in Miser & Quade, *op. cit.*

Sztompka, P., 1974. *System and Function. Toward a Theory of Society*, Academic Press, New York.

Tomlinson, R.L., and I. Kiss (eds.), 1984. *Rethinking the Process of Operational Research and Systems Analysis*, Pergamon, Oxford.

Unesco, 1986. *Perception and Analysis of World Problems. Major Programme I : Reflexion on World Problems and Future Oriented Studies. Synoptic Report 1984-1985.* Unesco, Paris.

Unesco, 1986. "Socio-economic analysis and planning : critical choice of methodologies", *Socio-economic Studies*, Vol. 12, Unesco, Paris.

Waddington, C.H., 1969. "Concepts and theories of growth, development, differentiation and morphologenesis", in C.H. Waddington, *Towards a Theoretical Biology*, Aldin Publ., Chicago.

Weiss, P., 1961. "From cell to molecule", in J.N. Allen, *The Molecular Control of Cellular Activity*, McGraw Hill, New York.

Zaslavskaya, T.I., 1981. "On the concept and techniques of systems analysis of the countryside", in A.G. Aganbegyan (ed.), *op. cit.*

Integrated development planning using socio-economic and quality of life indicators

Alex C. Michalos

1. AUTHOR'S BIASES

Broadly speaking, my work is guided by a vision that is egalitarian and pragmatic in content and in method. The philosophic tradition popularized by the American pragmatists beginning with the Progressive Era (1880-1915) was characterized by a concern with consequences. The writings of C.S. Peirce, William James, R.B. Berry and John Dewey are notorious for their emphasis on appraising particular beliefs and actions on the basis of the total consequences of accepting the beliefs and performing the actions. Peirce's insistence that the scientific enterprise was essentially a social activity, the benefits and costs of which finally had to be assessed from the point of view of a community of researchers, became even more generalized in Dewey's insistence that life itself is a social activity and that the quality of life must be assessed from the point of view of the human community. A human action is morally good insofar as it is intended to and does impartially maximize the average well-being of everyone affected by it, and a belief or set of beliefs (e.g. a scientific theory) is morally good insofar as its acceptance tends to produce the same result. Proper origins, breeding, credentials, foundations and traditional authorities are set aside as the crucial tests of beliefs and actions, and the centre stage is given to the impact of beliefs and actions on the fundamental aim of improving the human condition.

Besides an emphasis on the consequences specified above, the pragmatists characteristically rejected artificial dualisms that tended to divide, oversimplify, reduce and finally destroy the possibilities of understanding, appreciating and developing reliable, valid and useful knowledge about the world and its inhabitants. They emphasized the hazards inherent in the alleged separation between thinking and feeling, facts and values, science and humanities, matter and form, means and ends, thought and action. Although it might be useful for this or that purpose to use a dualistic construct, the great contribution of the pragmatists was steadfastly to keep their fundamental purpose always in view. Whatever contributes to the improvement of the human condition should be preserved and promoted. Everything else is at best frivolous and at worst evil. Hence, Bertrand Russell's complaint about John Dewey's philosophy, namely that it leaves us no moral holidays.

As I have specified the basic aim of pragmatism above, it is clearly egalitarian. Feminists and socialists share the view that throughout history some people have been exploited by others, and they share the vision of a better world in which there is little or no exploitation. They share the view that a world inhabited by people motivated primarily by co-operation and goodwill is better than a world inhabited by people motivated primarily by competition and selfishness. And finally, they share the view that a better world can be developed through the conscious, continuous and vigorous efforts of progressive people all over the world and throughout all time. It was this optimistic and melioristic view-point that informed and motivated Albion Small in his development of pragmatic sociology at the University of Chicago at the turn of the century. Indeed, the North American branch of the contemporary social indicators movement can be traced back fairly directly to the vision of the philosophical and sociological pragmatists of the Progressive Era, especially those of the Chicago School.

2.   BASIC TERMINOLOGY

Although there seems to be little confusion these days about basic terminology in the social indicators movement, different people use different definitions of some key words. So it is worthwhile to provide some brief definitions. More detailed accounts may be found in Michalos (1980). Generally speaking, all statistics may be divided into two mutually exclusive and exhaustive classes on the basis of whether or not they are supposed to have some clear significance for the quality of people's lives. I use the term 'social indicator' to designate statistics that are supposed to have significance for the quality of life, and refer to all other statistics simply as 'statistics'. I use the term 'social report' to designate organized sets of social indicators. Social indicators that refer to personal feelings, attitudes, preferences, opinions, judgments or beliefs of some sort will be called 'subjective indicators' (e.g. satisfaction with one's education), while all others will be called 'objective indicators' (e.g. a national illiteracy rate). Social indicators are similar to variables in logic and mathematics, and just as we speak of the values of variables in formal sciences, we may speak of the indicator-values of social indicators (e.g. an illiteracy rate of 5 per cent).

'Positive indicators' are such that if their indicator-values increase, then some facet of the quality of life is improving. 'Negative indicators' are such that if their indicator-values increase, then some facet of the quality of life is deteriorating. Of course, particular individuals and groups may disagree about exactly which indicators are positive and which are negative, and in the final analysis decisions about such matters are inextricably wrapped up in one's vision of a good life and a good world. Although I tried to make the case for all such decisions in my North American Social Report and many of the indicators that are used below are also used in that earlier treatise, it would require too much time and space to attempt comprehensive discussions here. Instead, I have simply outlined my biases in the previous section and hope that the reader can see how this or that indicator might be regarded as positive or negative from the point of view of an egalitarian vision. (Interested readers may consult the third volume of *North American Social Report* (1981) for detailed discussions concerning indicators of science, technology and education.)

'Input indicators' provide statistics regarding the means used to obtain certain ends or objectives, and 'output indicators' provide statistics regarding the latter. For example, student enrolment figures are input indicators, while student graduation figures are output indicators. Again, of course, decisions must be made about what is to be regarded as means and ends, proximate and final ends, and so on. I assumed, for instance, that enrolment is a means to the end of getting an education and that graduation indicates achievement of that aim. In certain circumstances the most pressing problem may be enrolment itself, or perhaps financing. Obviously, I cannot cover all cases with a single set of designations, but it should be possible to provide a set that is useful for most cases.

A 'social counting system', as I understand it, is a social report patterned after ordinary economic accounting with balance sheets specifying debits and credits, or costs and benefits. I view the task of designing such a system as equivalent to designing an integrated system of social accounts to be used in development planning.

3.   INTEGRATED DEVELOPMENT

Unesco has sponsored some splendid workshops on the nature of integrated development, the most useful of which for me was published as *Different Theories and Practices of Development* (1982). In his contribution to this volume, Iraida Alechina (1982, p. 25) quotes an unidentified Unesco document as follows :

> "Development is **integrated** : it is an organic process involving a number of economic, social and cultural factors which overlap and constantly influence one another.
> Development is **endogenous** : each country carries out its development according to its own choice, and in conformity with the real values, aspirations and motivations of the population.
> Development is **global** : its objectives and problems are determined with relation to world problems and reflect the general nature of development... The society in which development is carried out is not isolated, but forms part of the network of relations and forces that cover the entire world, including the most economically advanced societies as well as those which, from the economic point of view, are the most deprived."

Briefly, what is being specified in this quotation is a system of social accounts that is internally and externally coherent and comprehensive. Internally the various aspects indicated in the system should be comparable, and externally the systems of different countries should also be comparable. Furthermore, the requirement of endogenous development apparently directs our attention to the particular human values, wants and needs characteristic of different societies. In my own terminology, this is a requirement for subjective as well as objective indicators. One attempt to integrate subjective and objective indicators in a single system was illustrated in my *North American Social Report*, and another in the *German Social Report* (1987) written by Wolfgang Zapf and his colleagues at Mannheim University. Nikolai Lapin and Radovan Richta (1982, p. 200) seem to have been endorsing a similar view when they wrote the following lines.

"The emergence of the whole person is a complex historical process. It does not take place automatically, as a consequence of existing external 'conditions', but has deep-rooted historical preconditions. Yet it depends to a large extent on the subjective factor, on our goals and values and on free choice. Only the unity of objective social conditions and the subjective aspirations of people can lead to the harmonious development of the whole person."

Fig. 1 shows a set of social statistics with the particular subsets distinguished above. To simplify matters, I am using the word 'social' here in a broad sense in which it includes issues that might with greater precision be regarded as economic, political and cultural.

Unclear Significance for Quality of Life	Clear Significance for Quality of Life = Social Indicators		
		Positive (P)	Negative (N)
	Input (I) Objective (O) Subjective (S)	IOP ISP	ION ISN
	Output (U) Objective (O) Subjective (S)	UOP USP	UON USN

Fig. 1 - Social Statistics

    The easiest way to get a general assessment of the quality of
life in a country or set of countries from such a matrix is by
applying the Principle of Cost-Benefit Dominance (CBD). The Principle is described in some detail in Michalos (1970) and applied
extensively in my *North American Social Report*. It is essentially
comparative or relative, rather than absolute. One begins by
selecting a set of positive and negative indicators, preferably with
similar numbers of objective and subjective, input and output indicators. Next, one obtains a set of indicator-values to serve as
baseline figures for each indicator, preferably for a single year.
For any subsequent year, the quality of life has improved if any of
the three cases obtain : (1) the indicator-values of all positive
and negative indicators have changed in the desired direction ;
(2) the indicator-values of at least one positive or negative indicator have changed in the desired direction and all others have
stayed the same ; (3) the indicator-values of more positive than
negative indicators have changed in the desired direction.
    The third case is potentially more complicated and demanding
from the point of view of the sophistication of the information or
data it requires. For this third case one must have some ideas
about the relative importance of one's social indicators. In the
simplest situation, every indicator would be equally valuable and
equally weighted. So losses on one indicator could be traded off
against gains on another. However, depending on the particular
indicator-values of various indicators, it might be possible to get
a clear view of trade-offs involving indicators that are rank ordered in importance or value. For example, university graduates
might be valued so much more highly than expenditures for public
libraries, or vice-versa, that slight increases on one indicator
might be regarded as more valuable than larger increases on the
other. *A priori* one cannot say how important everyone should find
every indicator relative to every other indicator. In principle, I
think it should be possible to develop a quite general scientific
theory of value based on the theory of multiple discrepancies that
will be explained below, and such a theory would allow one to make
the required judgments. But in fact we are years away from what
seems to be possible in principle. For present purposes, I am
merely proposing the introduction of a conceptually integrated set
of indicators, with some guidelines as to how the total set might be
appraised collectively to obtain a single judgment regarding the
quality of life.

4.   PROPOSED SET OF SOCIAL INDICATORS AND STATISTICS

My original plan involved separate reviews of the current Unesco
database, assessments of its strengths and weaknesses, and the
suggestion of new indicators and statistics to improve the total
system. As I worked through this plan, it became clear that although I had to go through these steps to a finished product, it
would not be necessary or efficient to take my readers through the

118

same steps. It seems more efficient to present the finished product immediately and to indicate its main features and departures from Unesco's original database. Concrete proposals can be much more efficiently reviewed and disposed of favourably or unfavourably than very general remarks.

Annex 1 contains my proposed new data-set, including some explanatory remarks regarding various of its aspects. It is a relatively long Annex, 30 pages long to be exact. Broadly speaking, the original data-set has been expanded by the addition of about 100 output indicators, including 70 subjective output indicators. The subjective items have been written out completely, but the response categories have all been limited to three categories just to identify the main anchor points. Final versions of these items would probably use five or seven response categories. Unesco's original data-set had only two output indicators, both objective. In general, my specific proposals operationalize some of the basic recommendations of two recent United Nations documents, namely *Compiling Social Indicators on the Situation of Women* (1984) and *Improving Concepts and Methods for Statistics and Indicators on the Situation of Women* (1984). In particular, I have proposed breakdowns by sex for every indicator ; educational time series by years to supplement the ambiguous series by first, second and third levels of education ; attendance and completion series by years to supplement enrolment and graduation series by levels of education ; completion series based on standardized tests ; series involving rates and ratios to supplement series involving only total numbers (which are largely reflections of population sizes and impossible to interpret as having positive or negative impacts on the quality of life) ; and productivity series in which inputs are specifically related to outputs in order to measure the relative effectiveness and efficiency of various systems, e.g. of the education and training systems, and of the scientific and technological research and development systems.

5. MULTIPLE DISCREPANCIES THEORY (MDT)

Objective indicators are useless unless they can be plausibly interpreted as providing reliable, valid and important information about some state of affairs or changes in some state of affairs. In other words, objective indicators are useless unless someone is satisfied with their levels of reliability, validity and importance. Thus, even those who reject subjective indicators (for any reason) must admit that an acceptable theory of satisfaction would improve our understanding of judgments about which indicators do have satisfactory levels of reliability, validity and importance. Those who think that one very direct and important way to find out how people feel about their lives is to ask them have always been interested in the development of an acceptable theory of satisfaction. Some people prefer to use the word 'happiness' rather than 'satisfaction', and others use the two words practically as synonyms.

Virtually all research has shown that the two words share some common meaning, e.g. see Diener (1984), Veenhoven (1984) and Michalos (1985). So a theory of satisfaction would also be a theory of happiness.

As I understand it, a fully developed scientific theory of satisfaction or happiness would be cast in an axiomatic form and would provide precise explanations and predictions regarding the fundamental question : 'What makes people satisfied or happy ?'. It would be applicable to satisfaction or happiness with life as a whole (i.e. global satisfaction or happiness) as well as to satisfaction or happiness with specific domains of life (i.e. domain satisfaction) such as marital satisfaction, job satisfaction and so on. The theory that will be described below, which I call Multiple Discrepancies Theory, or MDT for short, is just such a theory. (A more detailed discussion of MDT may be found in Michalos (1985).)

A review of *Psychological Abstracts* and *Sociological Abstracts* for the past decade reveals that researchers around the world have been publishing articles and books on satisfaction and happiness at a rate of over a thousand titles a year. Our library at the University of Guelph includes such things as *The Art of Happiness*, *The Conquest of Happiness*, *The Right to be Happy*, *The Happy Ascetic*, *The Happy Adolescent*, *The Happy Captive*, *The Happy Critic*, *The Happy Man*, *Happy Warrior*, *Happy People*, *A Happy Pair*, *Happiness in Marriage*, *The Happy Family*, *Happy World*, *The Happy Hunter*, *The Happy Glutton*, *The Happy Kitchen*, *The Happy Hypocrite*, *Happy Days*, *Happy Year*, *Happy Holidays*, *Happy Christmas*, *The Happy Journey*, *The Happy Time*, *The Happy Life*, *A Happy Death*, *Happy Gardener*, *The Happy Garden*, *Happy Dog/Happy Owner Book*, *The Happy Dolphins*, *Happy Eagle*, *Happy Enough*, *Happy Thoughts*, and *The Happy Profession*.

Considering the wide variety of theories that have appeared in the literature on satisfaction and happiness, one group has impressed me the most. I refer to this group of theories as 'discrepancy theories' or 'gap theories'. The basic idea behind these sorts of theories, of which MDT is one example, is that satisfaction or happiness is an emergent property resulting from the particular relationships or mixtures of other properties. In other words, in these theories satisfaction or happiness is analyzed and understood as the effect or result of something else, something more primitive. While utilitarian philosophers and economists have used satisfaction or happiness as the basis or basic building block of their theories, gap theories in general and MDT in particular are theories designed to analyze and explain that basis. MDT is a theory designed to go beyond satisfaction or happiness, to get to its sources or causes.

Annex 2 is a list of 78 publications (excluding my own work) from 1979 to 1985, in which some sort of a gap or discrepancy hypothesis was tested.

At least 80 per cent of the tests were reported to be successful. That is, at least 80 per cent of the times when someone hypothesized a connection between some sort of a discrepancy and satisfaction or happiness, such a connection was found. Some people are inclined to discount such statistics because they believe that people prefer to publish positive rather than negative results. I think that most academic researchers publish any results they get because any kind of publication contributes to their own resumés, which in turn contribute to their chances for promotion and tenure. Besides, most people would agree with Karl Popper's view that we learn and the body of scientific knowledge grows at least as much from our failures as from our successes.

Before moving on to a detailed discussion of MDT, two other features of Annex 2 should be mentioned. First, one should notice the wide variety of dependent variables employed in these studies. They include satisfaction with jobs, personal skill development, group performance, leader's behaviour, housing, neigbbourhood, health, health care, therapy and surgery, income and personal finances, personal relationships, physical attractiveness, sex, marriage, family and love life, life as a whole, recreation, religion, government services, student test results and grades, auto repair services, video disc players, potted plants and canned peaches. Then one should notice the variety of explanatory and predictive discrepancies, including the gap between an expected and actual environment, desired and actual job tasks, ideal and actual leader behaviour, goals and achievement, preferred and perceived physical characteristics, needs and achievements, one's own and other's job complexity, equitable versus actual relationships, one's own and partner's social style, one's own abilities and job requirements, one's own and spouses beliefs, expected and actual performance, one's own attractiveness and that of others, actual versus deserved housing, wanted and actual product quality. In brief, this is a record of significant success for an incredible variety of dependent satisfaction or happiness variables and hypothesized discrepancies.

The basic hypotheses of Multiple Discrepancy Theory (MDT) are as follows :

H1: Reported net satisfaction is a linear function of perceived discrepancies between what one has and wants, relevant others have, the best one has had in the past, expected to have three years ago, expects to have after five years, deserves and needs.

H2: All perceived discrepancies, except that between what one has and wants, are linear functions of objectively measurable discrepancies, which also have direct effects on satisfaction and actions.

H3: The perceived discrepancy between what one has and wants is a mediating variable between all other perceived discrepancies and reported net satisfaction.

H4: The pursuit and maintenance of net satisfaction motivates human action in direct proportion to the perceived expected levels of net satisfaction.

H5: All discrepancies, satisfaction and actions are directly and indirectly affected by age, sex, education, ethnicity, income, self-esteem and social support.

H6: Objectively measurable discrepancies are linear functions of human action and conditioners.

Although nobody has bound together as many hypotheses or articulated a theory of multiple discrepancies as systematically as I have, a number of people have worked with two or more discrepancy hypotheses in conjunction. As I have mentioned in all my earlier publications, I originally followed Campbell, Converse and Rodgers (1976), and Andrews and Withey (1976) fairly directly. Crosby (1982) used several gap hypotheses in conjunction, and cited seven other people who had also used multiple discrepancies in one way or another, namely Davis (1959), Runciman (1966), Gurr (1970), Williams (1975), Berkowitz (1968), Adams (1965) and Patchen (1961). Goodman (1974), Oldham et al. (1982) and Carp, Carp and Millsap (1982) should also be listed as labourers in the same vineyard.

H1 refers to seven different perceived discrepancies. The idea that net satisfaction is a function of the perceived discrepancy or gap between what one has and wants is at least as old as the Stoic philosophy of Zeno of Citium around 300 B.C. In the form of aspiration theory, Lewin et al. (1944) gave the idea a new start. More recent confirmations of the basis hypothesis have been reported by Bledsoe, Mullen and Hobbes (1980) ; Canter and Rees (1982) ; Cherrington and England (1980) ; Campbell, Converse and Rodgers (1976) ; Andrews and Withey (1976) ; Michalos (1980a, 1982, 1983, 1985, 1986a) ; and Crosby (1976, 1982).

The idea that net satisfaction is a function of the perceived discrepancy between what one has and relevant others have can also be found before the birth of Christ, namely in Aristotle's *Politics* in the fourth century B.C. In the form of reference group theory, Merton and Kitt (1950) gave the hypothesis a provocative new start. Recent confirmations have come from Oldham and Miller (1979) ; Appelgryn and Plug (1981) ; Hatfield and Huseman (1982) ; Duncan (1975) ; Campbell, Converse and Rodgers (1976) ; Andrews and Withey (1976) ; Crosby (1976, 1982) ; Oldham et al. (1982) ; Goodman (1974) ; and Michalos (1980a, 1982, 1983, 1985, 1986a). Wills (1981, 1983) considers this sort of theory (by its other popular name, 'social comparison theory') from the point of view of its usefulness in explaining people's behaviour and attitudes regarding help-seeking decisions, self-evaluation and self-enhancement. He also reviews several publications in which support is found for 'downward comparison theory', i.e. the theory that says people select folks who are relatively worse off than themselves to make comparisons which in turn make themselves look and then feel better.

Confirmations of the hypothesis that net satisfaction is a function of the perceived gap between what one has now and the best one has ever had in the past have been reported by Campbell, Converse and Rodgers (1976) and Michalos (1980a, 1982, 1983, 1985, 1986a). Suls and Sanders (1982) present evidence supporting a developmental model in which evaluations based on this sort of perceived discrepancy occur in children around the ages of four to five, while "social comparisons with similar others" occur a bit later around the age of nine.

Equity theorists have found considerable support for the hypothesis that net satisfaction is a function of the perceived gap between what one has and what one deserves. For examples, see Hatfield, Greenberger, Traupman and Lambert (1982) ; Walster, Berscheid and Walster (1976) ; Adams and Freedman (1976) ; Cook (1975) ; and Goodman and Friedman (1971). Although some respondents in virtually all the surveys I have run using this hypothesis have complained that they have a hard time judging what it is that they deserve, merit or have due to them when all things are considered, the hypothesis frequently explains a significant proportion of the variance in our dependent variables, e.g. see Michalos (1980a, 1982, 1983, 1985, 1986a).

The hypothesis that net satisfaction is a function of the perceived discrepancy between what one has and expected to have was given a fairly systematic treatment by Festinger (1957). As indicated by several authors in Abelson et al. (1968), Festinger's theory of cognitive dissonance mixed several kinds of discrepancies together, although there was a tendency to emphasize the gap between expected and actual states of affairs. Support for this hypothesis has been reported by Campbell, Converse and Rodgers (1976) ; Weintraub (1980) ; Oliver (1980) ; Ross, Mirowski and Duff (1982) ; Michalos (1980a, 1982, 1983, 1985, 1986a) ; and many others cited in Abelson et al. (1968).

Person-environment fit theorists have hypothesized that, among other things, net satisfaction is a function of the perceived fit or match between what a person has (resources, abilities) and what a person needs, or alternatively, what a person has and what that person's environment (job, social situation, etc.) requires. Considerable support for this hypothesis has been reported in review articles by Harrison (1978, 1983) and Caplan (1979, 1983). Kurella (1979), Booth, McNally and Berry (1979), and Michalos (1980a, 1982, 1983, 1985, 1986a) have also reported support for a similar sort of hypothesis.

The seventh gap hypothesis incorporated into H1 involves the perceived discrepancy between what one has now and expects to have in the future (after five years). One would expect that optimism about the future would bring satisfaction, and there is some experimental evidence supporting this idea, e.g. in Goodman (1966) and Michalos (1980a, 1982, 1983, 1985, 1986a). However, relative to the other gap hypotheses, the influence of this one tends to be fairly weak.

H1 refers to reported satisfaction because the survey research procedures used to test MDT rely on personal reports. Although I often omit the word 'reported', strictly speaking it is essential. Since nobody can open up anyone's head to find out how well or poorly anything reported matches anything actually experienced, MDT is no worse off than any other socio-psychological theory on this score.

Usually, I think, things are regarded and reported as satisfying if, and only if, on balance they are satisfying. So, typically 'satisfaction' has the force of 'net satisfaction', and 'dissatisfaction' has the force of 'net dissatisfaction'. Scales running from 'very satisfied' to 'very dissatisfied' presuppose that respondents are reporting net assessments.

H2 affirms ontological realist or objectivist assumptions, namely that there is a world relatively independent of this or that person, containing things with more or less objectively measurable properties, which are more or less objectively comparable. I think that all human artifacts, including methods, practices principles, and bodies of knowledge are constructed by people with a variety of interests and purposes, and that there is no way to decide once and for all exactly which features of our world are merely constructed and which are found. It seems highly unlikely that the whole universe has somehow been constructed out of our imagination, but there is no way, I think, to say just how much has been constructed. Metaphysics aside, however, the point of H2 is fairly straightforward. It implies, for example, that the perceived discrepancy between what one earns and some relevant other person earns is to some extent a function of a real or objectively measurable discrepancy ; the perceived discrepancies between needs for nourishment or warmth and their attainment are to some extent functions of real or objectively measurable discrepancies ; and so on. While I strongly suspect, and there is some evidence, that the mixture of objectively measurable and perceived discrepancies is a bit like a horse and rabbit stew, with perceived discrepancies represented by the horse, I shall have little more to say on the matter here. (Evidence may be found in Campbell, Converse and Rodgers (1976) ; Michalos (1980a) ; Golant (1986) ; and Gauthier (1987).) For reasons explained in Michalos (1978, 1985), H2 does not apply to the gap between what people have and want. Besides affirming some sort of realism, H2 says that objectively measurable discrepancies have a direct impact on net satisfaction and human action.

H3 says that the perceived gap between what one has and wants serves as a mediator between all other perceived gaps and net satisfaction. This hypothesis was confirmed by Campbell, Converse and Rodgers (1976), and Michalos (1980a, 1982, 1983, 1985, 1986a). H1 and H3 taken together imply that perceived discrepancies have both direct and indirect (mediated) effects on reported net satisfaction.

H4 connects net satisfaction to human action in a fairly traditional utilitarian way. (For examples, see Luce and Raiffa (1957) ; Edwards and Twersky (1967) ; and Harsanyi (1982).)

According to H5, discrepancies are directly and indirectly affected by certain demographic elements and conditioners. Although such elements have not been found to be relatively powerful predictors of satisfaction or happiness, they do have some impact. On average, perhaps as much as 10 per cent of the variance in reported net satisfaction or happiness can be explained by demographic variables. Generally speaking, the best and most recent literature regarding the impact of demographic elements on satisfaction and happiness are in Diener (1984) ; Veenhoven (1984) ; and McNeil, Stones and Kozma (1986). Diener (1984, p. 558) cited eleven studies indicating that "High self-esteem is one of the strongest predictors of [subjective well-being]." Although it cannot be demonstrated here, in the presence of discrepancy variables, self-esteem is not a very strong predictor. The importance of a variety of species of

124

social support, measured in a variety of ways, is thoroughly docu-
mented in Caplan (1979) ; Turner, Frankel and Levin (1983) : and
Abbey and Andrews (1985).

The point of H6 is to indicate that human action, including
especially one's own, has a direct effect on the objectively
measurable discrepancies of one's life, as do the previously mentioned demographic and conditioning elements. It is assumed, of
course, that there is some time lag and directionality involved, and
that events and actions are not their own causes or motives.

Fig. 2 illustrates the relationships postulated in the six
basic hypotheses of MDT.

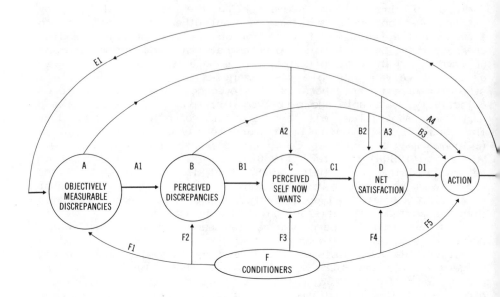

Fig. 2 – Multiple Discrepancies Theory

In this Figure, capital letters stand for items in boxes (e.g. 'A'
stands for objectively measurable discrepancies) and numbers following letters stand for paths connecting items in boxes (e.g. 'A1'
stands for the path connecting objectively measurable discrepancies
to perceived discrepancies). Thus, for example, Fig. 2 illustrates
H1 by showing that objectively measurable discrepancies (A) are a
function of an agent's own action along the path E1 and the conditioners along the path F1, and so on for the other features of the
six basic hypotheses.

Fig. 3 illustrates in greater detail the centre core of relationships expressed in Fig. 2, ignoring all references to objectively measurable discrepancies.

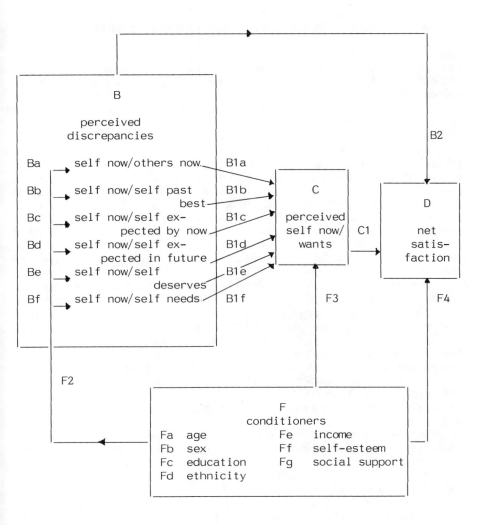

Fig. 3 - Perceptual Core of MDT

In Fig. 3, each perceived discrepancy in box B has an abbreviation, e.g. 'Ba' for "the perceived discrepancy between what
one has now and relevant others have". Similarly, each conditioner
in box F has an abbreviation, e.g. 'Fa' for "age". The path
labelled B1 in Fig. 2 is unpacked into its six constituents B1a-B1f
in Fig. 3. To keep the figure relatively simple, the seven items in
box F are not unpacked. Strictly speaking, every path labelled with
an F should be unpacked into seven constituents labelled, for example, F4a, F4b, and so on.

6. APPLICATIONS OF MDT TO UNIVERSITY STUDENTS IN 23 COUNTRIES

Results of applications of MDT have been published in Michalos (1985, 1986a), and have been reported in Michalos (1986b, 1986c, 1986d). Since 1984, an international survey research project has been in progress involving applications of MDT to about 20,000 university undergraduates in 67 universities, in 44 countries around the world. Translations of my English questionnaire have been made into 22 languages. About 40 data-sets have already been sent to Guelph and several preliminary analyses have been completed. Below I shall mainly report on results concerning satisfaction with one's own university education for about 6,000 students in 23 universities in 23 different countries. Since data-sets are still coming in and there are literally hundreds of specific analyses yet to be made, readers should regard all results reported as first words rather than last. I shall begin with a brief description of the survey methodology, including the design of the questionnaire used to operationalize my theory.

The questionnaire was an extended version of those described in Michalos (1980a, 1982, 1983, 1985, 1986a). It had a demographic page, an instruction page illustrating the kinds of questions that would be asked, a page defining the terms designating twelve particular domains of life, and eight pages containing items involving the assessment of domain and global satisfaction from eight different perspectives. A seven-point Likert-type scale was provided on each of these pages to obtain data relevant to the seven discrepancies mentioned in H1 of MDT and to the basic satisfaction ratings. An off-scale category was available in every case to allow people to opt out by checking 'No opinion'.

Basic satisfaction ratings were taken on my revised delightful-terrible scale. For example, the global item asked "How do you feel about your life as a whole right now ?" and the response categories ran from "terrible" (=1 point), through "mixed dissatisfying and satisfying" (=4) to "delightful" (=7).

Assessments of the discrepancies between what one has and wants were obtained in the next battery of questions. For example, the global item asked "Consider your life as a whole. How does it measure up to your general aspirations or what you want ?" and the response categories ran from "not at all" (=1), through "half as well as what you want" (=4) to "matches or is better than what you want" (=7).

Assessments of the discrepancies between what one has and relevant others have were obtained next. The global item asked "Consider your life as a whole. How does it measure up to the average for most people your own age and sex in this area ?" and the response categories ran from "far below average" (=1), through "average" (=4) to "far above average" (=7).

Assessments of the discrepancies between what one has and deserves were next. The global item asked "Consider your life as a whole. How does it measure up to the life you think you deserve ?" and the responses ran from "far below what is deserved" (=1), through "matches exactly what is deserved"(=4) to "far above what is deserved" (=7).

Assessments of the discrepancies between what one has and needs were next. The global item asked "Consider your life as a whole. How does it measure up to what you think you need ?" and the responses ran from "far below what is needed" (=1), through "matches exactly what is needed" (=4) to "far above what is needed" (=7).

Assessments of the discrepancies between what one has and expected to have three years ago at this point in life were next. The basic question was briefly "Compared to what you expected to have, does your life offer extremely less now (=1), about what you expected (=4) or extremely more (=7) ?".

Assessments of the discrepancies between what one has now and expects to have five years in the future were next. The question was briefly "Compared to what you expect five years from now, does your life offer much less now than you expect later (=1), about the same (=4) or much more now (=7) ?". In the analysis these scores were inverted so that bigger numbers indicated more and smaller numbers indicated less attractive states of affairs, which was consistent with all other item scores.

Assessments of the discrepancies between what one has and the best one has ever had in the past were next. The global item asked "Consider your life as a whole. How does it measure up to the best in your previous experience ?" and the responses ran from "far below the previous best" (=1), through "matches the previous best" (=4) to "far above the previous best" (=7).

Assessments of happiness with life as a whole were based on the question "Considering your life as a whole, would you describe it as very unhappy (=1), unhappy (=2 or 3), mixed (=4), happy (=5 or 6), or very happy (= 7) ?".

The conditioners measured directly were age, sex and years of education. The English questionnaire and some translations included measures of self-esteem and social support, while some others did not. In the former, self-esteem was measured using four positive items from the Rosenberg (1965) scale, and social support was measured using a six-item scale from Abbey and Andrews (1985). In order to be able to include 23 universities from different countries in this review, our analyses are based on questionnaires lacking the self-esteem and social support measures. Instead of collecting data on incomes, which I suspected would be similar for most students or misleading as a result of scholarships, grants or bursaries, average length of weekly employment time was measured. In Canada, if not everywhere else, it is not likely that full-time students take on part-time paid employment unless they have financial problems. So the time invested in such employment might be a reasonable indirect measure of economic status. Ethnicity was measured in three ways. For the present analyses, ethnicity was measured indirectly by the length of time (in years) that a student was residing in the country in which he or she was attending university.

An attempt was made to obtain samples of at least 300 undergraduates from each participating university. Most of the samples were drawn as convenience samples from large introductory classes, although some were random samples drawn from entire student populations at some universities. In most cases, questionnaires were filled out during class time, with most students in the class participating. So far all evidence indicates that a student's major course of study has no particular effect on reported satisfaction and happiness, i.e. whether one specializes in physical science, social science, philosophy, medicine, commerce or anything else does not significantly affect one's reported satisfaction or happiness. Apparently, then, it did not matter which introductory classes were used as samples.

Fig. 4 summarizes the students' delightful-terrible scale score means for reported net satisfaction with their current university education.

Fig. 4 – Satisfaction with one's university education

On a seven-point scale with 1 indicating terrible and 7 indicating delightful, the mean scores for each sample from each university are listed below.

	Males and Females	Males	Females
5.6	Philippines		F Philippines
5.5		M Philippines	
5.4	Puerto Rico	M PR, USA	F PR
5.3	USA		F USA
5.2	Portugal	M Canada	
5.1	Canada, Chile, New Zealand	M Chile, Portugal	F Canada, NZ
5.0		M NZ	F Chile
4.9	Bahrain, Belgium, Yugoslavia, Mexico	M UK, Yugoslavia, Mexico	F UK, Yugoslavia
4.8		M India, Thailand	
4.7	India, Switzerland, Thailand	M Switzerland	
4.6		M Germany	F Bangladesh, Switzerland, Thailand
4.5	Bangladesh, Germany		F Germany
4.3		M Egypt	
4.2	Egypt	M Bangladesh	
4.1			F Bahrain, Egypt
4.0	Spain		
3.9	Greece	M Greece, Spain	
3.8		M Korea	
3.7	Korea		
3.4	Japan, Turkey	M Japan, Turkey	

Fig. 4 (continued)

Universities from which samples were drawn :

U of Philippines, U of Puerto Rico, Illinois U, Lisbon Tech, Guelph, Austral, Massey, UC of Bahrain, Louvain, York, Zagreb, Baja Sur, Delhi, Freiburg, Chiang Mai, Dhaka, Mannheim, Ain Shams, Madrid, Thessaloniki, Korea U, Tokai, Uludag. (See Annex for detailed tables with sample sizes, etc.)

Although the scale ran from 1 to 7 points, the students' actual score means ran from 3.4 to 5.6. In very round figures, assuming sample sizes of at least 100 cases and standard deviations of 1 point, differences between the mean scores for any two groups should be about .5 to be statistically significant. For the 23 universities in this set, the groups of students sampled at the University of the Philippines, University of Puerto Rico, University of Illinois, Lisbon Institute of Technology, University of Guelph, Austral University and Massey University formed a cluster reporting relatively higher levels of satisfaction than students in the rest of the set. Students sampled at Tokai University, Uludag University, Korea University, University of Thessaloniki and the University of Madrid formed a cluster reporting relatively lower levels of satisfaction. In general, male and female mean scores for each university were not significantly different.

Fig. 5 below illustrates the rank order of total effects (i.e. direct plus indirect effects) for all of the explanatory variables used in these applications of MDT. It shows that the perceived gap between what students had and wanted out of their university education had the greatest relative impact on their reported net satisfaction. The second most influential variable was the perceived gap between what they had and other people of their own age and sex in their area had regarding university education. At the bottom end of influential variables, the figure shows that sex and number of hours of weekly part-time paid employment had the smallest relative impacts.

Fig. 6 illustrates the rank order of total effects for the same set of explanatory variables and the same students with males and females analyzed separately.

Although I began with a general rule of ignoring all results when the sample sizes dropped below 100, occasionally this rule was bent all the way down to, but absolutely never below, 90. Hence, because of the relative sizes of males and females in the various samples, there were a total of 21 universities in the male set and 16 in the female set. Fig. 6 shows that the two relatively most influential variables for males and females taken separately were the same two for males and females taken together. The third relatively most influential variable for males was the perceived gap between what students had and needed, while for females it was the perceived gap between what they had now compared to what three years ago they expected to have now.

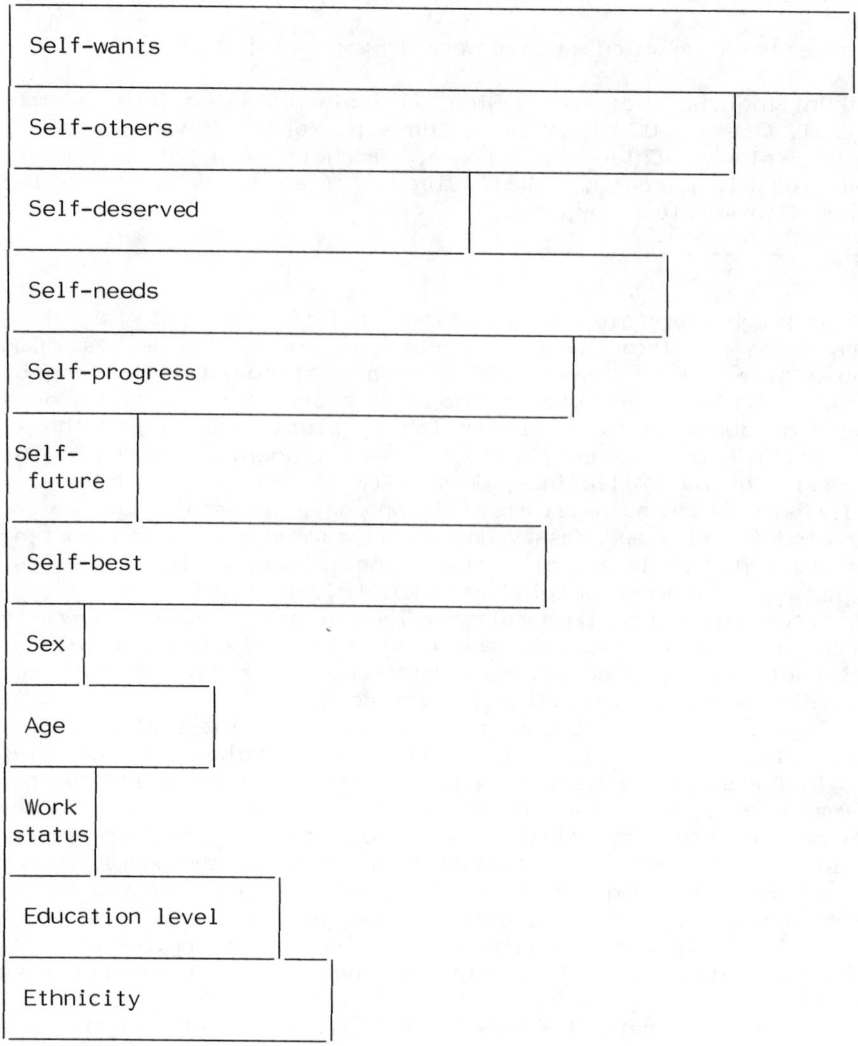

Fig. 5

Satisfaction with one's university education
(23 countries)

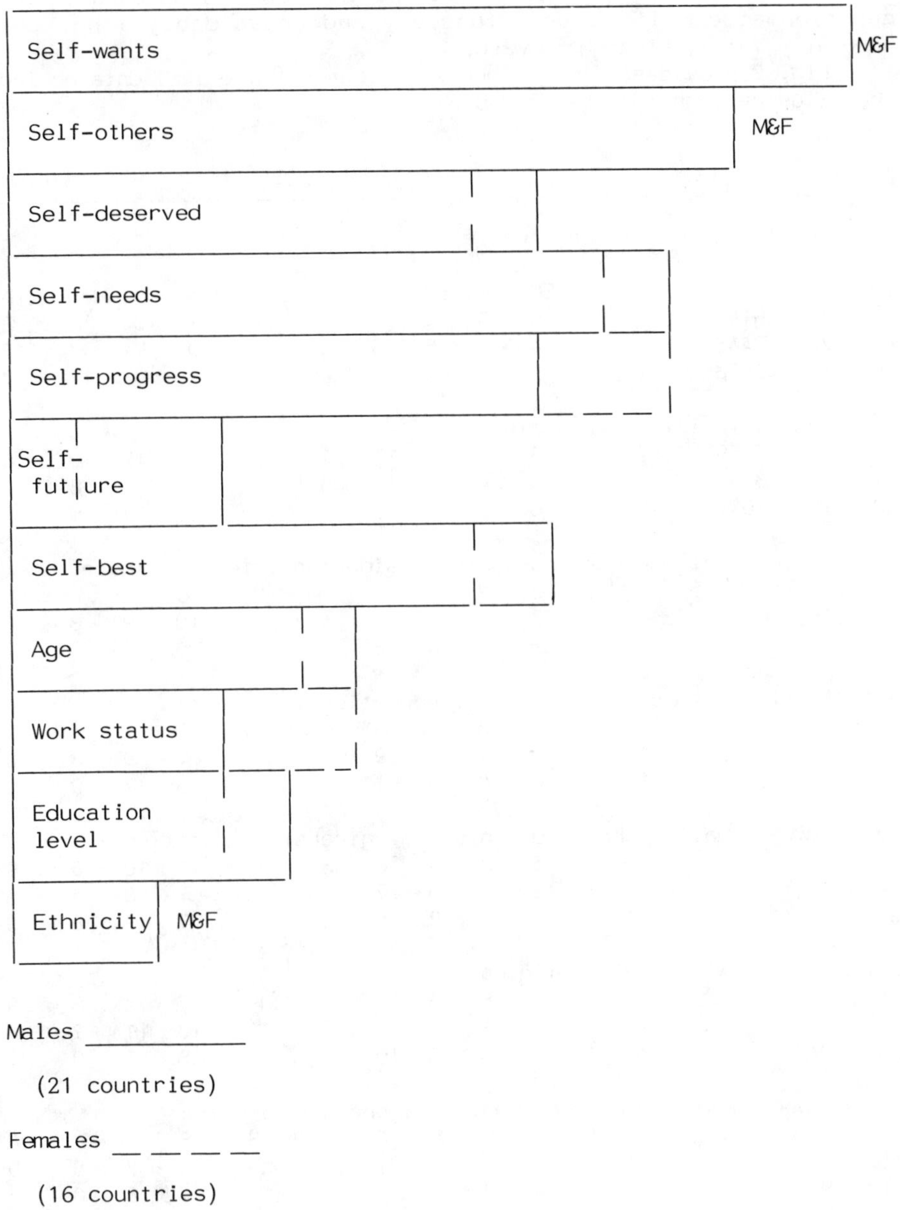

Self-wants | M&F

Self-others | M&F

Self-deserved

Self-needs

Self-progress

Self-
fut|ure

Self-best

Age

Work status

Education
level

Ethnicity | M&F

Males _____

   (21 countries)

Females _ _ _ _

   (16 countries)

Fig. 6

Satisfaction with one's university education

Annex 4 contains a set of abbreviations and definitions used in the questionnaire. It is unfortunately and unavoidably long, but hopefully fairly straightforward.

Fig. 7 provides, among other things, more numerical data behind the illustrations in Figs. 5 and 6.

Satisfaction with life as a whole :

%	UN	N	SW	SO	SD	SN	SP	SF	SB	Sex	Age	WS	Led	Eth
40	23	6143	1	2	6	5	4	9	3	7	11	10	12	8
40	20	3445	1	2	4	3	5	6	3		9	7	8	7
40	16	2678	1	2	5	6	3	10	4		8	9	11	7

Happiness with life as a whole :

%	UN	N	SW	SO	SD	SN	SP	SF	SB	Sex	Age	WS	Led	Eth
36	23	6159	2	3	6	4	5	11	1	7	9	12	10	8
35	20	3442	2	1	5	4	6	11	3		10	9	8	7
40	16	2697	2	3	6	5	4	8	1		10	7	9	8

Gap between what one has and wants considering life as a whole :

%	UN	N	SW	SO	SD	SN	SP	SF	SB	Sex	Age	WS	Led	Eth
34	23		1	3	2	5	9	4		6	8	9	7	8
35	20		1	3	2	5	7	4			10	9	8	6
34	16		1	2	3	4	8	5			6	9	7	

Satisfaction with one's university education :

%	UN	N	SW	SO	SD	SN	SP	SF	SB	Sex	Age	WS	Led	Eth
45	23		1	2	6	3	5	10	4	11	9	11	8	7
46	21		1	2	5	3	6	9	4		7	9	8	10
44	16		1	2	6	4	3	11	5		8	7	9	10

Gap between what one has and wants re. university education :

%	UN	N	SW	SO	SD	SN	SP	SF	SB	Sex	Age	WS	Led	Eth
34	23		1	5	2	4	8	3		7	11	10	6	9
34	21		1	3	2	6	7	5			7	8	4	8
33	16		1	5	3	2		4			7	9	6	8

Satisfaction with one's religion :

%	UN	N	SW	SO	SD	SN	SP	SF	SB	Sex	Age	WS	Led	Eth
56	22		2	1	4	5	6	10	3	11	7	12	8	9
57	13		1	2	3	4	6	8	5		10	11	7	9
53	9		2	1	6	4	5	10	3		8	11	9	7

Gap between what one has and wants re. one's religion :

%	UN	N	SW	SO	SD	SN	SP	SF	SB	Sex	Age	WS	Led	Eth
47	22		1	4	2	5	6	3		8	8	9	7	8
49	13		1	3	2	4	7	6				8	5	9
46	9		1	4	2	6		3			7	8	8	5

Fig. 7

Per cent of variance explained and total effects rank order of predictors for : University totals, males and females

It shows the percent of variance explained by MDT and the rank order of total effects for all explanatory variables. MDT accounted for an average of about 45 per cent of the variance in students' reported net satisfaction with their university education. This average included some very high figures, e.g. 73 per cent of the variance in females' reported satisfaction at the University of Freiburg, 69 per cent for females at the University of Mannheim, 65 per cent for the whole group at Dhaka University. It also included some very low figures, e.g. 20 per cent for females at Austral University of Chile, 25 per cent for females at the University of Illinois, 30 per cent for males at the University of Baja California (see Annex 3 for details).

About a third of the variance in the most influential variable, the perceived gap between what students had and wanted, was explained by the other variables in the set, and the perceived gap between what students had and relevant others had displayed the greatest impact on the self-wants gap. The latter point is particularly important. Having discovered that the self-wants gap has the greatest relative impact on satisfaction, it is worthwhile to know what has the greatest relative influence on the former. Again, it might have been the case that at this second level needs, equity or something else was most important in creating the perceived gap between what students had and wanted. In fact, the perceived gap between what students had and thought others of the same sex and age in their area had (i.e. the social comparison or self-others gap) had the greatest relative impact on their perceived self-wants gap.

Annex 3 includes data regarding students' satisfaction and happiness with life as a whole, and satisfaction with their own religion (defined briefly as "spiritual fulfilment"). I am not going to go into the details of this material here, but it is worthwhile to notice the percentage of variance explained for these different dependent variables. Broadly speaking, the most difficult thing to explain is the most general, namely, happiness or satisfaction with life as a whole. On average, about 35 to 40 per cent of the variance in these variables can be explained by MDT. Headey (1985) found support for some interesting models in which domain satisfaction served as a mediating variable between life events and general well-being. MDT is most successful, so far as explained variance of dependent variables is concerned, at explaining satisfaction with one's religion. On average, about 55 per cent of the variance in such satisfaction is explained by MDT. In fact, cursory inspection of results from other analyses clearly indicates that the more personal and specific the domain, the greater the per cent of explained variance by MDT. The average per cent of variance explained by MDT for satisfaction with one's living partner (spouse or other person sharing intimate relations) seems to be in the high 70s.

Annex 3 gives the detailed numerical data for all the applications of MDT to students' satisfaction with their own university education. For illustrative purposes, I shall discuss the Guelph sample in particular. (For the reader's convenience, we reproduce below the relevant page from Annex 3).

Canada
University of Guelph

	S	SW	SO	SD	SN	SP	SF	SB	TES	TESW
N	305	307	330	329	0	331	329	328	-	-
R2	39	30	4	1	0	4	3	2	-	-
Pred										
Age	0	0	0	0	0	16	0	0	4	3
WS	0	0	0	0	0	-14	0	0	-3	-2
LED	0	0	14	11	0	0	0	0	4	4
ETH	0	0	14	0	0	0	18	14	6	4
SO	17	30							29	30
SN	0	23							9	23
SP	14	19							22	19
SB	12	0							12	0
SW	40								40	

Males

	S	SW	SO	SD	SN	SP	SF	SB	TES	TESW
N	170	172	187	0	0	0	0	187	-	-
R2	50	29	7	0	0	0	0	4	-	-
LED	0	0	19	0	0	0	0	0	6	6
ETH	0	0	19	0	0	0	0	22	9	6
SO	15	32							34	32
SN	0	16							9	16
SP	0	25							15	25
SB	12	0							12	0
SW	59								59	

Females

	S	SW	SO	SD	SN	SP	SF	SB	TES	TESW
N	134	134	0	0	141	141	140	0	-	-
R2	36	34	0	0	3	6	8	0	-	-
Age	0	0	0	0	0	26	0	0	7	0
ETH	0	0	0	0	-20	0	29	0	0	-6
SO	0	26							0	26
SD	32	0							32	0
SN	0	32							0	32
SP	26	0							26	0
SB	21	23							21	23
SW	0								0	

Fig. 8

In the extreme left hand column, there are listed the numbers of students in the sample (N) for the whole group, and males and females taken separately. Each column from that labelled 'S' to that labelled 'SB' gives the results of a stepwise regression of the labelled item on the variables listed below it. The squared multiple correlation coefficient (R2) is given below each distinct N, indicating a separate regression equation. For example, in the column under 'S' (for "satisfaction with one's own university education") we find a total Guelph sample N of 305 students, including 170 males and 134 females. One student did not identify his or her sex. MDT explained 39 per cent of the variance in reported net satisfaction with university education for the whole group, 50 per cent for males and 36 per cent for females. (To simplify the tables, decimal points were omitted.) The zeros in the colums indicate that an explanatory variable either had no influence on the dependent variable that was statistically significant at the 5 per cent level or that its influence as measured by its beta value was smaller than .05. When an explanatory variable had no influence on anything, it was simply deleted from the table. For example, although work status (WS) has some role to play in explaining satisfaction for the whole group, it had no influence in the male or female samples taken separately. So 'WS' appears in the list of predictors for the whole group, but not in the list for males and females.

'SW' abbreviates "the perceived gap between what one has and wants regarding one's university education", and its regression on the explanatory or predictor variables is indicated below it. The same is true for the other gap variables used in MDT. 'TES' is short for "the total effects of the explanatory variables on reported net satisfaction with one's university education". These are the most important effects to consider for each table, the sum of direct and indirect effects. Notice, for example, that although age has no direct effect on reported satisfaction (column 1 at the left), its total effect is listed in the TES column as .04. That happens because age has a direct effect on the perceived gap between what one has and three years ago expected to have at this point in life (indicated in the column labelled 'SP' for "self-progress"), which in turn has a direct effect on the self-wants gap, which itself has a direct effect on satisfaction. Besides this chain of effects from age to satisfaction, there is the chain going from age to self-progress to satisfaction directly. If you multiply all these direct effects, you have $.16 \times .19 \times .40 = .01216$ for the first chain, and $.16 \times .14 = .0223$ for the second chain. Adding these effects together gives us .03456, or briefly, a total effect of .04 for age.

In my analyses, age was categorized into seven categories, namely, 16 years or less, 17-19, 20-22, 23-25, 26-30, 31-35, 36 or more. Figuratively speaking, a total age effect of .04 means that as an age category score increase one full step, the reported net satisfaction score tended to increase only 4 pour cent of a step. Contrast this with the impact of the self-wants gap : for every full step increase (from 1 to 7) closing the gap between what one has and wants regarding one's university education, the reported net satisfaction score tended to increase 40 per cent of a step. So the gap variable has a relative impact on reported net satisfaction that was about ten times greater than the relative impact of age.

It is indeed tedious to calculate total effects, and I shall not bore you with more examples of procedure. The important points are that total effects typically differ from mere direct effects, that the main virtue of path analysis (which is the statistical procedure on which these tables are based) is that it allows one to calculate such effects, and that total effects are listed in the columns of figures under 'TES' and 'TESW' (short for "the total effects on the perceived gap between what one has and wants regarding one's university education").

8. EXAMPLES OF PRACTICAL USES OF THE INTEGRATED FRAMEWORK FOR DEVELOPMENT PLANNING

In the first chapter of the first volume of my *North American Social Report* I explained 15 kinds of potential uses and abuses of social indicators. Briefly, the former included such things as predicting trends, making inequalities visible, facilitating planning, balancing social and economic assessments, evaluating current public programmes, determining priorities, facilitating comparisons, suggesting research areas and allowing continuous monitoring. I suppose readers of this document are already aware of plenty of examples of most of these kinds of uses. So I shall limit myself to giving some examples of how the new series being proposed here can provide important new information for development planning. In particular I want to suggest some uses of the data on sexual differences, yearly attendance rates, yearly completion rates, completions measured by standardized tests, costs per unit of output, and reported attitudes of key personnel in the fields of education, science, technology and culture. The examples will be hypothetical, but hopefully nonetheless useful for present purposes.

Before moving on to specific examples, however, it will be worthwhile to emphasize one practical consequence of the results illustrated in Fig. 5 above. Remember that it was shown there that the self-wants and self-others gaps had the greatest relative influence on students' reported net satisfaction with their university education. These results confirm an often articulated hypothesis that one reason apparently oppressed people do not feel oppressed is that their feelings are constrained by their own ignorance or lack of vision concerning alternatives. MDT is designed to reveal the relative impact of concerns with one's own perceived wants and needs, equity, status compared to relevant others and so on. Although there is an enormous body of mainly theoretical literature insisting that human needs have a crucial role to play in the determination of satisfaction and happiness, and a substantial literature emphasizing the importance of equity, the results of applications of MDT in the present case reveal that in fact needs and equity are less important than wants and social comparisons. (Most of the evidence accumulated so far from applications of MDT in a variety of domains and with a variety of population samples is consistent with these results.)

One practical consequence of these results cannot be emphasized too strongly, namely that education has a fundamental and demonstrable role to play in the pursuit of satisfaction and happiness. Before this is dismissed as a mere truism, notice that our results have allowed us to specify particular kinds of information that have

particular measurable impacts on reported net satisfaction and happiness. People's wants and the groups with which they make personal
comparisons must be affected by their information, and such information can be well or poorly founded. Evidently, necessary conditions
of personal and social development include the possession of well-
founded information and a progressive vision, rather than poorly-
founded information and a conservative vision. While a broad and
progressive vision may lead to vast perceived gaps, dissatisfaction
and unhappiness in the short run, such a vision is necessary for
growth, development, satisfaction and happiness in the long run.
(There is an obvious analogy here in the logically necessary conditions for the growth of scientific knowledge including the creation
of bold new hypotheses (Popper, 1934).) In other words, our results
support the view that well-founded information and a progressive
vision are necessary conditions of moving people from what might be
called a Fool's Paradise to a Real Paradise.

Assuming that if all other things are roughly equal then it is
better to be satisfied or happy than dissatisfied or unhappy, there
are only four possibilities to be considered. So it will not detain
us too long to examine them. They are as follows. One may have :

1. well-founded information and be satisfied or happy,
2. well-founded information and be dissatisfied or unhappy,
3. poorly-founded information and be satisfied or happy,
4. poorly-founded information and be dissatisfied or unhappy.

I suppose the first case is the most desirable, and might with
some hyperbole be regarded as Real Paradise. Here one has well-
founded information or reliable and valid knowledge on which to base
one's judgments, and one is satisfied or happy. The second case
might be regarded as Real Hell, i.e. feeling miserable and having
excellent reasons for feeling that way. The third case is a Fool's
Paradise, i.e. one's good feelings have no justification in the real
world. And I suppose the fourth case should be regarded as a Fool's
Hell, i.e. one is miserable for no good reason at all.

Results of applications of MDT reveal that satisfaction and
happiness are determined to a significant extent by, among other
things, perceived comparisons with other people. The other people
may be so similar to oneself, perhaps so similarly oppressed, that
there is virtually no possibility of a perceived discrepancy. However, when one's attention is called to people remarkably dissimilar
and better off than oneself, even if the new comparison group is
hypothetical, then a necessary condition of a perceived discrepancy
has been fulfilled. It is the function of educators and educational
institutions to provide students with a well founded, broader and
more progressive vision than they might otherwise have. The finer
vision will free them from their Fool's Paradise, frustrate and
dissatisfy them in the short run, and, hopefully, motivate them to
pursue and capture the Real Paradise of their finest dreams. The
scenario is ancient. The Old Testament prophet said that when
people lose their vision they perish, and the New Testament is the
story of eternal life following crucifixion. Although I am an

atheist and have no inclinations toward any kind of religion, MDT is a theory that is consistant with these ancient views.

Having completed our brief digression on the practical significance of MDT for growth and development, let us return to some more specific examples of the use of my proposed integrated system of social indicators. All of the examples will refer to the items in Fig. 2 by their section and item numbers. For example, '2:IOP.1' refers to Section 2, item number IOP.1 on pupil attendance ratios.

Because it is possible for students to be enrolled in school without attending classes for one reason or another, and attendance is more important than enrolment from the point of view of learning, attendance ratios are necessary for evaluating educational programmes, making comparisons and planning priorities. Hence, the need for items like 2:IOP.1, 2:IOP.2, 2:IOP.3 and 2:IOP.4.

Items like 2:IOP.5, gross enrolment ratios by year and sex, are necessary for determining equality of treatment with regard to males and females enrolled in school. These ratios give us the per cent of eligible people that are actually enrolled.

Completion rates by years, age and sex are fundamental output indicators, e.g. 2:UOP.2, 3:UOP.2 (pre-first level, first level, second level and third level). Completion rates allow us to perform virtually all the planning tasks mentioned in the first paragraph of this section, i.e. predicting trends, assessing inequalities, etc. Without comparable enrolment and attendance figures for the same sets of students, it would be impossible to discover the causes of diverse completion rates. There would be no way to determine if unequal male and female completion rates were the result of unequal enrolments or equal enrolments but unequal attendance. The point of recording yearly completion rates is to allow one to determine precise years of difficulty. It is possible, for example, that earlier or later years of secondary school are more crucial from the point of view of getting through the whole system. We should like to know if the chances (i.e. relative frequency probabilities) of completing, say, grade 9 are greater or smaller than the chances of completing grade 8 for males and females. In which years, if any, should special programmes or personnel be introduced to get the maximum benefit with regard to getting all enrolled people to complete their education ?

Obviously, in the preceding paragraph and elsewhere in this document it is assumed that completion of a course of study is equivalent to actually having learned a certain body of knowledge. That is generous, to say the least. We should be on much more solid ground if all students everywhere were given standardized tests covering various bodies of knowledge. Then we could get precise measures of the relative costs per unit of knowledge in certain fields, in certain societies, in certain schools, in certain years and so on. That would be incredibly useful for planning growth and development, and for setting priorities to get the maximum benefit for a given cost. Hence, items like 2:UOP.3, 2:UOP.4, 3:UOP.3, 3:UOP.4 (for pre-first, first, second and third levels of education) are included. All these items require the construction and administration of standardized tests of knowledge similar to those that have been used for several years by the International Association for Evaluation of Educational Achievement (IEA). Although Pedhazur (1982) has revealed some difficult problems in the interpretation of these tests, the latter provide unique approaches to the measurement of educational achievement and should be given serious attention by researchers.

Items like 2:ION.9, public expenditure on education per completions by year of education, provide comparable information regarding the financial inputs to education. While expenditures per inhabitant or as a per cent of GNP (2:ION.7) give us some measure of a society's general or relative level of payments for education no matter how many people are being educated, items like 2:ION.9 indicate costs with specific reference to the benefits of the system, namely with reference to numbers of people actually completing a year's worth of education. Items like 2:ION.10 and 2:ION.11, on expenditures per student completing standardized tests covering grades or courses of study, provide even more precise information regarding the costs per measurable benefits in terms of knowledge gained.

My general policy with regard to cost indicators is to regard them as negative. I assume that in the best of all possible worlds (or Paradise, for that matter), one would obtain maximum benefits for minimum or zero costs, and the closer we come to such a balance sheet in this world, the better off we are. Thus, ideally one would like to have all eligible people enrolled in school, attending all classes, completing desired courses of study and actually learning what they are supposed to be learning free of charge. Since in this world there are always costs, the most one can reasonably do is try to keep costs down and continually increase benefits. In economists' jargon, one must try to develop systems that are both maximally effective and efficient, or briefly, systems characterized by maximum productivity.

Items like 2:USP.1-2:USP.18, 2:USP.1-3:USP.18 (for second and third levels of education) are designed to get some information about educational systems and practices directly from students themselves. Unless the item is followed by a phrase indicating that the questions are to be put only to second and third level students, it is assumed that students at every level of education are to be surveyed by years. Each of these sets of subjective output items fits into an explanatory cluster according to results obtained from research with MDT. For example, items 2:USP.1-2:USP.4 form one such cluster. Item 2:USP.4 asks about a student's satisfaction with her or his own school attendance record in the past year. Items 2:USP.1 and 2:USP.2 ask about the student's perceived self-wants and self-others gaps, respectively, regarding school attendance. So, we have data on satisfaction with school attendance and on its two relatively most powerful explanatory variables. Item 2:USP.3 provides information on the perceived discrepancy between a student's own performance and that of average students of the opposite sex. This will give us an idea of students' perceptions of sexual discrimination, and might even by a useful predictor of satisfaction. Besides fitting together in an explanatory cluster according to MDT, these items will be useful in conjunction with actual attendance ratios. Although many countries have laws about school attendance, there is presumably some relation between students' own attitudes towards it and their behaviour. Items like 2:USP.5-2:USP.ŏ form explanatory clusters around the issue of the perceived kind of education obtained with respect to the types of subjects studied, and items like 2:USP.9 are concerned with the perceived quality of education.

Items like 2:USP.19-2:IUSP.22 are designed to get teachers' views about pupil-teacher ratios (items 2:2.7 and 2:ION.1). Again, these subjective output indicators are designed in the light of results from MDT research, and with the assumption that the evaluation of educational systems and practices should include some input from the main participants, namely students and teachers. It is also assumed that such input is essential for sound planning, the determination of priorities and development.

Items like 5:IOP.2 tell us the relative share of scientists and engineers in every group of 1000 available members of the civilian labour force, and 5:IOP.4 tells us the share actually employed in research and development (R&D). Since such trained personnel are necessary ingredients of development, sound planning requires that we know the shares of these people available and working. Item 5:A provides figures on the number of immigrant professional and technical people entering one's country, and item 5:IOP.5 provides information on their share of the total immigrant population. Although a country's indigenous population and educational systems are typically its greatest source of professionals, immigration has always served as an important source of additional brain power. In the third volume of my *North American Social Report*, it is shown that both Canada and the United States rely on the 'brain drain' from other countries to maintain desired levels of professionals, especially in the medical profession. I am not recommending that countries actively lure professionals away from other countries, but it is reasonable to be aware of such immigration and to take account of it in development planning. In Canada, as in some Third World countries, development planning has included the systematic effort to attract native-born professionals home from other countries, especially from the United States. Some relatively small countries, such as Israel, export brain drain power much the same way that other countries export natural resources.

Items like 5:ION.2, on R&D expenditures as a per cent of GNP, are standard objective input measures of a country's financial R&D effort. They must be supplemented by objective output items like 5:UOP.1 (patents issued to resident inventors per 1000 scientists and engineers employed in R&D) and 5:UOP.2 (number of papers published per 1000 scientists and engineers employed in R&D). The latter productivity measures should also be supplemented by measures of productivity that relate output directly to dollar costs, e.g. items 5:ION.3 (cost per patent issued) and 5:ION.4 (cost per paper published). In all cases it is recommended that productivity figures be obtained with as much detail as possible regarding specific research fields, and the age and sex of researchers. Of course, here as everywhere else, it is extremely important and difficult to get measures of quality properly to adjust apparently gross measures of productivity. (The Summer 1986 issue of *Science, Technology and Human Values* advertises an 88-page bibliography on indicators of scientific quality.) However, this just represents an opportunity for exciting and challenging research in the future. It is, after all, pointless to pour money into R&D without paying any attention to the quality of the outputs obtained, no matter how impressive the outputs appear quantitatively.

The subjective output indicators 5:USP.1-5:USP.14 have been designed in the light of research with MDT, and consist of clusters of explanatory variables. For example, 5:USP.1-5:USP.5 form a cluster regarding the per cent of a professional's workday actually spent on activities directly related to R&D. Item 5:USP.1 obtains the percentage figures and item 5:USP.5 obtains professionals' satisfaction ratings regarding these figures. Items 5:USP.2 and 5:USP.3 give us data on professionals' perceived self-wants and self-others gaps, respectively, regarding time spent directly on R&D, while 5:USP.4 tells us about perceived discrimination.

Items 5:USP.6-5:USP.10 concern professionals' perceptions of and attitudes toward their R&D facilities ; specifically, equipment, supplies, libraries and funds. For purposes of detailed planning, it would be useful to expand these items regarding specific kinds of equipment, supplies and so on. Items 5:USP.11-5:USP.14 assess professionals' views about the quality and quantity of their own output. Both of these sets of items form MDT-type explanatory clusters.

The items in Section 6, labelled "culture and communication", are certainly relevant to their subject's label, but they seem to have at least as much commercial as cultural significance. One has to assume that more is probably better, because more implies the possibility of greater distribution and equality of access. But it is well-known that such probabilities and possibilities frequently bear little relation to what actually happens in the real world.

Similarly, one must assume that it is preferable to have more rather than fewer libraries, books, newspapers, periodicals and so on, if all other things are roughly equal. Besides, for purposes of planning development programmes, it is virtually impossible to establish priorities without reliable and valid data regarding such cultural artifacts. However, it is also important to assess the impact of available artifacts on a country's inhabitants. In particular, one ought to have information on the perceived quantity, quality, variety and cost of a country's cultural heritage. That is the point of the items covering Sections 7-10, items USP.1-USP.28. These items form four subsets of seven self-wants types of questions regarding quantity, quality, variety and cost. The seven items first ask in turn about respondents' ability to purchase as many books as wanted (USP.1), to borrow as many (USP.2), to attend as many cinema performances (USP.3), to purchase as many newspapers and periodicals (USP.4), to borrow as many newspapers and periodicals (USP.5), to listen to the radio as often (USP.6) and to watch television as much as wanted (USP.7).

Next, there are seven similar questions asking, for example, if respondents have usually been able to purchase books the content of which was as good in quality as they wanted (USP.8). Then there are seven questions regarding respondents' ability to get the kinds or variety of books, etc., that they wanted. Finally, there are seven

142

questions regarding respondents' ability to purchase books, etc., at a cost that was close to what they wanted to pay. Although it would have been more informative to include a full set of MDT-type explanatory clusters in this group of subjective output indicators, this would have at least tripled their number. I therefore limited the group to self-wants items, on the assumption that these would be most useful for planning purposes.

REFERENCES

Abbey, A. and F.M. Andrews, 1985. "Modeling the psychological determinants of life quality", *Social Indicators Research*, 16, pp. 1-34.

Abelson, R.P., 1968. *Theories of Cognitive Consistancy : A Sourcebook*, Rand McNally and Co., Chicago.

Abdel-Halim, A.A., 1979. "Interaction effects of power equalization and subordinate personality on job satisfaction and performance", *Human Relations*, 32, pp. 489-502.

Adams, J.S., 1965. "Inequity in social exchange", in L. Berkowitz (ed.), *Advances in Experimental Social Psychology*, Academic Press, New York, pp. 43-90.

Alechina, I., 1982. "The contribution of the United Nations system to formulating development concepts", *Different Theories and Practices of Development*, Unesco, Paris, pp. 9-68.

Allmer, H., 1982. "Selbstverantwortlichkeit und Schulerzufriedenheit nach erwarteter und unerwarteter Leistungsbewertung", *Psychologie in Erziehung und Unterricht*, 29, pp. 321-327.

Andrews, F.M. and S.B. Withey, 1976. *Social Indicators of Well-Being*, Plenum Press, New York.

Appelgryn, A.E. and C. Plug, 1981. "Application of the theory of relative deprivation to occupational discrimination against women", *South African Journal of Psychology*, 11, pp. 143-147.

Bahr, S.J., C.B. Chappell and G.K. Leigh, 1983. "Age at marriage, role enactment, role consensus, and marital satisfaction", *Journal of Marriage and the Family*, 45, pp. 795-803.

Barrett, G.V., J.B. Forbes, E.J. O'Connor and R.A. Alexander, 1980. "Ability-satisfaction relationships : field and laboratory studies", *Academy of Management Journal*, 23, pp. 550-555.

Bearden, W.O. and J.E. Teel, 1983. "Selected determinants of consumer satisfaction and complaint reports", *Journal of Marketing Research*, 20, pp. 21-28.

Bell, B.D., 1978-79. "Life satisfaction and occupational retirement : beyond the impact year", *International Journal of Aging and Human Development*, 9, pp. 31-50.

Berkowitz, L., 1968. "The study of urban violence : some implications of laboratory studies of frustration and aggression", *American Behavioral Scientist*, 11, pp. 14-17.

Betz, E.L., 1984. "Two tests of Maslow's theory of need fulfillment", *Journal of Vocational Behavior*, 24, pp. 204-220.

Bledsoe, J.C., D.J. Mullen and G.J. Hobbs, 1980. "Validity of the Mullen diagnostic survey for leadership improvement", *Perceptual and Motor Skills*, 50 (3, Pt. 1), pp. 838-846.

Booth, R.F., M.S. McNally and N.H. Berry, 1979. "Hospital corpsmen perceptions of working in a fleet Marine Force environment", *Military Medicine*, 144, pp. 31-34.

Campbell, A.P., P.E. Converse and W.L. Rodgers, 1976. *The Quality of American Life*, Russell Sage Foundation, New York.

Canter, D. and K. Rees, 1982. "A multivariate model of housing satisfaction", *International Review of Applied Psychology*, 31, pp. 185-208.

Carp, F.M., A. Carp and R. Millsap, 1982. "Equity and Satisfaction among the elderly", *International Journal of Aging and Human Development*, 15, pp. 151-166.

Cash, T.F., D.W. Cash and J.W. Butters, 1983. "Mirror, mirror, on the wall...? : contrast effects and self-evaluation of physical attractiveness", *Personality and Social Psychology Bulletin*, 9, pp. 351-358.

Caplan, R.D., 1979. "Social support, person-environment fit, and coping", in L.A. Ferman and J.P. Gordus (eds.), *Mental Health and the Economy*, Upjohn Institute, Kalamazoo, pp. 89-137.

Caplan, R.D., 1983. "Person-environment fit : past, present and future", in C.L. Cooper (ed.), *Stress Research*, John Wiley and Sons, New York, pp. 353-77.

Cate, R.M., S.A. Lloyd, J.M. Henton and J.H. Larson, 1982. "Fairness and reward level as predictors of relationship satisfaction", *Social Psychology Quarterly*, 45, pp. 177-181.

Cherrington, D.J. and J.L. England, 1980. "The desire for an enriched job as a moderator of the enrichment-satisfaction relationship", *Organizational Behavior and Human Performance*, 25, pp. 139-159.

Chisholm, R.F., D.E. Gauntner and R.F. Munzenrider, 1980. "Pre-enlistment expectations/perceptions of army life, satisfaction, and re-enlistment of volunteers", *Journal of Political and Military Sociology*, 8, pp. 31-42.

Churchill, G.A. and C. Surprenant, 1982. "An investigation into the determinants of customer satisfaction", *Journal of Marketing Research*, 19, pp. 491-504.

Cook, K.S., 1975. "Expectations, evaluations and equity", *American Sociological Review*, 40, pp. 372-388.

Crosby, F.J., 1976. "A model of egoistical relative deprivation", *Psychological Review*, 83, pp. 85-113.

Crosby, F.J., 1982. *Relative Deprivation and Working Women*, Oxford University Press, New York.

Davis, J.A., 1959. "A formal interpretation of the theory of relative deprivation", *Sociometry*, 22, pp. 280-296.

Dickstein, L.S. and A. Whitaker, 1983. "Effects of task outcome and subjective standard on state depression for cognitive and social tasks", *Bulletin of the Psychonomic Society*, 21, pp. 183-186.

Diener, E., 1984. "Subjective well-being", *Psychological Bulletin*, 95, pp. 542-575.

Dorr, D., S. Honea and R. Posner, 1980. "Ward atmosphere and psychiatric nurses' job satisfaction", *American Journal of Community Psychology*, 8, pp. 455-461.

Drexler, J.A. and M.K. Lindell, 1981. "Training/job fit and worker satisfaction", *Human Relations*, 34, pp. 907-915.

Duncan, O.D., 1975. "Does money buy satisfaction", *Social Indicators Research*, 2, pp. 267-274.

Edwards, W. and A. Tversky (eds.), 1967. *Decision Making*, Penguin Books, Middlesex.

Emmons, R.A. and E. Diener, 1985. "Factors predicting satisfaction judgments : a comparative examination", *Social Indicators Research*, 16, pp. 157-168.

Feather, N.T., 1979. "Human values and the work situation : two studies", *Australian Psychologist*, 14, pp. 131-141.

Festinger, L., 1957. *A Theory of Cognitive Dissonance*, Stanford University Press, Stanford.

Fields, N.S., 1983. "Satisfaction in long-term marriages", *Social Work*, 28, pp. 37-41.

Frank, E., C. Anderson and D. Rubinstein, 1979. "Marital role strain and sexual satisfaction", *Journal of Consulting and Clinical Psychology*, 47, pp. 1096-1103.

Gauthier, B., 1987. "Client satisfaction in program evaluation", *Social Indicators Research*, 19, pp. 174-201.

Gerrard, C.K., M. Reznikoff and M. Riklan, 1982. "Level of aspiration, life satisfaction, and locus of control in older adults", *Experimental Aging Research*, 8, pp. 119-121.

Glatzer, W. and M. Volkert, 1980. "Living conditions and the quality of life of older people", *Zeitschrift für Gerontologie*, 13, pp. 247-260.

Golant, S.M., 1986. "Subjective housing assessments by the elderly : a critical information source for planning and program evaluation", *The Gerontologist*, 26, pp. 122-127.

Goodman, P.S., 1966. *A Study of Time Perspective : Measurement and Correlates*, Doctoral Dissertation, Cornell University.

Goodman, P.S., 1974. "An examination of referents used in the evaluation of pay", *Organizational Behavior and Human Perform- ance*, 12, pp. 170-195.

Goodman, P.S. and A. Friedman, 1971. "An examination of Adams' theory of inequity", *Administrative Science Quarterly*, 16, pp. 271-288.

Gurr, T.R., 1970. *Why Men Rebel*, Princeton University Press, Princeton.

Gutek, B.A., *et al.*, 1983. "The importance of internal referents as determinants of satisfaction", *Journal of Community Psychology*, 11, pp. 111-120.

Handal, P.J., P.W. Barling and E. Morrissy, 1981. "Development of perceived and preferred measures of physical and social charac- teristics of the residential environment and their relationship to satisfaction", *Journal of Community Psychology*, 9, pp. 118- 124.

Harrison, R.V., 1978. "Person-environment fit and job stress", in C.L. Cooper and R. Payne (eds.), *Stress at Work*, John Wiley, New York, pp. 175-205.

Harrison, R.V., 1983. "The person-environment fit model and the study of job stress", in T.A. Beehr and R.S. Bhagat (eds.), *Human Stress and Cognition in Organizations : An Integrated Perspective*, John Wiley, New York.

Harsanyi, J.C., 1982. "Morality and the theory of rational be- haviour", in A. Sen and B. Williams (eds.), *Utilitarianism and Beyond*, Cambridge University Press, Cambridge, pp. 39-62.

Hartlage, L.C. and E.V. Sperr, 1980. "Patient preferences with regard to ideal therapist characteristics", *Journal of Clinical Psychology*, 36, pp. 288-291.

Hatfield, E., D. Greenberger, J. Traupmann and P. Lambert, 1982. "Equity and sexual satisfaction in recently married couples", *Journal of Sex Research*, 18, pp. 18-32.

Hatfield, J.D. and R.C. Huseman, 1982. "Perceptual congruence about communication as related to satisfaction : moderating effects of individual characteristics", *Academy of Management Journal*, 25, pp. 349-358.

Headey, B., *et al.*, 1985. "Modeling change in perceived quality of life (PQOL)", *Social Indicators Research*, 17, pp. 267-298.

Hener, T. and E.I. Meir, 1981. "Congruency, consistency and differentiation as predictors of job satisfaction within the nursing occupation", *Journal of Vocational Behavior*, 18, pp. 304-309.

Humphrys, P., 1981. "The effect of importance upon the relation between perceived job attributes, desired job attributes and job satisfaction", *Australian Journal of Psychology*, 33, pp. 121-133.

Ickes, W.J., B. Schermer and J. Steeno, 1979. "Sex and sex-role influences in same-sex dyads", *Social Psychology Quarterly*, 42, pp. 373-385.

Joyce, W.F. and J. Slocum, 1982. "Climate discrepancy : refining the concepts of psychological and organizational climate", *Human Relations*, 35, pp. 951-971.

Kemelgor, B.H., 1982. "Job satisfaction as mediated by the value congruity of supervisors and their subordinates", *Journal of Occupational Behaviour*, 3, pp. 147-160.

Kopelman, R.E., 1979. "Directionally different expectancy theory predictions of work motivation and job satisfaction", *Motivation and Emotion*, 3, pp. 299-317.

Kurella, S., 1979. "The social needs of patients and their satisfaction with medical care : a survey of medical inpatients in the county hospitals of the German Democratic Republic", *Academy Postgraduate Medical Education*, 13A, pp. 737-742.

Lapin, N. and R. Richta, 1982. *Different Theories and Practices of Development*, Unesco, Paris, pp. 163-210.

Lee, C. and R.S. Schuler, 1982. "A constructive replication and extension of a role and expectancy perception model of participation in decision making", *Journal of Occupational Psychology*, 55, pp. 109-118.

Lewin, K., *et al.*, 1944. "Level of aspiration", in J.McV. Hund (ed.), *Personality and Behaviour Disorders*, Ronald Press Co., New York, pp. 333-378.

Lloyd, S., R. Cate and J. Henton, 1982. "Equity and rewards as predictors of satisfaction in casual and intimate relationships", *Journal of Psychology*, 110, pp. 43-48.

Luce, R.D. and H. Raiffa, 1957. *Games and Decisions*, John Wiley and Sons, New York.

Maguire, G.H., 1983. "An exploratory study of the relationship of valued activities to the life satisfaction of elderly persons", *Occupational Therapy Journal of Research*, 3, pp. 164-172.

Matthews, C. and R.D. Clark, 1982. "Marital satisfaction : a validation approach", *Basic and Applied Social Psychology*, 3, pp. 169-186.

Mayer, T. and H.B. Andrews, 1981. "Changes in self-concept following a spinal cord injury", *Journal of Applied Rehabilitation Counseling*, 12, pp. 135-137.

McNeil, J.K., M.J. Stones and A. Kozma, 1986. "Subjective well-being in later life : issues concerning measurement and prediction", *Social Indicators Research*, 18, pp. 35-70.

Meir, E.I. and M. Erez, 1981. "Fostering a career in engineering", *Journal of Vocational Behavior*, 18, pp. 115-120.

Merton, R.K. and A.S. Kitt, 1950. "Contributions to the theory of reference group behavior", in R.K. Merton and P.F. Lazarsfeld (eds.), *Continuities in Social Research*, John Wiley & Sons, New York, pp. 40-105.

Michalos, A.C., 1970. "Cost-benefit versus expected utility acceptance rules", *Theory and Decision*, 1, pp. 61-88.

Michalos, A.C., 1978. *Foundations of Decision-Making*, Canadian Library of Philosophy, Ottawa.

Michalos, A.C., 1979. "Life changes, illness and personal life satisfaction in a rural population", *Social Science and Medicine*, 13A, pp. 175-181.

Michalos, A.C., 1980. *North American Social Report*, Vol. 1 : *Foundations, Population and Health*, D. Reidel Pub. Co., Dordrecht.

Michalos, A.C., 1980a. "Satisfaction and happiness", *Social Indicators Research*, 8, pp. 385-422.

Michalos, A.C., 1980b. *North American Social Report*, Vol. 2 : *Crime, Justice and Politics*, D. Reidel Pub. Co., Dordrecht.

Michalos, A.C., 1981. *North American Social Report*, Vol. 3 : *Science, Education and Recreation*, D. Reidel Pub. Co., Dordrecht.

Michalos, A.C., 1981a. *North American Social Report*, Vol. 4 : *Environment, Transportation and Housing*, D. Reidel Pub. Co., Dordrecht.

Michalos, A.C., 1982, "The satisfaction and happiness of some senior citizens in rural Ontario", *Social Indicators Research*, 11, pp. 1-30.

Michalos, A.C., 1982a. *North American Social Report*, Vol. 5 : *Economics, Religion and Morality*, D. Reidel Pub. Co., Dordrecht.

Michalos, A.C., 1983. "Satisfaction and happiness in a rural northern resource community", *Social Indicators Research*, 13, pp. 224-252.

Michalos, A.C., 1985. "Multiple discrepancies theory (MDT)", *Social Indicators Research*, 16, pp. 347-413.

Michalos, A.C., 1986a. "An application of multiple discrepancies theory (MDT) to seniors", *Social Indicators Research*, 17, pp. 349-373.

Michalos, A.C., 1986b. "Satisfaction with one's university education ; survey results from 23 countries". Paper presented to the annual meeting of the Canadian Society for the Study of Higher Education, Winnipeg.

148

Michalos, A.C., 1986c. "Satisfaction with one's religion ; survey results from 21 countries". Paper presented to the annual meeting of the Canadian Society for the Study of Religion, Winnipeg.

Michalos, A.C., 1986d. "Satisfaction and happiness with life as a whole ; survey results from 23 countries". Paper presented to the 9th World Congress of Sociology, New Delhi.

Michalos, A.C., 1986e. "Job satisfaction, marital satisfaction and the quality of life : a review and a preview", in F.M. Andrews (ed.), *Research on the Quality of Life*, University of Michigan Press, Ann Arbor.

Morse, J.J. and D.F. Caldwell, 1979. "Effects of personality and perception of the environment on satisfaction with task group", *Journal of Psychology*, 103, pp. 183-192.

O'Brien, G.E., 1983. "Skill-utilization, skill-variety and the job characteristics model", *Australian Journal of Psychology*, 35, pp. 461-468.

O'Brien, G.E. and P. Dowling, 1980. "The effects of congruency between perceived and desired job attributes upon job satisfaction", *Journal of Occupational Psychology*, 53, pp. 121-130.

O'Brien, G.E. and P. Humphrys, 1982. "The effects of congruency between work values and perceived job attributes upon the job satisfaction of pharmacists", *Australian Journal of Psychology*, 34, pp. 91-101.

O'Brien, G.E. and M. Pembroke, 1982. "Crowding, density and the job satisfaction of clerical employees", *Australian Journal of Psychology*, 34, pp. 151-164.

Oldham, G.R., *et al.*, 1982. "The selection and consequences of job comparisons", *Organizational Behavior and Human Performance*, 29, pp. 84-111.

Oldham, G.R. and H.E. Miller, 1979. "The effect of significant other's job complexity on employee reactions to work", *Human Relations*, 32, pp. 247-260.

Oliver, R.L., 1980. "A cognitive model of the antecedents and consequences of satisfaction decisions", *Journal of Marketing Research*, 17, pp. 460-469.

Osherson, S. and D. Dill, 1983. "Varying work and family choices : their impact on men's work satisfaction", *Journal of Marriage and the Family*, 45, pp. 339-346.

Patchen, M., 1961. *The Choice of Wage Comparisons*, Prentice-Hall, Englewood Cliffs.

Pedhazur, E.J., 1982. *Multiple Regression in Behavioral Research*, Holt, Rinehart and Winston, New York.

Peplau, L.A., C. Padesky and M. Hamilton, 1982. "Satisfaction in lesbian relationships", *Journal of Homosexuality*, 8, pp. 23-35.

Peters, A.S. and R. Markello, 1982. "Job satisfaction among academic physicians : attitudes toward job components", *Journal of Medical Education*, 57, pp. 937-939.

Peterson, M.F., 1979. "Leader behavior, group size, and member satisfaction in university Christian growth groups", *Journal of Psychology and Theology*, 7, pp. 125-132.

Rahim, A., 1981. "Job satisfaction as a function of personality-job congruence : a study with Jungian psychological types", *Psychological Reports*, 49, pp. 496-498.

Reimer, C., *et al.*, 1981. "Psychodynamic considerations and findings concerning rehabilitation after open-heart surgery", *Psychiatria Fennica*, Sup. Vol., pp. 47-54.

Roessler, R.T. and S.E. Boone, 1979. "The relationship of person/environment fit to client perceptions and performance in a rehabilitation center", *Rehabilitation Psychology*, 26, pp. 145-154.

Rosman, P. and R.J. Burke, 1980. "Job satisfaction, self-esteem, and the fit between perceived self and job on valued competencies", *Journal of Psychology*, 105, pp. 259-269.

Ross, C.E., J. Mirowsky and R.S. Duff, 1982. "Physician status characteristics and client satisfaction in two types of medical practice", *Journal of Health and Social Behavior*, 23, pp. 317-329.

Ross, R.H. and F.B. Kraft, 1983. "Creating low consumer product expectations", *Journal of Business Research*, 11, pp. 1-9.

Runciman, W.G., 1966. *Relative Deprivation and Social Justice*, University of California Press, Berkeley.

Scarpello, V. and J.P. Campbell, 1983. "Job satisfaction and the fit between individual needs and organizational rewards", *Journal of Occupational Psychology*, 56, pp. 315-328.

Schroder, K.H., 1981. "Social styles and heterosexual pair relationships", *American Journal of Family Therapy*, 9, pp. 65-74.

Suls, J. and G.S. Sanders, 1982. "Self-evaluation through social comparison : A developmental analysis", *Review of Personality and Social Psychology*, 3, pp. 171-197.

Swan, J.E. and I.F. Trawick, 1981. "Disconfirmation of expectations and satisfaction with a retail service", *Journal of Retailing*, 57, pp. 49-67.

Taylor, M.C., 1982. "Improved conditions, rising expectations, and dissatisfaction : a test of the past/present relative deprivation hypothesis", *Social Psychology Quarterly*, 45, pp. 24-33.

Thomas, L.E. and P.I. Robbins, 1979. "Personality and work environment congruence of mid-life career changers", *Journal of Occupational Psychology*, 52, pp. 177-183.

Tjosvold, D., R. Andrews and H. Jones, 1983. "Cooperative and competitive relationships between leaders and subordinates", *Human Relations*, 36, pp. 1111-1124.

Traupmann, J., E. Hatfield and P. Wexler, 1983. "Equity and sexual satisfaction in dating couples", *British Journal of Social Psychology*, 22, pp. 33-40.

Turner, R.J., B.G. Frankel and D.M. Levin, 1983. "Social support : conceptualization, measurements, and implications for mental health", *Research in Community and Mental Health*, 3, pp. 67-111.

Tziner, A., 1983. "Correspondence between occupational rewards and occupational needs and work satisfaction : a canonical redundancy analysis", *Journal of Occupational Psychology*, 56, pp. 49-56.

Unesco, 1982. *Different Theories and Practices of Development*, Unesco, Paris.

United Nations, 1984. *Compiling Social Indicators of the Situation of Women*, Studies in Methods, Series F, No. 32, United Nations, New York.

United Nations, 1984. *Improving Concepts and Methods for Statistics and Indicators on the Situation of Women*, Studies in Methods, Series F, No. 33, United Nations, New York.

Veenhoven, R., 1984. *Conditions of Happiness*, D. Reidel Pub. Co., Dordrecht.

Walster, E., E. Berscheid and G.W. Walster, 1976. "New directions in equity research", in L. Berkowitz and E. Walster (eds.), *Advances in Experimental Social Psychology*, Academic Press, New York, pp. 1-42.

Weintraub, Z., 1981. "The relationship between job satisfaction and work performance", *Revista de Psihologie*, 27, pp. 59-67.

Wiggins, J.D., D.A. Lederer, A. Salkowe and G.S. Rys, 1983. "Job satisfaction related to tested congruence and differentiation", *Journal of Vocational Behavior*, 23, pp. 112-121.

Wiggins, J.D. and A.D. Moody, 1983. "Identifying effective counselors through client-supervisor ratings and personality-environmental variables", *The Vocational Guidance Quarterly*, 31, pp. 259-269.

Wiggins, J.D., A.D. Moody and D.A. Lederer, 1983. "Personality typologies related to marital satisfaction", *American Mental Health Counselors Association Journal*, 5, pp. 169-178.

Williams, R.M.Jr., 1975. "Relative deprivation", in L.A. Coser (ed.), *The Idea of Social Structure : Papers in Honor of Robert K. Merton*, Harcourt Brace Jovanovich, New York, pp. 355-378.

Wills, T.A., 1981. "Downward comparison principles in social psychology", *Psychological Bulletin*, 90, pp. 245-271.

Wills, T.A., 1983. "Social comparison in coping and help-seeking", in B.M. DePaulo, A. Nadler and J.D. Fisher (eds.), *New Directions in Helping*, Vol. 2 : *Help-Seeking*, Academic Press, New York, pp. 109-141.

Wood, D.A., 1981. "The relation between work values and the perception of the work setting", *Journal of Social Psychology*, 115, pp. 189-193.

Wright, D. and T.B. Gutkin, 1981. "School psychologists' job satisfaction and discrepancies between actual and desired work functions", *Psychological Reports*, 49, pp. 735-738.

Wright, S.J., 1985. "Health satisfaction : a detailed test of the multiple discrepancies theory model", *Social Indicators Research*, 17, pp. 299-314.

Zaleski, Z., 1981. "Consistency in value appreciation and marriage satisfaction", *Roczniki Filozoficzne*, 29, pp. 163-173.

Zapf, W., et al., 1987. "German social report : living conditions and subjective well-being, 1978-1984", *Social Indicators Research*, 19, pp. 1-173.

ANNEX 1

SOCIAL INDICATORS AND STATISTICS
(See Annex 4 for abbreviations and definitions)

The following list of social indicators and statistics is constructed around the Table of Contents of Unesco's 1985 *Statistical
Yearbook*. Special definitions and notes to Unesco's tables may be
found in the *Yearbook*. To the 100 items listed in the Contents, I
have added 250. Only thirteen of the original 100 items seemed to
be interpretable as social indicators. To these thirteen, I have
added about 160. The items from the Contents are numbered exactly
as they were, e.g. 1.1, 1.2, etc. New items are numbers by chapter
and letter (e.g. 2.A, 2.B, etc.) when they are only social statistics to be used in the construction of social indicators. Social
indicators are identified as input or output, objective or subjective, positive or negative and given a number. For example,
IOP.1 identified an input indicator that is objective and positive,
IOP.2 identifies a second indicator of the same sort, USP.1 identifies an output indicator that is subjective and positive, and so
on. There are summary tables for chapters and parts of chapters to
help the reader follow the development of the full set of
indicators.

1. Reference Tables

1.1 Population, area and density, 1970, 1975, 1980, 1982 and 1983.

1.2 Estimated total population and population 0-24 years old, by
continents, major areas and groups of countries, 1970-2000.

1.3 UON Illiterate population 15 years of age and over and percentage illiteracy by sex.

1.4. UOP Percentage distribution of poulation 25 years of age and
over, by educational attainment and by sex.

Summary of Social Indicators : UOP=1, UON=1.

2. Education

2.1 Education systems.

2.2   Estimated total enrolment and teaching staff by level of education. (Add by sex. Frequently Unesco's tables include breakdowns by sex although the table titles do not explicitly
mention sex. I have explicitly mentioned sex in the titles of
my new tables where it is appropriate, and have only mentioned
adding sex or age in the titles of Unesco's tables when the
given tables do not include breakdowns by sex.)

2.A   Average daily attendance by level of education and sex.

IOP.1   Pupil attendance ratios by level of education and sex.
(Ratio of 2.A to 2.2.)

2.B   Estimated total enrolment and teaching staff by year of education and sex.

2.C   Average daily attendance by year of education and sex.

IOP.2   Pupil attendance ratios by year of education and sex.
(Ratio of 2.C to 2.B.)

USP.1   Have you attended school this year as often as you
wanted ? By years, age and sex. (Response categories are :
1=much less often than wanted, 2=half as often as wanted, 3=at
least as often as wanted.)

USP.2   Have you attended school this year as often as average
people of your age and sex in your community ? By years, sex
and age. (Response categories are : 1=much less often than the
average, 2=half as often as the average, 3=at least as often as
the average.)

USP.3   Have you attended school this year as often as average
people of your age but of the opposite sex in your community ?
By years, sex and age. (Response categories are : 1=much less
often than the average of the opposite sex, 2=half as often as
the average of the opposite sex, 3=at least as often as the
average of the opposite sex.)

USP.4   How satisfied are you with your school attendance record
this year ? By years, sex and age. (Response categories are :
1=very dissatisfied, 2=as satisfied as not, 3=very satisfied.)

USP.5   Were you able to get the kind of education you wanted to
get this year with respect to the types of subjects studied ?
By years, age and sex. (Response categories are : 1=most of
the subjects wanted were not obtained, 2=about half the subjects wanted were obtained, 3=all or most of the subjects
wanted were obtained.)

USP.6   Were you able to get the kind of education this year that
average people of your age and sex in your community got with
respect to the types of subjects studied ? By years, age and

sex. (Response categories are : 1=did not get most of the subjects obtained by average people, 2=got about half the subjects obtained by average people, 3=got all or most of the subjects obtained by average people.)

USP.7   Were you able to get the kind of education this year that average people of your age but of the opposite sex in your community got with respect to the types of subjects studied ? By years, age and sex. (Response categories are : 1=did not get most of the subjects obtained by average people of the opposite sex, 2=got about half the subjects obtained by average people of the opposite sex, 3=got all or more of the subjects obtained by average people of the opposite sex.)

USP.8   How satisfied are you with the kind of education you got this year with respect to the types of subjects studied ? By years, age and sex. (Response categories are : 1=very dissatisfied, 2=as satisfied as not, 3=very satisfied.)

USP. 9   How satisfied are you with the quality of education you got this year, all things considered ? By years, age and sex. (Response categories are : 1=very dissatisfied, 2=as satisfied as not, 3=very satisfied.)

USP.10   Have you attended school this year as often as you wanted ? By second and third levels and sex. (Response categories are : 1=much less often than wanted, 2=half as often as wanted, 3=at least as often as wanted.)

USP.11   Have you attended school this year as often as average people of your age and sex in your community ? By second and third levels and sex. (Response categories are : 1=much less often than the average, 2=half as often as the average, 3=at least as often as the average.)

USP.12   Have you attended school this year as often as average people of your age but of the opposite sex in your community ? By second and third levels and sex. (Response categories are : 1=much less often than the average of the opposite sex, 2=half as often as the average of the opposite sex, 3=at least as often as the average of the opposite sex.)

USP.13   How satisfied are you with your school attendance record this year ? By second and third levels and sex. (Response categories are : 1=very dissatisfied, 2=as satisfied as not, 3=very satisfied.)

USP.14   Were you able to get the kind of education you wanted to get this year with respect to the types of subjects studied ? By second and third levels and sex. (Response categories are : 1=most of the subjects wanted were not obtained, 2=about half the subjects wanted were obtained, 3=all or most of the subjects wanted were obtained.)

USP.15   Were you able to get the kind of education this year that average people of your age and sex in your community got with respect to the types of subjects studied ? By second and third levels and sex. (Response categories are : 1=did not get most of the subjects obtained by average people, 2=got about half the subjects obtained by average people, 3=got all or most of the subjects obtained by average people.)

USP.16   Were you able to get the kind of education this year that average people of your age but of the opposite sex in your community got with respect to the types of subjects studied ? By second and third levels and sex. (Response categories are : 1=did not get most of the subjects obtained by average people of the opposite sex, 2=got about half the subjects obtained by average people of the opposite sex, 3=got all or more of the subjects obtained by average people of the opposite sex.)

USP.17   How satisfied are you with the kind of education you got this year with respect to the types of subjects studied ? By second and third levels and sex. (Response categories are : 1=very dissatisfied, 2=as satisfied as not, 3=very satisfied.)

USP. 18   How satisfied are you with the quality of education you got this year, all things considered ? By second and third levels and sex. (Response categories are : 1=very dissatisfied, 2=as satisfied as not, 3=very satisfied.)

2.3   Total enrolment and teaching staff : percentage distribution by level of education. (Add by sex.)

2.D   Average daily attendance, percentage distribution by level of education and sex.

IOP.3   Pupil average daily attendance ratios, percentage distribution by level of education and sex. (Ratio of 2.D to 2.3.)

2.E   Total enrolment and teaching staff percentage distribution by year of education and sex.

2.F   Average daily attendance, percentage distribution by year of education and sex.

IOP.4   Pupil average daily attendance ratios, percentage distribution by year of education and sex. (Ratio of 2.F to 2.E.)

2.4   Estimated female enrolment by level of education. (Redundant given addition of sex to 2.2, and 2.B.)

2.5   Estimated female teaching staff for first and second level education. (Redundant given addition of sex to 2.2, and 2.B.)

2.6   Index numbers of total and female enrolment and teaching staff by level of education (1970=100).   (Replace with index numbers for IOP.1 to IOP.4.)

2.7   ION Pupil-teacher ratios by level of education.

ION.1   Pupil-teacher ratios by year of education.

USP.19   Has the pupil-teacher ratio in your school this year been roughly as you wanted it to be ?   By year, age and sex. (Question put to teachers.   Response categories are : 1=ratios were much bigger than wanted, 2=ratios were bigger by a half than wanted, 3=ratios were about as wanted.)

USP.20   Has the pupil-teacher ratio in your school this year been roughly the same as that of the average for schools in your country ?   By year, age and sex. (Question put to teachers. Response categories are : 1=ratios were much bigger than the average, 2=ratios were bigger by a half than the average, 3=ratios were about the same as the average.)

USP.21   Has the pupil-teacher ratio in your school this year been roughly as you wanted it to be ?   By level of education, age and sex. (Question put to teachers.   Response categories are : 1=ratios were much bigger than wanted, 2=ratios were bigger by a half than wanted, 3=ratios were about as wanted.)

USP.22   Has the pupil-teacher ratio in your school this year been roughly the same as that of the average for schools in your country ?   By level of education, age and sex. (Question put to teachers.   Response categories are : 1=ratios were much bigger than the average, 2=ratios were bigger by a half than the average, 3=ratios were about the same as the average.)

2.8   Estimated teaching staff and enrolment by sex for education preceding the first level.

2.G   Estimated teaching staff and enrolment by sex for education by years preceding first level.

ION.2   Pupil-teacher ratios by years preceding first level.

ION.3   Pupil-teacher ratios preceding first level.

2.9   Percentage distribution of education at the second level by type : enrolment and teaching staff.

2.H   Percentage distribution of education by year and type : enrolment and teaching staff.

2.10 IOP   Gross enrolment ratios by level.

IOP.5   Gross enrolment ratios by year and sex.

2.11 IOP Enrolment ratios by age-groups and sex.

2.12 Estimated public expenditure on education, in United States dollars at current market prices.

2.I Number completing school by level of education, age and sex.

2.J Number completing years of school by age and sex.

UOP.1   Pupil completion rates by level of education, age and sex. (Ratio of 2.2 to 2.I.)

UOP.2   Pupil completion rates by years of education, age and sex. (Ratio of 2.B to 2.J.)

UOP.3   Number and per cent of students completing standardized tests covering grades or courses of study by level of education, age and sex.

UOP.4   Number and per cent of students completing standardized tests covering grades or courses of study by years of education, age and sex.

ION.4   Estimated public expenditure on education per enrolled pupil by level of education.

ION.5   Estimated public expenditure on education per enrolled pupil by year of education.

ION.6   Estimated public expenditure on education as a per cent of GNP by level of education.

ION.7   Estimated public expenditure on education as a percent of GNP by year of education.

ION.8   Estimated public expenditure on education per completions by level of education.

ION.9   Estimated public expenditure on education per completions by year of education.

ION.10   Estimated public expenditure on education per student completing standardized tests covering grades or courses of study by level of education.

ION.11   Estimated public expenditure on education per student completing standardized tests covering grades or courses of study by years of education.

Summary of social indicators
for all levels and years of education

	By Year	By Level		By Year	By Level
Pos.	N	N	Neg.	N	N
IOP	4	3	ION	6	6
ISP	0	0	ISN	0	0
UOP	2	3	UON	1	0
USP	11	11	USN	0	0
Total	17	17		7	6

3. Education by Level and Country

3.1 National educational systems.

3.2 IOP Enrolment ratios for the first, second and third levels of education.

IOP.1 Gross enrolment ratios by year and sex.

3.A Gross enrolment ratios by age-groups and sex.

3.3 Education preceding the first level : institutions, teachers and pupils.

3.B Education preceding the first level by year : institutions, teachers and pupils by sex.

ION.1 Pupil-teacher ratios for education preceding first level.

ION.2 Pupil-teacher ratios by years preceding first level.

3.C Average daily attendance for education preceding first level by age and sex.

IOP.2 Pupil average daily attendance ratio for education preceding first level. (Ratio of 3.C to 3.3.)

3.D Average daily attendance by years preceding first level by age and sex.

IOP.3 Pupil average daily attendance ratio by years preceding first level by age and sex. (Ratio of 3.D to 3.B.)

3.E Number completing pre-first level education by age and sex.

3.F Number completing pre-first level education by years, age and sex.

UOP.1   Pupil completion rates for pre-first level education by age and sex.   (Ratio of 3.3 to 3.E.)

UOP.2   Pupil completion rates for pre-first level education by years, age and sex.   (Ratio of 3.B to 3.F.)

UOP.3   Number and per cent of students completing standardized tests covering grades or courses of study for pre-first level education by age and sex.

UOP.4   Number and per cent of students completing standardized tests covering grades or courses of study for pre-first level education by years, age and sex.

ION.3   Estimated public expenditure on pre-first level education per enrolled pupil of education.

ION.4   Estimated public expenditure on pre-first level education per enrolled pupil by year of education.

ION.5   Estimated public expenditure on pre-first level education as a per cent of GNP of education.

ION.6   Estimated public expenditure on pre-first level education as a per cent of GNP by year of education.

ION.7   Estimated public expenditure on pre-first level education per completions of education.

ION.8   Estimated public expenditure on pre-first level education per completions by year of education.

ION.9   Estimated public expenditure on education per student completing standardized tests covering grades or courses of study for pre-first level education.

ION.10   Estimated public expenditure on education per student completing standardized tests covering grades or courses of study for pre-first level education by years.

Summary of social indicators
for pre-first level education

	By Year	By Level		By Year	By Level
Pos.	N	N	Neg.	N	N
IOP	2	2	ION	5	5
ISP	0	0	ISN	0	0
UOP	2	2	UON	0	0
USP	0	0	USN	0	0
Total	4	4		5	5

(First Level Education)

3.4 Education at first level : institutions, teachers and pupils.
     (Add by age.)

3.G Education by years for first level, by teachers, pupils, age
     and sex.

ION.1   Pupil-teacher ratios for first level.

ION.2   Pupil-teacher ratios by year for first level.

3.H Average daily attendance for first level by age and sex.

3.I. Average daily attendance by years for first level by age and
     sex.

IOP.1   Pupil average daily attendance ratios for first level by
     age and sex. (Ratio 3.H to 3.4.)

IOP.2   Pupil average daily attendance ratios by years for first
     level by age and sex. (Ratio of 3.I to 3.G.)

3.5 Education at the first level : percentage distribution of en-
     rolment by grade. (Add by age.)

3.J Average daily attendance, percentage distribution by grade and
     sex for first level of education.

IOP.3   Pupil average daily attendance ratios, percentage dis-
     tribution by grade and sex for first level of education.
     (Ratio of 3.J to 3.5.)

3.6 ION Education at the first level : percentage repeaters by
     grade. (Add by age.)

IOP.4   Gross enrolment ratios by sex for first level.

IOP.5   Gross enrolment ratios by years and sex for first level.

IOP.6   Enrolment ratios by age-groups and sex.

3.K Number completing first level of education by age and sex.

3.L Number completing years in first level of education by age and
     sex.

UOP.2   Pupil completion rates by years for first level of educa-
     tion by age and sex. (Ratio of 3.G to 3.L.)

UOP.3   Number and per cent of students completing standardized
     tests covering grades or courses of study for first level
     education by age and sex.

UOP.4   Number and per cent of students completing standardized tests covering grades or courses of study for first level education by years, age and sex.

ION.3   Estimated public expenditure on first level education per enrolled pupil of education.

ION.4   Estimated public expenditure on first level education per enrolled pupil by year of education.

ION.5   Estimated public expenditure on first level education as a per cent of GNP of education.

ION.6   Estimated public expenditure on first level education as a per cent of GNP by year of education.

ION.7   Estimated public expenditure on first level education per completions of education.

ION.8   Estimated public expenditure on first level education per completions by year of education.

ION.9   Estimated public expenditure on education per student completing standardized tests covering grades or courses of study for first level education.

ION.10   Estimated public expenditure on education per student completing standardized tests covering grades or courses of study for first level education by years.

Summary of social indicators
for first level education

	By Year	By Level		By Year	By Level
Pos.	N	N	Neg.	N	N
IOP	4	2	ION	6	5
ISP	0	0	ISN	0	0
UOP	2	2	UON	0	0
USP	0	0	USN	0	0
Total	6	4		6	5

(Second Level Education)

3.7 Education at the second level (general, teacher-training and vocational) : teachers and pupils.

3.M Education by years for second level by teachers, pupils age and sex.

ION.1   Pupil-teacher ratios for second level education.

ION.2   Pupil-teacher ratios by years for second level education.

3.N Average daily attendance for second level by age and sex.

3.O Average daily attendance by years for second level by age and sex.

IOP.1   Pupil average daily attendance ratios for second level by age and sex. (Ratio of 3.N to 3.7.)

IOP.2   Pupil average daily attendance ratios by years for second level by age and sex. (Ratio of 3.O to 3.M.)

USP.1   Have you attended school this year as often as you wanted ? By years, age and sex. (Response categories are : 1=much less often than wanted, 2=half as often as wanted, 3=at least as often as wanted.)

USP.2   Have you attended school this year as often as average people of your age and sex in your community ? By years, sex and age. (Response categories are : 1=much less often than the average, 2=half as often as the average, 3=at least as often as the average.)

USP.3   Have you attended school this year as often as average people of your age but of the opposite sex in your community ? By years, sex and age. (Response categories are : 1=much less often than the average of the opposite sex, 2=half as often as the average of the opposite sex, 3=at least as often as the average of the opposite sex.)

USP.4   How satisfied are you with your school attendance record this year ? By years, sex and age. (Response categories are : 1=very dissatisfied, 2=as satisfied as not, 3=very satisfied.)

USP.5   Were you able to get the kind of education you wanted to get this year with respect to the types of subjects studied ? By years, age and sex. (Response categories are : 1=most of the subjects wanted were not obtained, 2=about half the subjects wanted were obtained, 3=all or most of the subjects wanted were obtained.)

USP.6   Were you able to get the kind of education this year that average people of your age and sex in your community got with respect to the types of subjects studied ? By years, age and sex. (Response categories are : 1=did not get most of the subjects obtained by average people, 2=got about half the subjects obtained by average people, 3=got all or most of the subjects obtained by average people.)

USP.7   Were you able to get the kind of education this year that average people of your age but of the opposite sex in your community got with respect to the types of subjects studied ? By years, age and sex. (Response categories are : 1=did not get most of the subjects obtained by average people of the opposite sex, 2=got about half the subjects obtained by average people of the opposite sex, 3=got all or more of the subjects obtained by average people of the opposite sex.)

USP.8   How satisfied are you with the kind of education you got this year with respect to the types of subjects studied ? By years, age and sex. (Response categories are : 1=very dissatisfied, 2=as satisfied as not, 3=very satisfied.)

USP. 9   How satisfied are you with the quality of education you got this year, all things considered ? By years, age and sex. (Response categories are : 1=very dissatisfied, 2=as satisfied as not, 3=very satisfied.)

USP.10   Have you attended school this year as often as you wanted ? By second and third levels and sex. (Response categories are : 1=much less often than wanted, 2=half as often as wanted, 3=at least as often as wanted.)

USP.11   Have you attended school this year as often as average people of your age and sex in your community ? By second and third levels and sex. (Response categories are : 1=much less often than the average, 2=half as often as the average, 3=at least as often as the average.)

USP.12   Have you attended school this year as often as average people of your age but of the opposite sex in your community ? By second and third levels and sex. (Response categories are : 1=much less often than the average of the opposite sex, 2=half as often as the average of the opposite sex, 3=at least as often as the average of the opposite sex.)

USP.13   How satisfied are you with your school attendance record this year ? By second and third levels and sex. (Response categories are : 1=very dissatisfied, 2=as satisfied as not, 3=very satisfied.)

USP.14   Were you able to get the kind of education you wanted to get this year with respect to the types of subjects studied ? By second and third levels and sex. (Response categories are : 1=most of the subjects wanted were not obtained, 2=about half the subjects wanted were obtained, 3=all or most of the subjects wanted were obtained.)

USP.15   Were you able to get the kind of education this year that average people of your age and sex in your community got with respect to the types of subjects studied ? By second and third levels and sex. (Response categories are : 1=did not get most of the subjects obtained by average people, 2=got about half the subjects obtained by average people, 3=got all or most of the subjects obtained by average people.)

USP.16   Were you able to get the kind of education this year that average people of your age but of the opposite sex in your community got with respect to the types of subjects studied ? By second and third levels and sex. (Response categories are : 1=did not get most of the subjects obtained by average people of the opposite sex, 2=got about half the subjects obtained by average people of the opposite sex, 3=got all or more of the subjects obtained by average people of the opposite sex.)

USP.17   How satisfied are you with the kind of education you got this year with respect to the types of subjects studied ? By second and third levels and sex. (Response categories are : 1=very dissatisfied, 2=as satisfied as not, 3=very satisfied.)

USP. 18   How satisfied are you with the quality of education you got this year, all things considered ? By second and third levels and sex. (Response categories are : 1=very dissatisfied, 2=as satisfied as not, 3=very satisfied.)

3.8   Education at the second level (general) : percentage distribution of enrolment by grade. (Add by age.)

3.P   Average daily attendance, percentage distribution by grade and sex for second level of education.

IOP.3   Pupil average daily attendance ratios, percentage distribution by grade and sex for second level of education. (Ratio of 3.P to 3.8.)

3.9   ION Education at the second level (general) : percentage repeaters by grade. (Add by age.)

IOP.4   Gross enrolment ratios by sex for second level.

IOP.5   Gross enrolment ratios by years and sex for second level.

IOP.6   Enrolment ratios by age-groups and sex.

3.Q   Number completing second level of education by age and sex.

3.R   Number completing years in second level of education by age and sex.

UOP.1   Pupil completion rates for second level of education by age and sex. (Ratio of 3.7 to 3.Q.)

UOP.2   Pupil completion rates by years for second level of education by age and sex.   (Ratio of 3.M to 3.R.)

UOP.3   Number and per cent of students completing standardized
tests covering grades or courses of study for second level
education by age and sex.

UOP.4   Number and per cent of students completing standardized
tests covering grades or courses of study for second level
education by years, age and sex.

ION.3   Estimated public expenditure on second level education per
enrolled pupil of education.

ION.4   Estimated public expenditure on second level education per
enrolled pupil by year of education.

ION.5   Estimated public expenditure on second level education as
a per cent of GNP of education.

ION.6   Estimated public expenditure on second level education as
a per cent of GNP by year of education.

ION.7   Estimated public expenditure on second level education per
completions of education.

ION.8   Estimated public expenditure on second level education per
completions by year of education.

ION.9   Estimated public expenditure on education per student
completing standardized tests covering grades or courses of
study for second level education.

ION.10   Estimated public expenditure on education per student
completing standardized tests covering grades or courses of
study for second level education by years.

Summary of social indicators
for second level education

	By Year	By Level		By Year	By Level
Pos.	N	N	Neg.	N	N
IOP	4	2	ION	6	5
ISP	0	0	ISN	0	0
UOP	2	2	UON	0	0
USP	9	9	USN	0	0
Total	15	13		6	5

(Third Level Education)

3.10 IOP Education at the third level : number of students per 100.000 inhabitants. (Add by age.)

3.11 Education at the third level : teachers and students by type of institution. (Add by age.)

3.S Number of students and teachers beyond second level by years, age and sex.

IOP.1   Ratio of third level students to age cohort by years, age and sex.

ION.1   Student-teacher ratios for third level of education.

ION.2   Student-teacher ratios by year for third level of education.

USP.1   Have you attended school this year as often as you wanted ? By years, age and sex. (Response categories are : 1=much less often than wanted, 2=half as often as wanted, 3=at least as often as wanted.)

USP.2   Have you attended school this year as often as average people of your age and sex in your community ? By years, sex and age. (Response categories are : 1=much less often than the average, 2=half as often as the average, 3=at least as often as the average.)

USP.3   Have you attended school this year as often as average people of your age but of the opposite sex in your community ? By years, sex and age. (Response categories are : 1=much less often than the average of the opposite sex, 2=half as often as the average of the opposite sex, 3=at least as often as the average of the opposite sex.)

USP.4   How satisfied are you with your school attendance record this year ? By years, sex and age. (Response categories are : 1=very dissatisfied, 2=as satisfied as not, 3=very satisfied.)

USP.5   Were you able to get the kind of education you wanted to get this year with respect to the types of subjects studied ? By years, age and sex. (Response categories are : 1=most of the subjects wanted were not obtained, 2=about half the subjects wanted were obtained, 3=all or most of the subjects wanted were obtained.)

USP.6   Were you able to get the kind of education this year that average people of your age and sex in your community got with respect to the types of subjects studied ? By years, age and sex. (Response categories are : 1=did not get most of the subjects obtained by average people, 2=got about half the subjects obtained by average people, 3=got all or most of the subjects obtained by average people.)

USP.7   Were you able to get the kind of education this year that average people of your age but of the opposite sex in your community got with respect to the types of subjects studied ? By years, age and sex. (Response categories are : 1=did not get most of the subjects obtained by average people of the opposite sex, 2=got about half the subjects obtained by average people of the opposite sex, 3=got all or more of the subjects obtained by average people of the opposite sex.)

USP.8   How satisfied are you with the kind of education you got this year with respect to the types of subjects studied ? By years, age and sex. (Response categories are : 1=very dis-satisfied, 2=as satisfied as not, 3=very satisfied.)

USP. 9   How satisfied are you with the quality of education you got this year, all things considered ? By years, age and sex. (Response categories are : 1=very dissatisfied, 2=as satisfied as not, 3=very satisfied.)

USP.10   Have you attended school this year as often as you wanted ? By second and third levels and sex. (Response cate-gories are : 1=much less often than wanted, 2=half as often as wanted, 3=at least as often as wanted.)

USP.11   Have you attended school this year as often as average people of your age and sex in your community ? By second and third levels and sex. (Response categories are : 1=much less often than the average, 2=half as often as the average, 3=at least as often as the average.)

USP.12   Have you attended school this year as often as average people of your age but of the opposite sex in your community ? By second and third levels and sex. (Response categories are : 1=much less often than the average of the opposite sex, 2=half as often as the average of the opposite sex, 3=at least as often as the average of the opposite sex.)

USP.13   How satisfied are you with your school attendance record this year ? By second and third levels and sex. (Response categories are : 1=very dissatisfied, 2=as satisfied as not, 3=very satisfied.)

USP.14   Were you able to get the kind of education you wanted to get this year with respect to the types of subjects studied ? By second and third levels and sex. (Response categories are : 1=most of the subjects wanted were not obtained, 2=about half the subjects wanted were obtained, 3=all or most of the sub-jects wanted were obtained.)

USP.15   Were you able to get the kind of education this year that average people of your age and sex in your community got with respect to the types of subjects studied ? By second and third levels and sex. (Response categories are : 1=did not get most of the subjects obtained by average people, 2=got about half the subjects obtained by average people, 3=got all or most of the subjects obtained by average people.)

USP.16   Were you able to get the kind of education this year that average people of your age but of the opposite sex in your community got with respect to the types of subjects studied ? By second and third levels and sex. (Response categories are : 1=did not get most of the subjects obtained by average people of the opposite sex, 2=got about half the subjects obtained by average people of the opposite sex, 3=got all or more of the subjects obtained by average people of the opposite sex.)

USP.17   How satisfied are you with the kind of education you got this year with respect to the types of subjects studied ?   By second and third levels and sex. (Response categories are : 1=very dissatisfied, 2=as satisfied as not, 3=very satisfied.)

USP. 18   How satisfied are you with the quality of education you got this year, all things considered ? By second and third levels and sex. (Response categories are : 1=very dissatisfied, 2=as satisfied as not, 3=very satisfied.)

3.12 Education at the third level : enrolment by sex and field of study (1980, 1982, and 1983). (Add by age.)

3.13 Education at the third level : enrolment by ISCED level of programmes and field of study. (Add by age.)

3.14 UOP Education at the third level : graduates by ISCED level of programmes and field of study. (Add by age.)

3.15 Education at the third level : number of foreign students enrolled.

3.T IOP Foreign student enrolment ratios by age and sex.   (Ratio of 3.15 to 3.11.)

3.16 Education at the third level : foreign students by country of origin in 45 selected countries.

3.U Number completing years in third level education by age and sex.

UOP.1   Student completion rates by years for third level education by age and sex. (Ratio of 3.S to 3.U.)

UOP.2   Number and percent of students completing standardized tests covering grades or courses of study by years for third level education by age and sex.

IOP.2   Enrolment ratios by age-groups and sex.

ION.3   Estimated public expenditure on third level education per enrolled student.

ION.4   Estimated public expenditure on third level education as a per cent of GNP.

ION.5   Estimated public expenditure on third level education per degrees awarded.

ION.6   Estimated public expenditure on third level education per completions by years.

ION.7   Estimated public expenditure on education per student completing standardized tests covering grades or courses of study by years for third level education.

Summary of social indicators
for third level education

	By Year	By Level		By Year	By Level
Pos.	N	N	Neg.	N	N
IOP	1	2	ION	3	4
ISP	0	0	ISN	0	0
UOP	3	0	UON	0	0
USP	9	9	USN	0	0
Total	13	11		3	4

Summary of social indicators
by levels and years

Levels		By Year	By Level		By Year	By Level
Pre-	Pos.	N	N	Neg.	N	N
First	IOP	2	2	ION	5	5
Level	ISP	0	0	ISN	0	0
	UOP	2	2	UON	0	0
	USP	0	0	USN	0	0

Summary of social indicators
by levels and years (continued)

Levels		By Year	By Level		By Year	By Level
First	IOP	4	2	ION	6	5
Level	ISP	0	0	ISN	0	0
	UOP	2	2	UON	0	0
	USP	0	0	USN	0	0
Second	IOP	4	2	ION	6	5
Level	ISP	0	0	ISN	0	0
	UOP	2	2	UON	0	0
	USP	9	9	USN	0	0
Third	IOP	1	2	ION	3	4
Level	ISP	0	0	ISN	0	0
	UOP	3	0	UON	0	0
	USP	9	9	USN	0	0
Totals	IOP	11	8	ION	20	19
	ISP	0	0	ISN	0	0
	UOP	9	6	UON	0	0
	USP	18	18	USN	0	0

Total Positive 38   32   Negative   20   19

4. Educational Expenditure

4.1. ION Public expenditure on education : total and as percentage of the Gross National Product of all public expenditure.

4.2 Public current expenditure on education : distribution according to purpose.

4.3 Public current expenditure on education : distribution by level of education.

4.4 Public current expenditure on education : distribution by level of education and by purpose.

5. Science and Technology

5.1 Estimated number of scientists and engineers engaged in R&D for 1970 and 1980.

5.2 Estimated expenditure for R&D for 1970 and 1980, in United States dollars.

(Scientific and Technical Personnel) ('Personnel' has been substituted for 'manpower' in all its occurrences.)

5.3 Scientific and technical personnel potential.

IOP.1   Scientists and engineers as a per cent of civilian labour force, by age and sex.

IOP.2   Scientists and engineers per 1000 civilian labour force, by age and sex.

5.4 Number of scientists, engineers and technicians engaged in research and experimental development.

IOP.3   Scientists and engineers in R&D as a per cent of civilian employed, by age and sex.

IOP.4   Scientists and engineers in R&D per 1000 civilian employed, by age and sex.

5.A Immigrant professional and technological personnel, by age and sex.

IOP.5   Immigrant professional and technological personnel as a percent of all immigrants, by age and sex.

5.5 Number of scientists and engineers engaged in research and experimental development by their field of study.

5.6 Total personnel engaged in research and experimental development by sector of performance and by category of personnel.

5.7 Number of scientists and engineers engaged in research and experimental development performed in the productive sector, by branch of economic activity.

5.8 Number of scientists and engineers engaged in research and experimental development performed in the higher education and the general service sectors by field of science and technology.

(Expenditure on Research and Experimental Development)

5.9 Total expenditure for research and experimental development by type of expenditure.

ION.1   R&D expenditure per 1000 employed scientists and engineers.

ION.2   R&D expenditure as a per cent of GNP.

5.10 Total expenditure for the performance of research and experimental development by source of funds.

5.11 Current expenditure for research and experimental development by type of R&D activity.

5.12 Total and current expenditure for research and experimental development by sector of performance.

5.13 Total expenditure for the performance of research and experimental development in the productive sector, by branch of economic activity.

5.14 Total expenditure for the performance of research and experimental development in the higher education and the general service sectors by field of science and technology.

5.15 Expenditure for national research and experimental development activities by major socio-economic aim.

(Selected Indicators of Scientific and Technological Development)

5.16 Personnel engaged in research and experimental development : selected data for recent years.

5.17 Expenditure for research and experimental development : selected data for recent years.

5.18 Selected indicators for scientific and technical personnel potential and personnel engaged in research and experimental development.

5.19 Selected indicators for expenditure for research and experimental development.

(Selected output measures of Science and Technology)

5.B Number of patents filed, by fields.

5.C Number of patents filed by resident inventors, fields, age and sex.

UOP.1   Number of patents issued to resident inventors per 1000 scientists and engineers employed in R&D, by fields, age and sex.

ION.3   Cost per patent issued to resident inventors, by fields, age and sex.

5.D Number of scientific papers published in refereed journals by resident scientists and engineers, by fields, age and sex.

UOP.2 Number of papers published per 1000 scientists and engineers employed in R&D, by fields, age and sex.

ION.4 Cost per paper published, by fields, age and sex.

5.E UOP.3 Number of major technological devices per household (excluding radios and television sets), e.g. motor vehicles by type, telephones, refrigerators, stoves, washers, dryers, dishwashers, freezers, vacuum cleaners, indoor toilets, baths.

(Questions to be put to scientists and engineers engaged in R&D)

USP.1 What per cent of your workday is spent on activities directly related to R&D ? (For this and other questions, record answers by degrees held, age and sex.)

USP.2 Is the per cent of your workday spent on activities directly related to R&D as big as you want it to be ? (Response categories are : 1=much smaller than wanted, 2=about half as big as wanted, 3=at least as big as wanted.)

USP.3 Is the per cent of your workday spent on activities directly related to R&D as big as that of average professionals of your age and sex in your field of research in this country ? (Response categories are : 1=much smaller than the average, 2=about half as big as the average, 3=at least as big as the average.)

USP.4 Is the per cent of your workday spent on activities directly related to R&D as big as that of average professionals of your age but of the opposite sex in your field of research in this country ? (Response categories are : 1=much smaller than that of the average of the opposite sex, 2=about half as big as the average of the opposite sex, 3=at least as big as the average of the opposite sex.)

USP.5 How satisfied are you with the per cent of time you spend on activities directly related to R&D ? (Response categories are : 1=very dissatisfied, 2=as satisfied as not, 3=very satisfied.)

USP.6 Do the R&D facilities (equipment, supplies, libraries, funds) available to you measure up well to what you want ? (Response categories are : 1=much less than wanted, 2=about half of what is wanted, 3=at least as much as is wanted.)

USP.7 Do the R&D facilities available to you measure up well to those of average professionals of your age and sex in your field of research in this country ? (Response categories are :

1=much less than those of the average, 2=about half those of
the average, 3=at least as much as those of the average.)

USP.8   Do the R&D facilities available to you measure up well to
those of average professionals of your age but of the opposite
sex in your field of research in this country ?   (Response
categories are : 1=much less than those of the average of the
opposite sex, 2=about half of those of the average of the
opposite sex, 3=at least as much as those of the average of the
opposite sex.)

USP.9   If you could improve only one feature of your research
facilities, what particular feature would be improved ?   (Responses list desired improvements with marginal percentages.)

USP.10   How satisfied are you with the R&D facilities available to
you ? (Response categories are : 1=very dissatisfied, 2=as
satisfied as not, 3=very satisfied.)

USP.11   How does your own R&D output (however you measure it
qualitatively and quantitatively) measure up to what you want
it to be ? (Response categories are : 1=far below what is
wanted, 2=about half of what is wanted, 3=at least as good as
what is wanted.)

USP.12   How does your own R&D output measure up to that of average
professionals of your age and sex in your field in this country ? (Response categories are : 1=far below that of the
average, 2=about half that of the average, 3=at least as good
as the average.)

USP.13   How does your own R&D output measure up to that of average
professionals of your age but of the opposite sex in your field
in this country ? (Response categories are : 1=far below that
of the average of the opposite sex, 2=about half the average of
the opposite sex, 3=at least as good as that of the average of
the opposite sex.)

USP.14   How satisfied are you with your own R&D output, considering quality and quantity together ? (Response categories are :
1=very dissatisfied, 2=as satisfied as not, 3=very satisfied.)

Summary of social indicators
of science and technology

Pos.	N	Neg.	N
IOP	6	ION	4
ISP	0	ISN	0
UOP	3	UON	0
USP	14	USN	0

Total   23   4

6. Culture and Communication

6.1 Number of book titles published.

IOP.1   Number of book titles published per 1000 inhabitants.

6.2 Number and circulation of daily newspapers.   (Per 1000 inhabitants=IOP.2.)

6.3 Newsprint production and consumption.

6.4 Production and consumption of other printing and writing paper.

6.5 Production of long films.

IOP.3   Number of long films printed per 1000 inhabitants.

6.6 Number and seating capacity of fixed cinemas.   (Per 1000 inhabitants=IOP.4.)

6.7 Annual cinema attendance.

UOP.1   Annual cinema attendance per 1000 inhabitants.

6.8 Number of radio broadcasting transmitters.

UOP.2   Radio transmitters per 1000 inhabitants.

6.9 Number of radio receivers and receivers per 1000 inhabitants. (Per 1000 inhabitants=1OP.5.)

6.10 Number of television transmitters.

UOP.3   Television transmitters per 1000 inhabitants.

6.11 Number of television receivers and receivers per 1000 inhabitants.   (Per 1000 inhabitants=IOP.6.)

7. Libraries

7.1 Libraries and their holdings by category of library.

IOP.1   Number of volumes per inhabitant, for all libraries.

UOP.1   Number of borrowers per 1000 inhabitants, for all libraries.

7.2 National libraries : collections, borrowers, works loaned out, current expenditure, employees.

UOP.2   Number of works loaned out per inhabitant, for national libraries.

ION.1   Total library expenditures per inhabitant, for national libraries.

7.3 Public libraries : collections, borrowers, works loaned out, current expenditure, employees.

UOP.3   Number of works loaned out per inhabitant, for public libraries.

ION.2   Total library expenditures per inhabitant, for public libraries.

7.4 Libraries of institutions of higher education : collections, borrowers, works loaned out, current expenditure, employees.

UOP.4   Number of works loaned out per student enrolled in third level education.

ION.3   Total library expenditures per student enrolled in third level education.

7.5 School libraries : collections, borrowers, works loaned out, current expenditure, employees.

UOP.5   Number of works loaned out per pupil enrolled in first and second level education.

ION.4   Total library expenditures per pupil enrolled in first and second level education.

UOP.6   Weighted average number of works loaned out per inhabitant, student and pupil. (From UOP.2, 3, 4, 5.)

ION.5   Weighted average library expenditures per inhabitant, student and pupil. (From ION.1, 2, 3, 4.)

(Book Production)

7.6 Book production : number of titles by UDC classes.

IOP.2   Number of books produced per inhabitant.

7.7 Book production : number of titles by subject group.

7.8 Book production : number of titles by language of publication.

7.9 Book production : number of copies by UDC classes.

7.10 Book production : number of copies by subject group.

7.11 Production of school textbooks : number of titles and copies.

7.12 Production of children's books : number of titles and copies.

7.13 Translations by country of publication and by UDC classes.

7.14 Translations by original language and by UDC classes.

7.15 Translations by country of publication and by selected languages from which translated.

7.16 Translation by original languages and by selected languages into which translated.

7.17 Authors most frequently translated.

(Newspapers and Periodicals)

7.18 Daily general-interest newspapers : number and circulation (total and per 1000 inhabitants).

7.19 Non-daily general-interest newspapers and other periodicals : number and circulation (total and per 1000 inhabitants).

7.20 Periodicals, other than general-interest newspapers : number and circulation by subject group.

7.21 Newsprint, printing and writing paper : production, imports, exports and consumption (total and per 1000 inhabitants).

8.   Cultural Heritage

8.1 Archival institutions : holdings, accessions, reference service, personnel and current expenditure.

9.   Film and Cinema

9.1 Long films : number of films produced. (Source of 6.5.)

9.2 Long films : number of long films imported by country of origin.

9.3 Cinemas : number, seating capacity and annual attendance.

10.   Broadcasting

10.1 Radio broadcasting : number of transmitters and transmitting power by frequency band. (Source of 6.8.)

10.2 Radio broadcasting : number of receivers and receivers per 1000 inhabitants. (Source of 6.9.)

10.3 Television broadcasting : number of transmitters and transmitting power.   (Source of 6.10.)

10.4 Television broadcasting : number of receivers and receivers per
1000 inhabitants.   (Source of 6.11.)

10.5 Radio broadcasting : programmes by function and by type of
institution.

10.6 Television broadcasting : programmes by function and by type of
institution.

10.7 Radio and television broadcasting : personnel employed by type
of personnel and by type of institution.

10.8 Radio and television broadcasting : annual revenue by source
and by type of institution.

10.9 Radio and television broadcasting : annual current expenditure
by purpose and by type of institution.

Selected subjective indicators for culture and communications chapters

(These items are roughly co-ordinated to topics in chapters 7 to 10.
To indicate briefly the particular topics to which they are related,
each item is followed by an abbreviation in parentheses. For example, (7BP) is short for '7.Book Publishing', (10B) is short for
'10.Broadcasting', and so on.)

Now we should like to find out how you feel about the quantity,
quality, variety and cost of some cultural items available in your
country.

(Quantity)

USP.1   In the past year, have you been able to purchase as many
books as you wanted ? (Response categories are : 1=far fewer
than wanted, 2=about half as many as wanted, 3=at least as many
as wanted.) (7BP)

USP.2   In the past year, have you been able to borrow as many
books as you wanted ? (Response categories are : 1=far fewer
than wanted, 2=about half as many as wanted, 3=at least as many
as wanted.) (7L)

USP.3   In the past year, have you been able to attend as many
cinema performances as you wanted ? (Response categories are :
1=far fewer than wanted, 2=about half as many as wanted, 3=at
least as many as wanted.) (9FC)

USP.4   In the past year, have you been able to purchase as many newspapers and periodicals as you wanted ? (Response categories are : 1=far fewer than wanted, 2=about half as many as wanted, 3=at least as many as wanted.) (7NP)

USP.5   In the past year, have you been able to borrow as many newspapers and periodicals as you wanted ? (Response categories are : 1=far fewer than wanted, 2=about half as many as wanted, 3=at least as many as wanted.) (7L)

USP.6   In the past year, have you been able to listen to the radio as often as you wanted ? (Response categories are : 1=far less than wanted, 2=about half as much as wanted, 3=at least as much as wanted.) (10B)

USP.7   In the past year, have you been able to watch television as often as you wanted ? (Response categories are : 1=far less than wanted, 2=about half as much as wanted, 3=at least as much as wanted.) (10B)

(Quality)

USP.8   In the past year, have you usually been able to purchase books the content of which was as good in quality as you wanted ? (Response categories are : 1=usually a far lower quality than wanted, 2=usually about half the quality that was wanted, 3=usually at least as good as wanted.) (7BP)

USP.9   In the past year, have you usually been able to borrow books the content of which was as good in quality as you wanted ? (Response categories are : 1=usually a far lower quality than wanted, 2=usually about half the quality that was wanted, 3=usually at least as good as wanted.) (7L)

USP.10   In the past year, have you usually been able to attend cinema performances the content of which was as good in quality as you wanted ? (Response categories are : 1=usually a far lower quality than wanted, 2=usually about half the quality that was wanted, 3=usually at least as good as wanted.) (9FC)

USP.11   In the past year, have you usually been able to purchase newspapers and periodicals the content of which was as good in quality as you wanted ? (Response categories are : 1=usually a far lower quality than wanted, 2=usually about half the quality that was wanted, 3=usually at least as good as wanted.) (7NP)

USP.12   In the past year, have you usually been able to borrow newspapers and periodicals the content of which was as good in quality as you wanted ? (Response categories are : 1=usually a far lower quality than wanted, 2=usually about half the quality that was wanted, 3=usually at least as good as wanted.) (7L)

USP.13   In the past year, have you usually been able to listen to radio programmes the content of which was as good in quality as you wanted ?   (Response categories are : 1=usually a far lower quality than wanted, 2=usually about half the quality that was wanted, 3=usually at least as good as wanted.) (10B)

USP.14   In the past year, have you usually been able to watch television programmes the content of which was as good in quality as you wanted ?   (Response categories are : 1=usually a far lower quality than wanted, 2=usually about half the quality that was wanted, 3=usually at least as good as wanted.) (10B)

(Variety)

USP.15   In the past year, have you been able to purchase as many kinds of books as you wanted ?   (Response categories are : 1=far fewer kinds than wanted, 2=about half as many kinds as wanted, 3=at least as many kinds as wanted.) (7BP)

USP.16   In the past year, have you been able to borrow as many kinds of books as you wanted ?   (Response categories are : 1=far fewer kinds than wanted, 2=about half as many kinds as wanted, 3=at least as many kinds as wanted.) (7L)

USP.17   In the past year, have you been able to attend as many kinds of cinema performances as you wanted ?   (Response categories are : 1=far fewer kinds than wanted, 2=about half as many kinds as wanted, 3=at least as many kinds as wanted.) (9FC)

USP.18   In the past year, have you been able to purchase as many kinds of newspapers and periodicals as you wanted ?   (Response categories are : 1=far fewer kinds than wanted, 2=about half as many kinds as wanted, 3=at least as many kinds as wanted.) (7NP)

USP.19   In the past year, have you been able to borrow as many kinds of newspapers and periodicals as you wanted ?   (Response categories are : 1=far fewer kinds than wanted, 2=about half as many kinds as wanted, 3=at least as many kinds as wanted.) (7L)

USP.20   In the past year, have you been able to listen to as many kinds of radio programmes as you wanted ?   (Response categories are : 1=far fewer kinds than wanted, 2=about half as many kinds as wanted, 3=at least as many kinds as wanted.) (10B)

USP.21   In the past year, have you been able to watch as many kinds of television programmes as you wanted ?   (Response categories are : 1=far fewer kinds than wanted, 2=about half as many kinds as wanted, 3=at least as many kinds as wanted.) (10B)

(Cost)

USP.22   In the past year, have you usually been able to purchase books at a cost that was close to what you wanted to pay ? (Response categories are : 1=usually far higher than what I wanted to pay, 2=usually higher than what I wanted to pay by about a half, 3=usually close to what I wanted to pay.) (7BP)

USP.23   In the past year, have you usually been able to purchase books at a cost that was close to what you wanted to pay ? (Response categories are : 1=usually far higher than what I wanted to pay, 2=usually higher than what I wanted to pay by about a half, 3=usually close to what I wanted to pay.) (7L)

USP.24   In the past year, have you usually been able to attend cinema performances at a cost that was close to what you wanted to pay ? (Response categories are : 1=usually far higher than what I wanted to pay, 2=usually higher than what I wanted to pay by about a half, 3=usually close to what I wanted to pay.) (9FC)

USP.25   In the past year, have you usually been able to purchase newspapers and periodicals at a cost that was close to what you wanted to pay ? (Response categories are : 1=usually far higher than what I wanted to pay, 2=usually higher than what I wanted to pay by about a half, 3=usually close to what I wanted to pay.) (7NP)

USP.26   In the past year, have you usually been able to borrow newspapers and periodicals at a cost that was close to what you wanted to pay ? (Response categories are : 1=usually far higher than what I wanted to pay, 2=usually higher than what I wanted to pay by about a half, 3=usually close to what I wanted to pay.) (7L)

USP.27   In the past year, have you usually been able to listen to radio programmes at a cost that was close to what you wanted to pay ? (Response categories are : 1=usually far higher than what I wanted to pay, 2=usually higher than what I wanted to pay by about a half, 3=usually close to what I wanted to pay.) (10B)

USP.28   In the past year, have you usually been able to watch television programmes at a cost that was close to what you wanted to pay ? (Response categories are : 1=usually far higher than what I wanted to pay, 2=usually higher than what I wanted to pay by about a half, 3=usually close to what I wanted to pay.) (10B)

Summary of social indicators
of culture and communication

Chapter	Pos. N		Neg. N	
6	IOP	6	ION	0
	ISP	0	ISN	0
	UOP	3	UON	0
	USP	0	USN	0
	Total	9		0
7	IOP	2	ION	5
	ISP	0	ISN	0
	UOP	6	UON	0
	USP	16	USN	0
	Total	24		5
8-10	IOP	0	ION	0
	ISP	0	ISN	0
	UOP	0	UON	0
	USP	12	USN	0
	Total	12		0
Culture and Communication Totals	IOP	8	ION	5
	ISP	0	ISN	0
	UOP	9	UON	0
	USP	28	USN	0
	Total	45		5

The following table gives the total number of social indicators
in duplicate fashion. Because education indicators were constructed
using school years as well as school levels, the columns under years
and levels represent alternative sets of indicators. The indicators
of science, technology, culture and communications did not have
years and levels alternatives. Hence, the total number of indicators for these areas of concern were added into each of the four
columns below, with the appropriate positive and negative, objective
and subjective divisions. In other words, in the following table,
columns one and three constitute one collection of indicators,
namely that using years of education in the education indicators,
while columns two and four constitute an alternative collection
using levels of education.

Grand Total of All Social Indicators

	Positive			Negative	
	By Year	By Level		By Year	By Level
IOP	29	25	ION	32	31
ISP	0	0	ISN	0	0
UOP	22	20	UON	3	2
USP	71	71	USN	0	0
Totals	122	116		35	33

ANNEX 2

SUMMARY OF GAP THEORETIC STUDIES

Author(s)	Year	Sample Size	Sample Composition	Gap Type	Dependent Variable
Weintraub	1980	73	factory workers	expected/ actual environment	job satisfaction
Wright, Gutkin	1981	60	school psychologists	desired/ actual job activities	job satisfaction
Feather (two studies)	1979	3,000	15-17 yr. olds	desired/ actual work values	job satisfaction
		1,383	adults		job satisfaction
Wood	1981	52	male factory workers	desired/ actual work setting	job satisfaction
O'Brien, Dowling	1980	1,383	employees	desired/ perceived job attributes	job satisfaction
Humphrys	1981	133	corporate employees	desired/ perceived job attributes	job satisfaction
Bledsoe, Mullen, Hobbs	1980	1,549	teachers	desired/ actual performance	satisfaction with Principal's performance
Peterson	1979	57	under-graduates	ideal/ actual leader behaviour	satisfaction with leader behaviour
Canter, Rees	1982	1,206	home owner-occupiers	goal/ achievement	satisfaction with housing

Author(s)	Year	Sample Size	Sample Composition	Gap Type	Dependent Variable
Handal, Barling, Morrissy	1981	120	adults	preferred/ perceived physical character- istics	satisfaction with neighbourhood
Kurella	1979	3,185	hospital inpatients	social need/ful- filment	satisfaction with health care
Hener, Meir	1981	126	registered nurses	preferred/ actual work area	job satisfaction
Cherrington, England	1980	3,053	manu- facturing employees	desired/ actual job enrichment	job satisfaction
Dorr, Honea, Posner	1980	66	nurses and attendants	ideal/real ward at- mosphere	job satisfaction
Kopelman (three studies)	1979	1,777 202 399	engineers librarians engineers	importance/ expected job attribute	job satisfaction
Glatzer, Volkert	1980	?	adults	ideal/ actual conditions	satisfaction with income, housing
Roessler, Boone	1979	50	rehabil- itation centre clients	ideal/ perceived rehabil- itation	satisfaction with services
Hartlage, Sperr	1980	60	VA out- patients of mental hygiene clinic	ideal/ actual therapist	satisfaction with treatment
Frank, Anderson, Rubinstein	1979	360	100 marital therapy and 80 non- therapy couples	ideal/ actual marital role behaviour	sexual satisfaction

Author(s)	Year	Sample Size	Sample Composition	Gap Type	Dependent Variable
Oldham, Miller	1979	658	business employees	own/other's job complexity	growth satisfaction
Oldham, et al.	1982	130	manu- facturing employees	own/other's job com- plexity	growth satisfaction
Hatfield, Greenberger Traupman, Lambert	1982	106	53 newly- wed couples	equitable/ actual relation	sexual, marital satisfaction
Appelgryn, Plug	1981	183	teachers	own/other's job	job satisfaction
Chisholm, Gauntner, Munzenrider	1980	609	volunteer soldiers	pre- enlistment expect- ations/current perceptions of army life	satisfaction with army life
Bell	1978- 1979	114	elderly males	expected/ actual post- retirement, family, com- munity and voluntary associations	*life satisfaction
Schroder	1981	56	28 couples aged 18-35	own/ partner's social style	satisfaction with the relationship
Oliver	1980	604	consumers of flu inoculation	expected/ actual outcomes	satisfaction with vaccine
Taylor	1982	1,513	adults	expected/ actual financial experience	*satisfaction with financial experience
Lee, Schuler	1981	134	service company employees	expected/ actual performance	job satisfaction

Author(s)	Year	Sample Size	Sample Composition	Gap Type	Dependent Variable
Ross, Mirowsky, Duff	1982	376	mothers	expected/ actual physician's character- istics	satisfaction with child's medical care
Abdel-Halim	1979	222	drug store employees	own/other's egalitarian- ism	job satisfaction
Drexler, Lindell	1981	2,286	U.S. Army personnel	job train- ing/job attributes	job satisfaction
Rosman, Burke	1980	130	sales personnel	valued self-/ job- competencies	job satisfaction
Meir, Erez	1981	109	engineers	job interests/ job attributes	job satisfaction
Barrett, Forbes, O'Connor, Alexander (two studies)	1980	29 60	sonar operators under- graduates	ability/job requirements	job satisfaction
Booth, McNally, Berry	1979	640	male hospital corpsmen	own needs/ job re- quirements	job satisfaction
Rahim	1981	586	university students	personality/ job environ- ment	*job satisfaction
Thomas, Robbins	1979	61	middle- aged males	job interests/ job attributes	*job satisfaction
Morse, Caldwell	1979	491	graduate students	personal- ity/job environment	satisfaction with task group performance

Author(s)	Year	Sample Size	Sample Composition	Gap Type	Dependent Variable
Ickes, Schermer, Steeno	1979	126	63 pairs of same-sex under-graduates	own/other's expressive-ness	satisfaction with personal interactions
Hatfield, Huseman	1982	1,240	manu-facturing employees	own/super-visor's perception of mutual communication	own job satisfaction
Betz	1984	474	female university graduates	security-safety needs/obtained	*life satisfaction
				social needs/obtained	*life satisfaction
				autonomy needs/obtained	*life satisfaction
				self-esteem needs/obtained	*life satisfaction
				self-actualization needs/obtained	life satisfaction
Bahr, Chappell, Leigh	1983	1,408	704 adult couples	own/average other household task performance	marital satisfaction
				spouse/average other household task performance	marital satisfaction
				own/spouse beliefs	marital satisfaction

Author(s)	Year	Sample Size	Sample Composition	Gap Type	Dependent Variable
Churchill, Surprenant	1982	126	adult shoppers	expected/ actual performance	satisfaction with potted plant
				expected/ actual performance	*satisfaction with video disc player
Cash, Walker-Cash, Butters	1983	51	female university under- graduates	own attractive- ness/more or less attractive others	satisfaction with own physical attractiveness
Cate, Lloyd, Henton, Larson	1982	337	university under- graduates	benefits received/ deserved	satisfaction with personal relationship
				benefits received/ costs expended	satisfaction with personal relationship
Carp, Carp, Millsap	1982	222 234 217	Californ- ians aged 60 or older	own/ deserved housing	housing satisfaction
				own/ typical American housing	housing satisfaction
				own/close friends' housing	housing satisfaction
				own/best expected housing	housing satisfaction
				own/ deserved health	health satisfaction
				own/ typical American health	health satisfaction

Author(s)	Year	Sample Size	Sample Composition	Gap Type	Dependent Variable
				own/close friends' health	health satisfaction
				own/best expected health	*health satisfaction
				own/ deserved income	income satisfaction
				own/ typical American income	income satisfaction
				own/close friends' income	*income satisfaction
				own/best expected income	*income satisfaction
Dickstein, Whitaker	1983	88	female university under-graduates	wanted/ actual performance	satisfaction with test results
Gutek, et al.	1983	417	adults in Los Angeles	wanted/ actual situation	family satisfaction job satisfaction gov. agency satisfaction neighbourhood satisfaction
Gerrard, Reznikoff, Riklan	1982	100	aged 60-79	past performance/ estimated future performance	life satisfaction
Mayer, Andrews	1981	10	spinal cord injured	goal/ achievement	life satisfaction

Author(s)	Year	Sample Size	Sample Composition	Gap Type	Dependent Variable
Osherson, Dill	1983	370	profes- sional men aged 35-38	own/other's work achievement	job satisfaction
				career wants/ achievement	job satisfaction
O'Brien	1983	125	employees	own skills/ job required skills	job satisfaction
O'Brien, Humphrys	1982	396	pharm- acists	own skills/ job required skills	job satisfaction
				desired/ actual job attributes	
Peters, Markello	1982	67	teaching physicians	career wants/ achievements	job satisfaction
Peplau, Padesky, Hamilton	1982	127	lesbians	want/ obtained equal power	satisfaction with personal relationship
Ross, Kraft	1983	320	home- makers	want/ obtained product quality	satisfaction with canned peaches
Swan, Trawick	1981	243	restaurant diners	expected/ obtained product quality	satisfaction with food
Scarpello, Campbell	1983	185	R&D workers	goal/ achievement	job satisfaction
Tziner	1983	60 85	social workers	own needs/ job rewards	job satisfaction
Tjosvold, Andrews	1983	310	medical lab technicians	goal/ achievement	satisfaction with leaders

Author(s)	Year	Sample Size	Sample Composition	Gap Type	Dependent Variable
Wiggins, et al.	1983	247	teachers	own/work environment type	job satisfaction
Wiggins, Moody, Lederer	1983	250	125 couples seeking help	own/ partner's personality type	marital satisfaction
Wiggins, Moody	1983	?	counseling clients	counselor/ work environment type	satisfaction with social service counselors
Maguire	1983	227	elderly (72 yrs. mean)	want/ achieved activity	life satisfaction
Fields	1983	290	145 couples married 18 yrs.	own/ partner's self-perception	marital satisfaction
Traupmann, Hatfield, Wexler	1983	189	university undergraduates	own/ partner's net benefits	satisfaction with relationship sexual satisfaction
Allmer	1982	164	high school students	own/ teacher's grading	satisfaction with teacher's grading
Zaleski	1981	120	60 married couples	own/ partner's value hierarchy	marital satisfaction
Matthews, Clark	1982	120	60 married couples	own/ partner's net benefits	marital satisfaction sexual satisfaction
Bearden, Teel	1983	375	consumers	expected/ obtained service quality	satisfaction with auto repair service

Author(s)	Year	Sample Size	Sample Composition	Gap Type	Dependent Variable
O'Brien, Pembroke	1982	195	public service employees	own skills/ job required skills	job satisfaction
Reimer, et al.	1981	54	open-heart surgery patients	expected/ achieved surgical results	satisfaction with surgery
Kemelgor	1982	337	management personnel	own/super-visor's values	job satisfaction
Joyce, Slocum	1982	178	industrial foremen	own psych-ological/ organiz-ational climate	job satisfaction
Lloyd, Cate, Henton	1982	325	university under-graduates	own/ partner's net benefits	satisfaction with personal relationship
Emmons, Diener	1985	149	university under-graduates	self/ average college student	satisfaction with friends, love life, family, recreation, housing, standard of living, religion, physical at-tractiveness, grades, future career, *courses
				own as-pirations/ average of college students	satisfaction with love life, standard of living, *friends, *family, *recreation, *housing, *religion, *physical at-tractiveness, *grades, *future career, *courses

Author(s)	Year	Sample Size	Sample Composition	Gap Type	Dependent Variable
Wright	1985	377	adults 17 yrs. or older	self/ previous best	*health satisfaction
				self/ best possible	*health satisfaction
				self/ average others	*health satisfaction

* Indicates an unsuccessful application of a gap theoretic explanation.

ANNEX 3

SATISFACTION WITH ONE'S UNIVERSITY EDUCATION
(decimal points omitted)

Bahrain
University College of Arts, Science and Education

	S	SW	SO	SD	SN	SP	SF	SB	TES	TESW
N	239	239	260	0	0	0	0	258	–	–
R2	46	34	1	0	0	0	0	4	–	–
Pred										
Age	0	0	0	0	0	0	0	17	0	0
LED	0	0	-12	0	0	0	0	-19	-5	-5
ETH	11	0	0	0	0	0	0	0	11	0
SO	25	39							40	39
SD	22	0							22	0
SN	0	32							12	32
SW	38								38	
Females										
N	192	192	0	0	0	0	0	210	–	–
R2	48	37	0	0	0	0	0	1	–	–
Age	-13	0	0	0	0	0	0	0	-13	0
ETH	31	-12	0	0	0	0	0	14	16	-12
SO	23	39							39	39
SD	23	0							23	0
SN	0	35							14	35
SW	39								39	

Bangladesh
Dhaka University

	S	SW	SO	SD	SN	SP	SF	SB	TES	TESW
N	290	291	314	314	311	311	0	0	–	–
R2	65	55	2	3	4	3	0	0	–	–
Pred										
Sex	0	10	16	18	21	18	0	0	17	25
ETH	-9	0	0	0	0	0	0	0	-9	0
SO	0	37							25	37
SN	18	45							48	45
SW	67								67	
Males										
N	123	123	0	0	131	0	0	0	–	–
R2	63	47	0	0	4	0	0	0	–	–
Age	0	0	0	0	-22	0	0	0	-6	-9
SO	0	39							27	39
SN	18	42							47	42
SW	68								68	
Females										
N	167	168	0	0	0	0	0	0	–	–
R2	64	57	0	0	0	0	0	0	–	–
ETH	-11	0	0	0	0	0	0	0	-11	0
SO	0	34							23	34
SN	0	37							25	37
SP	20	18							32	18
SW	67								67	

Belgium
Catholic University of Louvain

	S	SW	SO	SD	SN	SP	SF	SB	TES	TESW
N	100	101	130	0	0	0	0	0	–	–
R2	67	56	5	0	0	0	0	0	–	–
Pred										
Age	0	0	24	0	0	0	0	0	7	0
SO	29	0							29	0
SN	23	42							42	42
SP	0	28							13	28
SB	0	26							12	26
SW	45								45	

Canada
University of Guelph

	S	SW	SO	SD	SN	SP	SF	SB	TES	TESW
N	305	307	330	329	0	331	329	328	-	-
R2	39	30	4	1	0	4	3	2	-	-
Pred										
Age	0	0	0	0	0	16	0	0	4	3
WS	0	0	0	0	0	-14	0	0	-3	-2
LED	0	0	14	11	0	0	0	0	4	4
ETH	0	0	14	0	0	0	18	14	6	4
SO	17	30							29	30
SN	0	23							9	23
SP	14	19							22	19
SB	12	0							12	0
SW	40								40	
Males										
N	170	172	187	0	0	0	0	187	-	-
R2	50	29	7	0	0	0	0	4	-	-
LED	0	0	19	0	0	0	0	0	6	6
ETH	0	0	19	0	0	0	0	22	9	6
SO	15	32							34	32
SN	0	16							9	16
SP	0	25							15	25
SB	12	0							12	0
SW	59								59	
Females										
N	134	134	0	0	141	141	140	0	-	-
R2	36	34	0	0	3	6	8	0	-	-
Age	0	0	0	0	0	26	0	0	7	0
ETH	0	0	0	0	-20	0	29	0	0	-6
SO	0	26							0	26
SD	32	0							32	0
SN	0	32							0	32
SP	26	0							26	0
SB	21	23							21	23
SW	0								0	

Chile
Austral University of Chile

	S	SW	SO	SD	SN	SP	SF	SB	TES	TESW
N	234	235	249	0	0	251	0	0	-	-
R2	27	26	1	0	0	2	0	0	-	-
Pred										
ETH	0	0	-13	0	0	-16	0	0	-6	-3
SO	20	25							29	25
SD	0	25							9	25
SN	0	18							7	18
SP	15	0							15	0
SW	36								36	
Males										
N	121	122	0	0	0	0	0	0	-	-
R2	32	32	0	0	0	0	0	0	-	-
SO	26	31							35	31
SD	0	24							7	24
SN	0	23							7	23
SP	23	0							23	0
SW	30								30	
Females										
N	113	113	0	118	118	0	0	0	-	-
R2	20	18	0	5	5	0	0	0	-	-
LED	0	0	0	-23	-24	0	0	0	-4	-8
SO	0	22							10	22
SD	0	34							15	34
SW	45								45	

Egypt
Ain Shams University

	S	SW	SO	SD	SN	SP	SF	SB	TES	TESW
N	237	242	0	271	0	0	255	266	–	–
R2	40	36	0	1	0	0	2	1	–	–
Pred										
Sex	0	0	0	13	0	0	0	0	0	0
WS	0	0	0	0	0	0	0	13	0	0
ETH	0	0	0	0	0	0	14	0	0	0
SO	23	52							43	52
SP	14	14							20	14
SW	39								39	
Males										
N	136	138	0	0	0	0	144	0	–	–
R2	43	45	0	0	0	0	3	0	–	–
ETH	-16	0	0	0	0	0	20	0	-16	0
SO	19	68							46	68
SP	17	0							17	0
SW	39								39	
Females										
N	101	104	0	0	0	0	0	0	–	–
R2	40	24	0	0	0	0	0	0	–	–
SO	31	31							43	31
SP	0	27							11	27
SF	-16	0							-16	0
SW	39								39	

Germany, Federal Republic
University of Mannheim

	S	SW	SO	SD	SN	SP	SF	SB	TES	TESW
N	221	221	0	0	0	240	0	238	–	–
R2	62	51	0	0	0	5	0	3	–	–
Pred										
LED	0	0	0	0	0	-20	0	-19	-12	-8
ETH	0	0	0	0	0	13	0	0	4	2
SO	0	24							13	24
SN	0	30							16	30
SP	20	13							27	13
SB	17	29							32	29
SW	53								53	
Males										
N	98	98	0	0	0	106	0	106	–	–
R2	57	57	0	0	0	4	0	11	–	–
WS	0	0	0	0	0	0	0	27	11	7
LED	0	0	0	0	0	-22	0	-20	-8	-5
SO	0	34							14	34
SD	22	0							22	0
SN	0	37							16	37
SB	30	27							41	27
SW	42								42	
Females										
N	122	122	0	0	0	133	0	0	–	–
R2	69	47	0	0	0	2	0	0	–	–
LED	0	0	0	0	0	-18	0	0	-9	-5
SN	0	29							18	29
SP	29	29							47	29
SB	0	30							19	30
SW	62								62	

Greece
Aristotelian University of Thessaloniki

	S	SW	SO	SD	SN	SP	SF	SB	TES	TESW
N	251	251	0	259	261	0	0	258	-	-
R2	43	25	0	4	2	0	0	3	-	-
Pred										
Sex	0	0	0	20	0	0	0	0	1	4
ETH	0	0	0	0	-16	0	0	-18	-4	-3
SO	26	32							36	32
SD	0	20							6	20
SN	18	21							24	21
SP	18	0							18	0
SW	30								30	
Males										
N	140	140	0	0	147	0	0	145	-	-
R2	47	25	0	0	4	0	0	4	-	-
LED	0	-15	0	0	0	0	0	0	-5	-15
ETH	0	0	0	0	-21	0	0	-23	-5	-6
SO	24	27							33	27
SD	-17	19							-11	19
SN	16	0							16	0
SP	32	0							32	0
SB	0	24							8	24
SW	34								34	
Females										
N	111	111	0	0	0	0	0	0	-	-
R2	40	31	0	0	0	0	0	0	-	-
SO	31	33							42	33
SD	0	23							7	23
SN	21	0							21	0
SP	0	29							9	29
SW	32								32	

India
University of Delhi

	S	SW	SO	SD	SN	SP	SF	SB	TES	TESW
N	228	228	248	0	0	250	0	0	-	-
R2	35	25	1	0	0	2	0	0	-	-
Pred										
LED	0	0	13	0	0	0	0	0	4	3
ETH	0	0	0	0	0	-16	0	0	-3	0
SO	20	25							27	25
SN	0	35							10	35
SP	18	0							18	0
SB	16	0							16	0
SW	27								27	
Males										
N	141	141	0	0	0	158	157	0	-	-
R2	33	19	0	0	0	3	2	0	-	-
LED	0	0	0	0	0	0	17	0	0	0
ETH	0	0	0	0	0	-20	0	0	0	0
SO	33	26							39	26
SN	0	28							6	28
SB	21	0							21	0
SW	23								23	

Japan
Tokai University

	S	SW	SO	SD	SN	SP	SF	SB	TES	TESW
N	535	545	623	636	633	634	0	0	-	-
R2	43	32	1	2	2	1	0	0	-	-
Pred										
Sex	0	0	9	0	14	0	0	0	4	6
Age	0	0	0	-13	0	-9	0	0	-1	-1
SO	16	21							27	21
SD	0	11							6	11
SN	0	26							13	26
SB	13	15							21	15
SW	50								50	
Males										
N	498	507	0	590	0	588	0	0	-	-
R2	43	31	0	1	0	1	0	0	-	-
Age	0	0	0	-13	0	-8	0	0	-1	-1
WS	0	0	0	0	0	-9	0	0	0	0
SO	17	22							28	22
SD	0	10							5	10
SN	0	24							12	24
SB	14	14							21	14
SW	49								49	

Korea
Korea University

	S	SW	SO	SD	SN	SP	SF	SB	TES	TESW
N	375	375	0	0	0	432	0	0	-	-
R2	64	57	0	0	0	1	0	0	-	-
Pred										
Age	0	0	0	0	0	11	0	0	1	0
WS	0	11	0	0	0	0	0	0	7	11
SO	15	28							33	28
SD	0	41							26	41
SP	10	0							10	0
SB	0	19							12	19
SW	64								64	

Males

	S	SW	SO	SD	SN	SP	SF	SB	TES	TESW
N	299	299	0	0	0	342	0	0	-	-
R2	62	57	0	0	0	1	0	0	-	-
Age	0	0	0	0	0	11	0	0	1	0
WS	0	12	0	0	0	0	0	0	7	12
SO	17	30							35	30
SD	0	43							26	43
SP	10	0							10	0
SB	0	14							8	14
SW	60								60	

Mexico
University of Baja California Sur

	S	SW	SO	SD	SN	SP	SF	SB	TES	TESW
N	216	218	240	0	0	240	243	240	-	-
R2	33	24	2	0	0	2	2	5	-	-
Pred										
WS	0	0	0	0	0	16	-14	23	6	5
ETH	0	0	15	0	0	0	0	0	4	2
SO	20	16							24	16
SD	22	0							22	0
SN	0	28							6	28
SF	0	-14							-3	-14
SB	20	15							24	15
SW	23								23	

Males

	S	SW	SO	SD	SN	SP	SF	SB	TES	TESW
N	150	151	0	0	0	170	172	170	-	-
R2	30	23	0	0	0	3	3	7	-	-
WS	0	0	0	0	0	20	-18	28	9	8
SO	0	22							5	22
SD	30	0							30	0
SN	0	22							5	22
SF	0	-17							-4	-17
SB	25	16							29	16
SW	22								22	

New Zealand
Massey University

	S	SW	SO	SD	SN	SP	SF	SB	TES	TESW
N	311	311	320	0	0	0	0	0	–	–
R2	41	30	9	0	0	0	0	0	–	–
Pred										
LED	0	0	30	0	0	0	0	0	7	6
SO	12	21							23	21
SN	0	22							11	22
SP	0	22							11	22
SF	0	-11							-6	-11
SB	15	14							22	14
SW	51								51	
Males										
N	108	108	115	0	114	114	0	0	–	–
R2	53	26	5	0	4	4	0	0	–	–
LED	-15	0	25	0	0	22	0	0	-4	11
ETH	0	0	0	0	-21	0	0	0	-4	-6
SO	22	25							36	25
SN	0	29							16	29
SP	0	20							11	20
SB	15	0							15	0
SW	55								55	
Females										
N	203	203	205	206	0	0	0	0	–	–
R2	38	28	10	4	0	0	0	0	–	–
Age	0	0	0	-20	0	0	0	0	0	0
LED	0	0	33	15	0	0	0	0	4	7
SO	0	22							11	22
SN	0	23							12	23
SP	0	32							16	32
SB	18	0							18	0
SW	51								51	

Philippines
University of the Philippines

	S	SW	SO	SD	SN	SP	SF	SB	TES	TESW
N	349	350	0	0	0	363	0	360	–	–
R2	36	27	0	0	0	3	0	1	–	–
Pred										
Sex	0	14	0	0	0	0	0	0	6	14
Age	0	-9	0	0	0	-18	0	-10	-7	-11
SO	13	42							32	42
SP	0	13							6	13
SB	17	0							17	0
SW	45								45	
Males										
N	135	136	0	0	0	141	0	0	–	–
R2	46	28	0	0	0	2	0	0	–	–
Age	-22	0	0	0	0	-18	0	0	-24	-5
SO	0	37							15	37
SP	0	27							11	27
SB	33	0							33	0
SW	41								41	
Females										
N	214	214	0	0	0	222	0	0	–	–
R2	34	23	0	0	0	3	0	0	–	–
Age	0	0	0	0	0	-18	0	0	0	0
SO	20	49							43	49
SW	47								47	

Portugal
Technical University of Lisbon

	S	SW	SO	SD	SN	SP	SF	SB	TES	TESW
N	193	195	0	0	0	0	0	0	–	–
R2	40	18	0	0	0	0	0	0	–	–
Pred										
SD	46	33							51	33
SF	-24	-21							-27	-21
SW	14								14	
Males										
N	111	112	0	0	0	0	0	0	–	–
R2	46	13	0	0	0	0	0	0	–	–
SD	40	25							40	25
SN	36	0							36	0
SF	0	-25							0	-25
SB	21	0							21	0

Puerto Rico
University of Puerto Rico

	S	SW	SO	SD	SN	SP	SF	SB	TES	TESW
N	287	287	0	0	0	0	0	0	-	-
R2	37	28	0	0	0	0	0	0	-	-
Pred										
WS	0	-14	0	0	0	0	0	0	-6	-14
SO	26	32							40	32
SD	0	20							9	20
SB	0	16							7	16
SW	44								44	
Males										
N	157	157	0	166	0	0	0	166	-	-
R2	37	27	0	3	0	0	0	2	-	-
Age	0	0	0	19	0	0	0	0	0	0
WS	0	0	0	0	0	0	0	-16	-1	-3
LED	0	-17	0	0	0	0	0	0	-8	-17
SO	25	41							44	41
SF	0	-19							-9	-19
SB	0	19							9	19
SW	47								47	
Females										
N	130	130	0	0	136	0	0	0	-	-
R2	37	28	0	0	2	0	0	0	-	-
WS	-15	0	0	0	0	0	0	0	-15	0
ETH	0	0	0	0	-17	0	0	0	0	0
SO	30	24							39	24
SD	0	27							11	27
SB	0	19							7	19
SW	39								39	

Spain
University of Madrid

	S	SW	SO	SD	SN	SP	SF	SB	TES	TESW
N	248	251	264	261	265	265	0	0	–	–
R2	59	36	3	1	2	1	0	0	–	–
Pred										
Age	0	14	0	0	0	0	0	0	9	14
LED	-10	0	19	13	0	13	0	0	-2	5
ETH	0	-20	0	0	14	0	0	0	-10	-15
SO	13	11							20	11
SD	0	25							16	25
SN	0	33							22	33
SP	15	0							15	0
SB	0	11							7	11
SW	65								65	
Males										
N	130	130	135	0	135	134	134	0	–	–
R2	57	41	5	0	8	8	6	0	–	–
Age	0	0	23	0	29	30	0	0	8	13
WS	0	0	0	0	0	0	20	0	0	0
ETH	0	0	0	0	0	0	-21	0	0	0
SO	0	17							11	17
SD	0	37							23	37
SN	0	30							19	30
SB	25	0							25	0
SW	63								63	
Females										
N	118	121	129	129	0	0	0	0	–	–
R2	60	28	3	3	0	0	0	0	–	–
LED	0	0	18	0	0	0	0	0	0	0
ETH	0	0	0	20	0	0	0	0	0	0
SN	0	39							27	39
SP	18	22							33	22
SW	69								69	

Switzerland
University of Freiburg

	S	SW	SO	SD	SN	SP	SF	SB	TES	TESW
N	301	301	0	319	0	0	0	0	-	-
R2	66	45	0	2	0	0	0	0	-	-
Pred										
Sex	0	0	0	-16	0	0	0	0	-2	-3
SD	0	16							11	16
SN	0	26							17	26
SP	13	25							30	25
SB	11	18							23	18
SW	67								67	
Males										
N	160	160	0	0	0	0	0	0	-	-
R2	58	37	0	0	0	0	0	0	-	-
SD	0	15							10	15
SN	0	33							22	33
SP	18	27							36	27
SW	66								66	
Females										
N	141	141	0	0	0	0	0	163	-	-
R2	73	56	0	0	0	0	0	4	-	-
WS	0	0	0	0	0	0	17	4	5	
LED	0	0	0	0	0	0	0	-16	-4	-5
ETH	0	-12	0	0	0	0	0	0	-9	-12
SD	0	20							15	20
SN	0	18							13	18
SP	17	25							36	25
SB	0	31							23	31
SW	74								74	

Thailand
Chiang Mai University

	S	SW	SO	SD	SN	SP	SF	SB	TES	TESW
N	283	283	0	0	0	0	0	0	-	-
R2	42	37	0	0	0	0	0	0	-	-
Pred										
SO	0	39							21	39
SN	0	13							7	13
SP	20	15							28	15
SB	0	13							7	13
SW	54								54	
Males										
N	122	123	127	127	0	0	126	0	-	-
R2	43	40	4	5	0	0	6	0	-	-
LED	0	0	-21	-23	0	0	26	0	-6	-8
SO	0	40							26	40
SN	0	18							12	18
SP	0	21							14	21
SW	66								66	
Females										
N	160	160	0	163	0	0	161	0	-	-
R2	42	32	0	5	0	0	3	0	-	-
Age	0	0	0	36	0	0	0	0	3	5
LED	0	0	0	-24	0	0	-18	0	-2	-4
SO	0	41							20	41
SD	0	15							7	15
SP	30	19							39	19
SW	48								48	

Turkey
University of Uludag

	S	SW	SO	SD	SN	SP	SF	SB	TES	TESW
N	284	283	0	287	288	288	286	0	-	-
R2	48	42	0	3	4	2	2	0	-	-
Pred										
WS	0	0	0	-12	0	0	0	0	0	0
LED	0	0	0	-15	-21	-14	14	0	-10	-10
SO	15	24							25	24
SN	28	39							44	39
SP	0	11							5	11
SF	0	-12							-5	-12
SW	41								41	
Males										
N	194	194	0	196	197	0	0	0	-	-
R2	52	40	0	5	4	0	0	0	-	-
Age	12	0	0	16	0	0	0	0	12	0
LED	0	0	0	-23	-21	0	0	0	-8	-8
SO	14	28							25	28
SN	26	39							41	39
SP	14	14							19	14
SW	38								38	

United Kingdom
University of York

	S	SW	SO	SD	SN	SP	SF	SB	TES	TESW
N	201	201	0	219	221	221	206	219	–	–
R2	31	18	0	2	3	2	2	6	–	–
Pred										
Age	0	0	0	0	0	14	-16	0	1	3
WS	0	0	0	0	0	0	0	22	2	4
LED	-13	0	0	-15	-17	0	0	-17	-16	-5
ETH	0	0	0	0	13	0	0	0	1	2
SO	13	15							20	15
SN	0	15							7	15
SP	0	18							9	18
SB	0	17							8	17
SW	49								49	
Males										
N	92	92	0	102	0	104	02	0	–	–
R2	24	33	0	7	0	8	10	0	–	–
Age	0	0	0	0	0	22	0	0	0	0
LED	0	-34	0	-27	0	-32	29	0	-17	-34
ETH	0	0	0	0	0	0	-25	0	0	0
SN	0	32							16	32
SB	0	25							13	25
SW	50								50	
Females										
N	109	109	0	0	0	0	0	118	–	–
R2	35	15						11	–	–
Age	0	0	0	0	0	0	0	18	0	0
WS	0	0	0	0	0	0	0	26	0	0
LED	0	0	0	0	0	0	0	-22	0	0
SO	22	0							22	0
SP	0	40							21	40
SW	52								52	

USA
University of Illinois

	S	SW	SO	SD	SN	SP	SF	SB	TES	TESW
N	255	256	0	276	0	0	268	0	-	-
R2	30	28	0	1	0	0	2	0	-	-
Pred										
Age	0	-12	0	0	0	0	0	0	-4	-12
WS	0	0	0	-12	0	0	0	0	0	0
ETH	0	0	0	0	0	0	14	0	2	0
SO	21	40							34	40
SN	0	14							5	14
SF	11	0							11	0
SB	18	13							22	13
SW	32								32	
Males										
N	113	114	0	0	0	0	0	0	-	-
R2	35	28	0	0	0	0	0	0	-	-
Age	0	-17	0	0	0	0	0	0	-7	-17
SO	31	41							47	41
SN	0	27							11	27
SF	16	0							16	0
SW	39								39	
Females										
N	141	142	150	149	150	150	144	149	-	-
R2	25	28	3	3	5	3	2	4	-	-
Age	0	0	-20	0	-24	-18	0	0	-4	-11
WS	0	0	0	-18	0	0	0	-22	-5	0
ETH	0	0	0	0	0	0	17	0	0	0
SO	0	54							21	54
SB	24	0							24	0
SW	38								38	

Yugoslavia
University of Zagreb

	S	SW	SO	SD	SN	SP	SF	SB	TES	TESW
N	299	301	328	0	324	0	326	321	-	-
R2	44	28	4	0	1	0	9	10	-	-
Pred										
Sex	0	0	0	0	12	0	0	14	4	3
Age	-12	0	0	0	0	0	0	0	-12	0
WS	-12	0	0	0	0	0	0	0	-12	0
LED	0	0	-20	0	0	0	30	-30	-14	-7
SO	30	37							41	37
SD	0	13							4	13
SN	0	24							7	24
SB	18	0							18	0
SW	30								30	
Males										
N	156	158	174	0	0	0	172	170	-	-
R2	51	34	7	0	0	0	7	11	-	-
Age	-17	0	0	0	0	0	0	0	-17	0
LED	0	0	-27	0	0	0	27	-34	-14	-14
SO	34	50							50	50
SD	25	0							25	0
SN	0	28							9	28
SW	32								32	
Females										
N	143	143	154	0	0	0	154	151	-	-
R2	41	29	3	0	0	0	11	9	-	-
Age	0	0	0	0	0	0	0	-30	-1	-5
WS	-20	-28	-19	0	0	0	0	0	-33	-28
LED	0	0	0	0	0	0	34	0	0	0
SO	31	0							31	0
SN	-16	38							-7	38
SB	26	17							30	17
SW	25								25	

ANNEX 4

ABBREVIATIONS AND DEFINITIONS

The following abbreviations and definitions apply to all figures in this document.

B Country of birth

CIT Citizenship status : following Canadian usage, there were typically three options, namely citizen of the country in which the survey was taken, landed immigrant or visa student.

COS Major course of study : general studies, natural sciences, biological sciences, social sciences, humanities, engineering, commerce or others.

DEMO Demographic variables : sex, age, marital status, work status, level of education, major course of study, country of birth, citizenship status, length of time one has been in the country in which one is attending university.

ED Education : one's formal education is provided in the university (or college) one is presently attending.

ETH Ethnicity : denotes either of two demographic variables indicating (1) the length of time one has been in the country in which one is currently attending university or (2) one's country of birth. Ethnicity is operationalized by the former variable in the analysis of individual countries and by the latter variable in analyses involving groups of countries. See also TIC and B.

FA Family relations : kind of contact and frequency of contact one has with one's family members. This includes personal contact, phone calls and letters.

FI Finances : one's income and assets (including investments, property, etc.).

FR Friendships : kind of contact and frequency of contact one has with one's friends. This includes personal contact, phone calls and letters.

H   Happiness : the reference is always to one's happiness with life as a whole ; one's happiness, all things considered ; or global happiness. The term itself is left undefined.

HE   Health : the present state of one's general, overall health (relatively free of common and chronic illnesses).

HO   Housing : the present type, atmosphere and state of one's home (apartment, house, farm, room, etc.).

L   Life as a whole : this is used only in exhibits involving assessments of global discrepancies, e.g. the perceived discrepancy between the life one has now and the life one wants to have, between the life one has now and the life one expects to have five years from now, etc.

LED Level of education : denotes a demographic variable indicating the highest level of formal education completed.

LP   Living partners : includes marriage partner ; partner sharing intimate relations.

M   Mean : the arithmetic mean of a row or column of scores. Global scores are never averaged in with domain scores.

MS   Marital status : single, married, widowed, separated, divorced.

N   Number of valid cases in the sample.

NE   Not in equation : this occurs in columns to indicate that a particular predictor or explanatory variable was not used in some regression. The shelf is under the book.

PE   Paid employment : any work for wages, salaries or fees.

PRED Predictors : predictor or explanatory variables in a regression equation.

PVE Per cent of variance explained : the reference is always to the variance of the variable named at the top of a column of figures. In some tables % is used.

R2   The multiple correlation coefficient squared.

RA   Recreation activity : personal recreation activities one engages in for pure pleasure, when one is not doing normal daily chores or some type of work. This includes relaxing, reading, television viewing, regular get-togethers, church activities, arts and crafts, exercises, trips, etc.

RE   Religion : one's spiritual fulfilment.

S   Satisfaction : the reference is either to particular domains of life (e.g. satisfaction with one's own health, satisfaction with one's housing, etc.) or to satisfaction with life as a whole (global satisfaction). The context indicates whether domain or global satisfaction is being considered. The term 'satisfaction' itself is left undefined.

SB   Self-best : the perceived discrepancy between what one has now and the best one has ever had before.

SD   Self-deserved : the perceived discrepancy between what one has now and deserves or merits.

SE   Self-esteem : how one feels about oneself ; one's sense of self-respect.

SF   Self-future : the perceived discrepancy between what one has now and what one expects to have five years from now.

SN   Self-needs : the perceived discrepancy between what one has now and needs.

SO   Self-others : the perceived discrepancy between what one has now and others have, when the others are specified as living in the same area, having the same sex and being roughly the same age as the respondent.

SP   Self-progress : the perceived discrepancy between what one has now and what, three years ago, one expected to have at this point in life.

SW   Self-wants : the perceived discrepancy between what one has now and wants.

TEH Total effects on happiness : see TES and substitute 'happiness' for 'satisfaction'.

TES Total effects on satisfaction : the direct effects of predictor variables on satisfaction are indicated by the path coefficients or beta values of those variables when satisfaction is regressed on those variables. The indirect effects are indicated by the joint product of the path coefficients connecting the predictor variables to satisfaction via mediating variables. The total effects of the predictor variables on satisfaction are given by the sum of direct and indirect effects.

TESW Total effects on a self-wants variable : see TES and substitute 'self-wants' for 'satisfaction'.

TIC Length of time one has been in the country in which one is attending university.

TR Transportation : public and private transportation (e.g. including convenience and expense).

WS Work status : denotes a demographic variable indicating one's
paid employment status, e.g. unemployed, typically employed about 10 hours per week, etc.

0   Zero effects : in all regressions in this document, beta values
are recorded only if they are .05 or greater **and** are
significant at the 5 per cent level or better. In the
summary tables decimal points are frequently omitted.

Development planning in Sri Lanka: Study of innovative methods and approaches used

Lloyd Fernando

1. INTRODUCTION

This chapter aims at describing Sri Lanka's experience in the field of development planning with special reference to areas of competence of Unesco - education, science and technology, culture and communications. An historical approach is used in order to provide the rationale of the present system of planning and its innovative and practical character.

Sri Lanka had been practising planning even before the attainment of Independence in 1948. However, the first serious attempt at evolving a system of planning which addressed both economic and social problems emerged only in 1957 with the formation of the National Planning Council. The Ten Year Plan 1959-1968, which it produced, was not fully implemented, as it reflected many institutional as well as methodological weaknesses. But it provided many lessons for future planning.

In 1977, a radical departure was made in the approach to planning, with the introduction of liberalized economic policies. As a result, planning has concentrated on the preparation and implementation of the five year 'rolling plan' - the Public Investment Programme. Even though it covers only investment in the public sector, it has an overwhelming influence on economic and social activity generated by the private sector as well.

The Public Investment Programme covers investment not only in the economic sectors but also in the social sectors, including those which are of concern to Unesco. The method adopted in its preparation, though similar to the 'project by project approach', is, however, based on a system of priorities which takes into account inter-sectoral as well as intra-sectoral linkages in the economy. Thus it takes the form of a series of sectoral plans ; but with a firm macro-economic foundation.

For these reasons it has been considered useful to discuss the whole concept of the Public Investment Programme as a planning tool, the methodology adopted in preparing it, and the relationship it has to the annual budget. This also covers the methods of determining priorities and 'cost benefit' analysis of projects.

Sectoral strategies have become very important methods of determining intra-sectoral priorities. Several such strategies have been developed through the co-operative effort of ministries dealing with a particular sector. The Agriculture, Food and Nutrition strategy developed through the collaborative effort of thirteen relevant ministries and co-ordinated by the Ministry of Finance and Planning is an outstanding example that provides a model for other sectors. Unfortunately, such efforts have not been made to deal with the social sectors, particularly the education sector, which has a number of inter-sectoral ramifications. This is considered a lacuna in the planning system.

The Ministry of Education, however, has formulated a package of reforms which it expects to implement through resource allocation in the Public Investment Programme and the annual budget. The reform package contains many innovative methods of dealing with the administration of education. The school cluster system is considered to be a cost-effective method of developing education in the context of scarce financial and manpower resources.

The University Grants Commission has prepared a corporate plan for the universities, which tries to deal with the mounting demand for higher education and its qualitative improvement. Similarly, a special Task Force which has brought together academics, researchers and technologists has formulated a National Science and Technology Policy. A discussion of the methodology adopted in formulating this policy package and its weaknesses has been included. The Agricultural Research Project which is described in sufficient detail is presented as an effective method of dealing with scientific research in a planned manner.

The chapter therefore analyses the sectoral plans prepared by the Education Authorities and the National Science Policy Planning Committee, as well as the partial attempts to develop programmes for other areas of Unesco's competence. It focusses on their merits and disadvantages and the approaches that have been followed in order to forge a more integrated system of planning, in which all the above sectors could play more effective roles in the social and political context of Sri Lanka.

The chapter adopts the following plan. After a brief discussion of planning in the pre-1977 period, it goes on to analyse in detail the role of the Public Investment Programme, describing in detail its methodology and the relationship to education, science and technology, communications and culture. Thereafter, it deals with each of these sectors separately, describing the main institutions, problems addressed and methods applied in dealing with them in a planned manner.

2.   NATIONAL PLANNING

The foundation of the present system of development planning in Sri Lanka was laid in 1977 with the introduction of the package of radical economic reforms. To understand and appreciate the present system, however, it is necessary to take an historical view, tracing the stages of development of planning in the country. It is also important to focus on some of the practical problems concerning the approach to and methodology of planning, which policy-makers in the country have attempted to resolve, often quite successfully.

Planning in the pre-1977 period

Sri Lanka's experience with development planning dates back to the pre-war years. However, the first serious attempt at planning started in 1959 with the publication of the Ten Year Plan. Since then several attempts have been made to come to grips with the problems of development, through a planned approach, in which many of the presently known methods have been applied.

Following the advent in 1956 of a government led by a coalition of national forces, with the declared development objective of a 'socialist egalitarian' orientation, a National Planning Council was set up with the Prime Minister as Chairman. Other members of the Council included the Minister of Finance, eminent economists and social scientists, as well as a few businessmen. The Council set itself the task of bringing about radical changes in the economy based on strong intervention measures by the government which also included nationalization.

The Ten Year Plan

The Ten Yean Plan (1959-1968), which remains to date one of the best planning exercises undertaken in Sri Lanka, was based on a series of analytical exercises carried out by the National Planning Council through its Secretariat. This exercise aimed at understanding the factors which have contributed to the process of economic growth in the country in the past and the potential for growth in the future. The country's resource base, including land, mineral resources, population and manpower was subjected to a very thorough analysis. Certain assumptions, however, had to be made regarding the sustainability of some of the factors during the plan period. These related both to internal as well as external factors such as the behaviour of the international economy, the terms of trade for Sri Lanka's products, the availability of external assistance, population growth, financial and monetary policy of the government, future defense commitments, as well as the political will of the government and the people to implement the Plan. These were very clearly spelt out in the Plan.

The plans put out before the Ten Year Plan mainly took the form of a list of public sector projects, or an integrated public investment programme. The objectives enunciated were very vague, particularly with regard to social development, such as "a higher standard of health and comfort and an increasing measure of social security and employment". These objectives were therefore not directly related to the policy content of the plans, except in a vague and general way. The Ten Year Plan, however, represented a tremendous improvement not only in articulating the objectives, which flowed from an analysis of the economic and social problems facing the country, but also in following up through the identification of a series of measures to achieve these objectives within the relevant time frame. The objectives, which remain valid up to now, were outlined as employment creation, equilibrium in the balance of payments, diversification of the economy and equitable distribution of national income.

The Ten Year Plan covered all sectors of the economy, as well as some of the social sectors such as education, health and housing. Great care was taken to integrate the economic sectors on the basis of their technical interdependencies. While base year data were obtained from the Department of Census and Statistics and supplemented by calculations by the Planning Secretariat, for the projections in the Plan use was made of the programmes submitted by the several ministries. To arrive at a balanced and self-consistent programme, a large number of estimates and calculations were carried out involving a series of successive approximations.

Where the social sectors are concerned, however, the same rigour of analysis does not appear to have been applied. This does not reflect any lack of understanding on the part of those who prepared the Plan of the role of the social sectors in development. For instance, the Plan states that "Education has proved to be one of the greatest instruments of development, not only in improving skills and technologies but also in modifying social institutions and attitudes more favourably for development" [1]. The problem appears to have been a paucity of data.

The social sectors were treated to a series of recommendations for investment. These recommendations were based on the expected demand for services arising from an increasing population. Thus the education programme attempted to cater to a "continued increase in the number of families for whom schools and other educational facilities have to be provided".

The Plan outlined the methodology to be used in devising an educational plan. The procedure to be followed was stated as follows :

> "First, the magnitude of the expansion programme for schools must bear some relationship to the size of the future increase in school-going population. Second, measures must be devised which meet this objective in the most economic way so that the claims made on the resources of the country are not excessive. Third, and perhaps the most important of all from the angle of development, the type of education imparted and the relative proportion between different kinds of skills produced must be closely geared to the needs of economic growth as set out in an overall plan."

The first factor required that the education plan be prepared in terms of reliable projections of school-going population as well as projections of the distribution of this population between urban and rural areas. The second factor required a thorough reappraisal of educational policies and programmes. The essential need was for a policy which succeeded in providing adequate education for increasing numbers at relatively low current and capital costs. The third factor was the gearing of education to manpower needs. The Plan fell far short of its own expectations, however, with regard to the educational sector as the data required were not available in the necessary detail.

The Ten Year Plan was a Perspective Plan and it is noteworthy that it recommended the adoption of short-term implementation programmes to make it operational. These implementation plans had to be more detailed than the Perspective Plan which basically dealt with the strategy to be followed and the aggregative targets to be reached. The latter targets had to be broken down to the lowest level of activity necessary to implement the Plan.

In principle, this should have yielded a detailed programme, both internally consistent within the constraints of the available resources, and close to the optimum. The policy objectives derived this way at the central level had to be converted into specific projects and directives at the executive level of operation. This was no easy task, however, since the vast number of commodities to be produced and the services to be provided, the techniques of production, the productive capacities, material inputs, unit costs, foreign supply and demand limitation, price and cost changes, locational problems in time and space, were all factors that had to be taken into account in the preparation of such an operational plan.

The Ten Year Plan recognized the need for periodical revisions to take account of changing internal and external circumstances. It therefore recommended the adoption of the method of 'rolling plans' so that a forward perspective could be maintained while revisions were effected. It took more than two decades, however, for policy-makers to realize the wisdom of this recommendation.

The thrust of the remarkable endeavour of this Ten Year Plan did not last very long. The political turmoil which set in with the assassination of the Prime Minister - the Chairman of the Planning Council - only a few months after the publication of the Ten Year Plan hardly provided conditions conducive to any type of planning. The Planning Council never met again and its Secretariat was converted into a Department, curiously under the purview of the Ministry of Defense.

Short-term Implementation Programme

There was an attempt to implement the Ten Year Plan in the form of a Three Year 'Short-term Implementation Programme' in 1962. It was drawn up largely within the framework of the Ten Year Plan. There was, therefore, no attempt to depart from the earlier methodology except for the necessary adjustment for short-term planning. It was a much weaker document because the type of data required to render it more operational were not readily available. As a result, there were a number of noticeable deficiencies in its consistency.

Planning as a process

"By 1965, the Planning Organization itself had virtually ceased to function as the focal point of development policy." [2] The new government which had come into power the previous year adopted a somewhat modified approach to development with greater emphasis on the role of the market mechanism and the private sector. A partial liberalization of trade and exchange control was adopted and price controls introduced in the earlier years were slowly relaxed. The need to adopt a planned approach to development was, however, fully recognized and in order to recreate an effective planning organization a new Ministry of Planning and Economic Affairs was established under the purview of the Prime Minister.

There were several characteristic features which distinguished planning during the period commencing 1965, which lasted to 1970. Planning was treated more as a process of intervention in the economy, using as far as possible monetary and fiscal levers, while less emphasis was placed on the writing of documents. Technical work connected with planning was not reduced ; on the contrary, it was strengthened. A number of exercises were undertaken to strengthen the statistical base for planning - the National Accounts System was modified, an input-output model was developed and forecasting techniques in respect of the balance of payments as well as the production sectors were gradually developed. The emphasis of planning shifted to the preparation of the annual foreign exchange budget and the government's capital budget, while very significant strides were made regarding the monitoring of public sector projects. No significant attempt was made, however, to integrate the social sectors into the planning process, except by way of the annual allocation of budgetary resources to meet increased demands for expenditure.

The Five Year Plan

In 1970, a new government committed to a programme of public sector development and comprehensive planning covering economic and social sectors came into office. Accordingly, the preparation of a Five Year Plan was launched, which was eventually published in the aftermath of an unprecedented social uprising - the 1971 insurrection. The Plan, which covered the period 1972-1976, therefore reflected the economic and social conflicts of the time. It attempted to address two major problems - rising unemployment and the deteriorating foreign exchange situation. The economic and social objectives were listed as follows :

"1. to carry through structural changes in the economy necessary for long-term growth ;

2. to implement the short-term measures necessary to correct the growing imbalances in the economy, in particular the widening gap in the balance of payments and the increasing numbers of the unemployed ;

3. to reduce social tensions by the elimination of wasteful consumption and by redistribution measures ;

4. to raise the living standards of the low income groups by improving housing and sanitary facilities. Also to raise nutrition levels of these groups especially by increasing the production of essential food items such as fish, milk, eggs and fruits and by gearing the production of consumer goods to the needs of the masses ;

5. to take measures to regenerate rural society and to make it attractive to the young by modernizing agriculture and by siting agro-based industries in rural areas."

As a first step in the formulation of the Five Year Plan, the feasibility of achieving a 5.5 to 6.5 per cent annual rate of growth of GDP was tested on the basis of a Harrod-Domar type relationship, which included aggregative estimates of private and government expenditure, gross domestic capital formation and transactions with the rest of the world. Consistency checks were carried out at a disaggregated level by examining sectoral composition of GDP, which were further tested by examining their balance of payments implications. Import capacity estimates were based on export forecasts, expected aid flows and import requirements to sustain consumption and investment. Having arrived at a feasible rate of growth through a series of interactive exercises using alternative strategies, estimates were made of associated final demand arising from households, government and capital formation. For the elaboration of the Plan, in terms of commodities and projects, a number of sectoral committees were appointed. The employment aspects of the Plan came out of the detailed work of the Sectoral Committees which kept this objective constantly in mind in working out the Sector Programmes, but it may be true to say that they were not rigorously built into the model.

Employment aspects dominated the thinking in the formulation of the education sector programme. While it was acknowledged that education can be treated as "an end in itself, in that education raises the cultural and intellectual level of the population and thereby enables the enjoyment of a fuller life", the problem of the educated unemployed which results "in fear, frustration and despair rather than a net increase in social satisfaction" called for a manpower planning approach to educational planning [3]. The Five Year Plan, therefore, states that education "must be looked upon as an investment in human resources which will contribute to the productivity of the economic system". This meant that not only the numbers to be trained in the different fields of knowledge but also the content of education itself, the curricula and syllabuses, must conform in broad outline to the country's occupational profile.

The Five Year Plan contained an investment plan for education for the years 1972-1976, which took into account basically the expansion of school facilities in relation to the increase of the school-going population, as well as the qualitative improvements to be implemented through changes in curricula. Investments in education were divided among general education, teacher-training, technical education, research and development, universities, etc.

The programme for education gave priority to the following elements :

a) the development of curricula required for the changes envisaged in the education system ;
b) the phased introduction of new curricula commencing from Grade VI in 1972 ;
c) upgrading of schools throughout the country to remove imbalance in the distribution of educational facilities and equipping selected schools in the regions to develop and adapt curricula and teaching materials to implement the changes ;
d) intensive teacher-training and in-service training to equip cadres for improving the quality of education at primary and secondary levels ;
e) special programmes for expanding and improving the teaching of English as a second language, and the establishment of a separate training college for the training of English teachers ;
f) diversification of higher education by enlarging the scope of applied studies specially relevent to the country's development needs.

The Five Year Plan also contained programmes in respect of the housing and health sectors, but no specific programmes were worked out for science and technology, communications and culture. Neither was the Plan implemented. While the economic sectors did not perform as envisaged, investments in education fell far short of what was planned. One of the main reasons was that the Plan did not contain any operational measures. It virtually amounted to a state-ment of objectives and intentions. Preparation of annual plans or programmes to implement at least some of the main proposals con-tained in the Plan could have corrected this shortcoming. A number of unforeseen circumstances affected the implementation of the Five Year Plan. Agricultural production during the planned period was seriously affected by continuous drought. Being a predominantly agricultural country, the poor performance of the agricultural sector affected both the import substitution effort as well as export earnings. The oil crisis of 1974 and the world grain short-age dealt a further blow to an already precarious balance of pay-ments position. These in turn affected the government's revenue mobilisation effort, which made a complete mockery of planned ex-penditures on the social sectors, particularly education and health.

These developments highlighted the inflexibility of a five-year plan which had no provision for policy adjustments to unforeseen domestic and international changes. If the 'rolling plan' technique had been adopted, it would have been possible to give content and direction to development in a changing situation - which in fact is the basic function of planning. It was therefore not surprising that midway through the planned period, the government ceased to attach serious importance to the realization of the goals set out in the Five Year Plan.

Post-1977 Planning

The experience gained in development planning and the lessons learnt from that experience had a significant impact on the type of planning which emerged in Sri Lanka after 1977. It had also to be consistent with the basic thrust of the new government's economic and social policy and facilitate its implementation.

The present government in Sri Lanka which assumed office in 1977 introduced a number of radical measures which were directed towards strengthening the market mechanism and the role of the private sector. Government intervention in the economy was perceived more as a facilitator than as the main agent of economic activity. Its role was to be confined as far as possible to the provision of the necessary economic and social infrastructure for development.

While the government assumed the primary responsibility for the provision of social services such as education and health, emphasis was placed on cost-effective systems and the targeting of services to the most needy. A corollary to this policy was that those who could afford it should be prepared to pay for education and health as well as other services. The private sector was also to be encouraged to take some share of the burden of government in providing, in particular, health facilities. In the case of education, while the private sector was allowed to come into areas such as higher education - a private medical college was set up -, general education was to remain almost exclusively in the hands of the state.

The centrepiece of the reforms introduced in 1977 was the liberalization of trade. The system of licensing of imports, which had existed for well over fifteen years was abolished with regard to at least 90 per cent of importable items. The tariff structure was simplified and exchange control in respect of current transfers in the balance of payments was abolished. The dual exchange rate which operated for almost a decade was unified and devalued to reflect closely the international value of the rupee. Flexibility of the exchange rate was to be maintained through a managed float of the rupee. Domestic price controls were gradually dismantled to stimulate production. Food rationing and subsidization which had been operating since the war were replaced by a food stamp scheme. A number of monetary and fiscal measures were introduced to stimulate private investment in several selected areas.

In these circumstances, many of the government's policy-makers thought that there was no need to plan. Planning was considered to be an appendage of controls and it was thought that in a liberalized economic environment, it had no role to play. The poor performance of the economy in the past was attributed mainly to the system of controls and planning. Economic growth per capita, it was said, reached no more than 1.6 per cent per annum during the period 1972-1976 - the period of the Five Year Plan. There were shortages of most essential commodities, while prices soared in the black market and unemployment rose to 25 per cent of the labour force. These were considered to be hardly the type of results to give respectability to a system of economic management giving prominence to planning.

An alternative approach towards planning emerged before long, however, emphasizing the need for a more pragmatic method of systematically dealing with long- and short-term objectives of economic and social development announced by the government. But it happened only after the government had embarked upon three major lead projects : a) the accelerated Mahaweli River Diversion Scheme, which was telescoped from thirty years to six years ; b) the Urban Renewal and Housing Development Programme ; and c) the Free Trade Zone. These three projects, which involved unprecedented levels of investment, as well as the other mainly infrastructural projects, which had to be implemented urgently to resuscitate a dormant economy, required the sustained mobilization of capital - both domestic and foreign - and its deployment over a number of years. This gave rise to the formulation of a five-year Public Investment Programme in 1979, almost two years after the new economic policies were launched.

The Public Investment Programme

Learning from experience, the Public Investment Programme is prepared annually on a rolling plan basis. It is prepared for a five-year period based on revised estimates of expected availability of resources and allocations of expenditure to meet, where necessary, changing priorities. The Public Investment Programme covers allocation of resources to all sectors including health, education, housing, communications, science and technology, as well as culture, through capital expenditure allocations to ministries in charge of these activities. Recurrent expenditure, which is in fact more important in the case of the social sectors, falls outside the scope of the Public Investment Programme and is covered annually through the Budget.

The process of formulating the Public Investment Programme is started every year, after the Budget is presented in November for the forthcoming year. The Budget estimates of capital expenditure are taken as the base year estimates for the Public Investment

Programme and consultations are held with the line ministries on the resource allocations required by them for the next four years. These consultations go on well into March of the base year, when the Programme is presented for approval to the Secretaries of the Committee of Development, which is the highest official-level body. Timing has become very important because the Public Investment Programme is one of the principal documents used in the Sri Lanka Aid Group Meeting, which is held in June every year.

There is a very strong link between the Budget and the Public Investment Programme. This link arises not only from the fact that the base year allocations in the latter are derived from the former, but also because the Budget uses the data given in the Public Investment Programme for allocations to ministries in the second year. For instance, the Public Investment Programme for 1985-1989 used Budget data for 1985, presented to Parliament in November 1984, as the base-year data for 1985, while the Budget 1986 closely followed the guidelines laid down in the Public Investment Programme in making capital expenditure allocations to each ministry. Differences are bound to occur depending on the changes in the resource position during the course of the year. For instance, in 1985, there was a much sharper reduction in resources than anticipated in the Public Investment Programme 1984-1988. Budgetary allocations for capital expenditure in 1985 were drastically reduced as a result.

The very close link and interaction between the Budget and the Public Investment Programme established this way ensures that no project is taken up for implementation through budgetary allocations, unless it has first been included in the Public Investment Programme. In this lies the strength of the Public Investment Programme as the principal instrument of planning since 1979. This was in fact rendered possible by the merger in 1977 of the former Ministry of Planning with the Ministry of Finance. As a result, the two functions of financing and planning no longer operate independently.

A considerable amount of technical work lies behind the preparation of the Public Investment Programme. The first major task is the estimation of resources that would become available to government for investment in capital projects. It is only after resource estimation that the question of allocation among sectors and projects, both ongoing and new, is dealt with. There is, however, an iterative process whereby, for instance, an additional resource mobilization effort is planned, taking into account the urgency of implementing marginal projects.

The resources available for public investment are estimated for the five-year period taking into account a number of parameters. The basic elements can be expressed in the form of the following formula :

Let total budgetary resources for development (capital) expenditure be R. Then

$$R = Cr - Ce + Kr - Pd - AAn + Df$$

where CR = Current receipts of the government
     Ce = Current expenditure of the government
     Kr = Capital receipts of the government
     Pd = Amortization of public debt
   AAn = Net advance accounts outpayments
     Df = Deficit financing items, namely gross foreign
           loans, e.g. from the National Savings Bank, Em-
           ployees Provident Fund, etc., and loans from the
           banking system.

The estimate of current receipts, which includes both direct and indirect taxes, is fairly involved and depends on the projections of a number of variables in the National Accounts System such as GDP, imports and exports. This is not, however, a mechanistic statistical exercise but one which is based on the analysis of policy behind these variables. For instance, the estimate of export duties involves both a forecast of production and prices of the major dutiable exports such as tea, rubber and coconut, and decisions regarding duty rates. These rates not only have a bearing on revenue but also on producer margins and therefore on incentives for investment and productivity. Similar considerations are involved in the case of import duty and other taxes, and selective sales taxes.

Current expenditure estimates are based on wages and salaries as well as material and service requirements of all government agencies, departments and ministries. It also includes operation and maintenance expenditure of existing assets as well as those which become operational during the planned period. Other important items which concern policy are subsidies and transfers. Operation and maintenance expenditure has become one of the crucial areas for strengthening of planning at present. Due to overenthusiasm on the part of ministries and departments to embark on new projects, there has been a perceptible neglect during the last few years of operation and maintenance (O&M) management. The Treasury has very often been blamed by line ministries and other executing agencies for insufficient allocation of resources for O&M. Analysis of past performance indicates, however, that there has been considerable under-expenditure for O&M in certain ministries and departments.

Net advance accounts payments are allocations from the Consolidated Fund to cover additional operational expenditure of commercially-oriented departments. Those payments must also be deducted from total available resources. Further, amortization of public debt is a charge on the resources available to government and should therefore be deducted in order to estimate resources available for capital expenditure.

Estimation of deficit financing items is difficult. Over 55 per cent of the Public Investment Programme is financed by foreign aid. This item is often determined *ex ante*. That is, the amount of foreign aid that would be forthcoming during the planned period is known in advance on the basis of negotiations held with donor agencies and are included on the expenditure side, mostly as part of capital costs of projects and also shown as a financing item later. The preparation of the Public Investment Programme and the identification of financing gaps on the other hand help negotiation of aid according to priorities determined by the government.

National Savings Bank deposits and loans from the Employees Provident Fund (EPF), Insurance Corporation, etc., are normally a captive source of deficit financing. Their indiscriminate use, however, leads to a pre-emption of resources to the private sector and could also result in wasteful expenditure by the government. There must be a conscious effort, therefore, to keep the total government expenditure down to levels compatible with total revenue, so that funds from the Savings Bank and the EPF can be released for private sector financing. Loans from the banking systems are inflationary and it is government policy to make use of this facility only as a last resort and at the very minimum level.

Priorities

The resources estimated on the above lines must first be allocated for the completion of ongoing projects. It is quite possible that they are insufficient for this purpose, which means that a rephasing or expenditure pruning exercise has to be undertaken. In recent years, it has become the practice to use, for this purpose, sector committees appointed by the Committee of Development Secretaries. The reason for this is that expenditure reduction or rephasing must be a collective effort in which urgent needs of various ministries and departments in respect of different projects are taken into account. Sector committees help these decisions to be taken on the basis of intra-sectoral priorities.

Where sector committees fail to decide on priorities, across-the-board, proportionate cuts become inevitable in order to bring total expenditure in line with the resources available. This method, though simple, creates various distortions in resource allocation and consequently in production. Across-the-board cuts reduce expenditure irrespective of whether it is financed from the Consolidated Fund or foreign aid. In the case of projects with a larger proportion of foreign aid (most of the larger projects are of this type), across-the-board cuts result in a significant reduction of foreign aid, entailing other problems as well, such as non-compliance with implementation schedules agreed upon with donors, which may affect future prospects for aid. For this reason, across-the-board cutting of expenditure is avoided as far as possible.

There are strong reasons for giving priority to the completion of ongoing projects. There are sunk costs - costs already incurred - which usually mean a higher return on the additional investment needed for completion. This does not mean that all completed projects or those under construction are sound or should always be given priority over new projects. There are many instances where low priority projects have crept in or projects with low net social returns have been launched, which should in fact be abandoned, rather than rephased. However, in general, an outright waste of resources occurs when capital lies idle because the investment is spread too thinly among too many projects.

The government of Sri Lanka has decided that in the case of new projects, no government investment should take place in areas where the private sector can operate better. This is basically taken to mean that the government should not embark on any commercially-oriented projects, notwithstanding their social desirability, unless it appears that the private sector is unable to handle them on its own. Even in such instances, the government is expected to go in for joint ventures with provision for future investment rather than contribute the entire capital required.

Following this principle it has been decided that in the medium term, public investment will concentrate on the following areas :

a) quick-yielding production-oriented projects which would reduce the balance of payments problem either through export expansion or efficient import substitution and which the private sector cannot undertake on its own ;

b) essential infrastructure needs in power, irrigation, transport and communication ; and

c) urgent needs in health, education, housing and nutritional standards of the people.

Procedures

The government has also laid down the procedures to be followed with regard to the admission of new projects into the Public Investment Programme. Accordingly, once a project is identified, based on the economic and social objectives of the government and the accepted investment priorities, its broad outline with at least a tentative estimate of the costs and benetifs should be submitted to the Committee of Development Secretaries for approval in principle, before proceeding to the next stage of project development.

After approval in principle is received from the Committee of Development Secretaries, the next stage of project development, the preparation of a detailed techno-economic feasibility study, commences. Appraisal of the project is carried out by the Committee of Development Secretaries after initial screening by the National Planning Division of the Ministry of Finance and Planning. It is then submitted to the Cabinet for final approval. Final negotiations with the appropriate aid agency are conducted by the External Resources Department after approval by the Cabinet. The project is thereafter included in the Public Investment Programme for annual resource allocation and implementation.

The determination of priorities is a very complex one. The Cabinet decision only lays down broad principles which could guide planners in determining priorities between sectors (inter-sectoral) and within sectors (intra-sectoral). Inter-sectoral priorities are normally determined through the macro frame developed by the National Planning Division. They reflect basically the desirable linkages which should be promoted in order to accelerate growth and employment creation. The most important areas to interlink in planning are the infrastructure field, where, for instance, the development of power, telecommunications and transport facilities must keep pace with development in other sectors.

Intra-sectoral priorities can be determined only by analysing more micro aspects at the level of projects that should be promoted. In view of the fact that no single ministry is today in charge of a sector, the determination of intra-sectoral priorities and development programmes based on them must necessarily be a collective effort. Thus, in order to determine priorities within the agricultural sector, the Agriculture, Food and Nutrition Strategy was launched involving fourteen line ministries and was co-ordinated by the National Planning Division. The strategy formulation stage being completed, the task forces which were set up in every participant ministry are now engaged in the formulation of projects for inclusion in the Public Investment Programme. Similar exercises were carried out in respect of the plantation sector, which brought forth the Medium-term Investment Programme (MTIP) for state plantations. At present, an MTIP is being formulated for private estates. Work on a Transport Master Plan has been launched, while a Road Rehabilitation Project is now being implemented through resource allocation in the Public Investment Programme and the Budget. Investments in the energy sector are determined strictly according to priorities set out in the Least Cost Energy Generation Programme prepared by the Ministry of Power and Energy. No such co-ordinated sector strategies have yet been devised in regard to the social sectors.

A number of references have been made to the role of the Committee of Development Secretaries. There is no Planning Commission in Sri Lanka. The Committee of Development Secretaries, which has in its membership the secretaries of all ministries considered to be dealing with development problems, performs *de facto* the functions of a planning commission. It includes not only Secretaries of Agriculture, Industry and Trade, but also Health, Education, Higher Education and State (dealing with the media). The National Planning Division of the Ministry of Finance and Planning, which is charged with the responsibility of preparing the Macro-Economic Framework and the Public Investment Programme, functions as its secretariat. The most important contribution of the Committee of Development Secretaries, which meets every week, is in the co-ordination of government development activities and the determination of priorities on the basis of sector studies mentioned earlier as well as technical advice provided by the National Planning Division. The Committee deals regularly with the 'approval in principle' of projects based on appraisal reports provided by the National Planning Division. These projects are included in the Public Investment Programme after final approval by the Cabinet, depending on the availability of resources for implementation.

Project appraisal

Project appraisal is a crucial element in the preparation of the Public Investment Programme. Well-known methods of cost benefit analysis are used in the appraisal of economic development projects. There is, however, no standard technique through which social sector projects can be appraised. The basic principle applied in this case is cost-effectiveness once the social objective and the priority of the project are clear, which is often a political judgment. Where sector strategies exist, the determination of priorities is much easier. Otherwise, the criterion used is the urgency of the project according to some acutely felt social need.

A social sector project may be distinguished from a commercially-oriented project in that the beneficiairies are not charged a market price for the services received. The benefits in these cases cannot easily be quantified in monetary terms. They are expected in general to lead to better income distribution and the reduction of poverty. The following basic questions are answered in the appraisal of social sector projects in general. Their significance, however, can vary according to the nature of the project and supplementary questions may have to be answered in order to fulfil the requirements of project appraisal.

a) Project objectives - it is very important to relate these to national objectives and targets. The location of the project must be determined according to the selection of the target group to be served. For instance, the location of a non-fee-paying primary school in a poverty stricken area where large numbers lack facilities for schooling may enhance the significance of the project. This may be justified in terms of the national objective of universal primary education. Where monetary value cannot be given to the benefits, the number of children to be served becomes a proxy.

b) Technical description of the project is necessary to justify its size and capacity, which must be related to the target group to be served. The choice of technology has a bearing on the cost structure and should therefore be justified in terms of alternatives available. Other considerations, such as the special operational needs of the project, for instance the availability of necessary infrastructure facilities such as roads, water, power, technical links with other projects, etc., must be satisfied in order to render the project viable.

c) Where labour and technical skills are lacking, arrangements for training and retention of staff are important considerations. Management capacity and administrative arrangements to implement the project are equally important.

d) Project costs must be identified in terms of capital costs and recurrent costs at full capacity and the availability of resources, both local and foreign, to finance these costs must be carefully assessed. In Sri Lanka, a common cause of failure, particularly of social sector projects, is the lack of resources for recurrent expenditure once the project has been completed with foreign aid.

Sectoral planning

Responsibility for sectoral planning in education, science and technology, communications and culture is very much a line ministry matter. Co-ordination among sectors is effected through the Committee of Development Secretaries and the National Planning Division of the Ministry of Finance. This is however carried out on an *ex post* basis.

The line ministry concerned initiates a project proposal taking into account perceived needs and submits it to the Committee of Development Secretaries, through the National Planning Division. It is then examined for its inter-sectoral implications. Determination of intrasectoral objectives and priorities is left to the individual ministry. For instance, if the Ministry of Higher Education submits a proposal to set up a faculty of agriculture in a particular university, the Ministry of Agriculture is expected to comment with regard to the demand for different types of agriculture graduates in the country, as well as in the area where the university is located. In the best instance, this would have been carried out at the project preparation stage.

An integrated approach, however, would require that the number of agriculture graduates to be trained , their areas of specialization, the universities to be selected for this purpose and the resources to be made available be determined in co-ordination with the Agriculture Development Strategy. Nowhere is this lack of co-ordination felt as sharply as in the areas of science and technology and education. In the following sections, we present a detailed account of the methods of management and planning in the areas of education, science and technology, communications and culture.

3.   EDUCATION

The system of education in Sri Lanka is broadly divisible into three sub-systems, namely a) general education, b) vocational/technical education, and c) higher education. General education is provided mainly within the formal school system. Pre-school education is not a component of state-managed general education. Facilities for preschool education are provided by local government authorities and non-governmental organizations. In addition to formal education programmes, there are also non-formal programmes to provide vocational/technical and general education.

General education within the formal system is divisible into primary education (grades 0-5), junior secondary education (grades 6-10) and senior secondary education (grades 11-12). The primary cycle consists of six grades (Kindergarten to grade 5). Kindergartens provide play-oriented activities of a non-formal nature designed to initiate children to the more formal cycle beginning with grade 1.

Promotion from one grade to the next is based on continuous evaluation of the general performance of the pupil. There are no compulsory examinations at the end of primary school. An accumulative record sheet is used to indicate and evaluate the progress of a child.

Sri Lanka has a rather youthful population, nearly 35 per cent of which is under fifteen years of age. According to the Population Census of 1981, the population in the age-span 5-14 is nearly 3.4 million and projections indicate that by 1990, the population in this age group would increase to about 3.8 million. The growth of the 5-14 population is of particular significance to educational planners for two reasons. First, the greater part of the school population is drawn from the 5-14 population. Secondly, universalization of elementary education for the 5-14 population is a policy objective of the government. Even if the participation rate remains at the current level, the school population will increase as a consequence of population increase. Present indications are that the enrolment ratio will continue to increase.

Pupils in the upper grades of the junior secondary and those in the senior secondary cycle of general education are generally in the 15-19 age group. The 15-19 population numbered nearly 1.6 million in 1981 and its enrolment ratio was around 34.1. According to projections made by the Ministry of Plan Implementation, the 15-19 population would increase to 1.7 million by 1990. The increase in the elementary enrolment will bring about an increase in the junior and senior secondary enrolments. In other words, the rise in the participation rate of the 15-19 year population is a corollary of the expansion of the primary/elementary enrolments. If the present trends continue, school enrolments in the different cycles will increase by about 60,000 to 70,000 per annum. The absorption of an enrolment increase of this size without a proportionate increase in the provision of infrastructural facilities will add to the quantum of deficits accumulated over the years which by their sheer magnitudes are quite staggering.

The responsibility for the design and implementation of non-formal programmes lies with the non-formal education branch of the Ministry of Education. Presently, there are four programmes which are conducted to benefit children, youths and adults. These are as follows :

1. skills development programmes for school leavers ;
2. literacy programmes for those not attending school and for primary school drop-outs ;
3. adult education/community education programme ;
4. English classes for adults.

Teacher training

Teachers recruited to the teaching service are untrained at the time of recruitment. They are subsequently trained while in service. The teacher-training programme lasts three years. The first two years take the form of institutionalized training which is offered at 25 teacher-training colleges. The third year is devoted to on-the-job training in selected schools.

The present practice of recruiting untrained teachers is now being progressively replaced by a scheme under which only trained teachers will be absorbed into the service. For this purpose, eight of the existing 25 teacher-training colleges have been developed to conduct fully residential pre-service teacher education courses. These pre-service training institutions are called colleges of education. Each has residential facilities for 500 trainees and offers a two-year institutionalized course.

Institutionalized training is followed by one year's internship at selected schools. On satisfactory completion of the internship, the trainees are awarded a certificate which is a pre-requisite to joining the teaching profession as a non-graduate teacher.

Graduate teachers in service are recognized as professionally competent teachers only after they have obtained a post-graduate diploma in education. Post-graduate courses in education are provided at three of the eight existing universities. Teachers are selected for admission to the post-graduate diploma course on the basis of a competitive examination.

Organizational structure

The Ministry of Education is charged with the responsibility of planning and implementing the educational policy of the government. The organization within the Ministry for this purpose is structured under the supervision of four additional secretaries working under the Secretary. Each is responsible for providing the staff services in the fields coming within their purview as well as the supervision of each of the divisions of the country under which the implementation programme is organized. The additional secretaries are assisted by deputy directors of school works, senior assistant secretaries, assistant secretaries, chief education officers and accountants. Two other institutions, namely the Department of Examinations and the Department of Educational Publications, are headed by two commissioners.

A project ministry has been created under the title Ministry of Education Services for the provision of buildings, furniture, equipment, school books and mid-day meals to school children. The Secretary for Education Services is responsible for the implementation of the functions of the project ministry, under the control and direction of the project Minister.

The actual implementation of educational programmes is carried out by the regional departments of education, which cover each of the 24 administrative districts of the country. Each regional department is managed by a regional director of education. The director is assisted by a chief education officer, education officers, an accountant, a school works engineer and supervisors.

The work of the regional education department is organized into five divisions, namely a) educational administration, b) educational development and planning, c) general administration, d) finance, and e) school works (buildings). The regional director himself controls the education development and planning division, while being responsible for efficient management of the whole regional department.

Each district is divided into several circuits which are more or less co-extensive with the electorates. On average, each circuit consists of 30 to 40 schools. A circuit is under the control of a circuit education officer whose main function is the supervision of schools in the circuit. He also provides a link between the schools and the regional department of education officers who are in charge of supervision of various subject areas.

General education planning

The White Paper on Education, which was the outcome of the work of a committee appointed by the government to investigate shortcomings in the education system, defined the objectives of the changes proposed as those "intended to promote more effectively the harmonious growth of the child and to prepare him more purposefully than before for life and work in society". This closely represents the broad objectives of general education in Sri Lanka.

The responsibility for planning general education rests with the Ministry of Education which aims at achieving the above objects. This planning activity is conducted by a planning and programming division under the direct supervision of a director, who reports to the additional director. The capital investment programme of the Ministry is harmonized with and incorporated into the Public Investment Programme of the government according to the procedures outlined earlier. The annual implementation programmes of the Ministry of Education, which also include recurrent expenditure, are prepared on the basis of the programme activities of the different branches of the Ministry and the regional departments of education.

Educational planning at the regional level is of recent origin. According to a scheme prepared by the Ministry of Education, the regional director of education is required to prepare a three-year rolling plan for the educational development of the region. This plan once approved by the Ministry of Education provides the basis for the preparation of the annual implementation plan.

At the school level, the head of the school is entrusted with the responsibility of drawing up the annual plan for his school. He is assisted in this task by the deputy principal, grade co-ordinators and subject co-ordinators. The effectiveness of planning at the different levels depends on the nature and viability of the linkage between school level planning and zonal planning, on the one hand, and between zonal planning and district-level planning, on the other.

Until recently, planning for the provision of resource inputs focussed on the development of individual schools. According to the Ministry of Education, such a focus of planning only served to accentuate the differences among the schools which competed for a share of the limited resources. The reduction of disparities within and among districts in a situation where the available resources are limited has to be based on a strategy which views schools not as isolated elements but as a component of a network.

For systematization of resource utilization, the Ministry of Education has now launched a scheme to divide each district into a number of school zones on the basis of contiguous *grama sevaka* divisions (the smallest local government unit). In demarcating school zones, such parameters as the road network, natural barriers, topographical features, flow of pupils, the location of existing schools and other related matters are examined in detail by the regional directors of education, according to the guidelines provided by the Ministry of Education. A school zone which consists of two or more contiguous *grama sevaka* divisions has ten to fifteen schools. Demarcation by the end of 1984 was the first phase of a process directed towards rationalization of the school network.

Rationalization of the school network in each school zone is part of the strategy to optimize the use of resources available to education. In order to determine the structure of the network required for each zone, the regional directors of education consider in detail such questions as :

a) upgrading of schools ;
b) opening of new schools ;
c) re-organization/amalgamation of existing schools and other resources ;
d) closure/shifting of existing schools.

Guidelines for the rationalization of the school network are set out by the Ministry of Education for the regional directors of education. According to the Ministry's definition, rationalization is the optimization of resource utilization to provide primary, junior secondary and senior secondary educational facilities for meeting the needs of the population in a given geographical area. Rationalization is therefore based on a detailed consideration of the following questions :

1. the size of the present school-age population in the *grama sevaka* divisions ;
2. the size of the school-age population in the coming years ;
3. whether there will be new settlement areas in a zone ; if so, the size of the school-age population in each such settlement area ;

(Data on school-age population in new settlement areas are obtained from the settlement authority.)

4. whether adequate facilities exist in a zone for primary/junior secondary/senior secondary education ;
5. which areas are under-served in relation to primary/junior secondary/senior secondary education ;
6. which schools are overcrowded ;
7. which schools are under-utilized ;
8. which schools need to be amalgamated.

These questions are considered in detail with a view to achieving the following objectives :

1. to provide access to all primary school-age children ;
2. to provide junior secondary education for those completing the primary cycle ;
3. to provide senior secondary education for those completing junior secondary education ;
4. to prepare zonal and district plans for development of education.

The Planning Unit of the Regional Education Department is responsible for rationalizing the school network and preparing the zonal plans/district plans.

The main purpose of demarcation of school zones and rationalization of the school network within each zone is the preparation of a three-year district investment plan based on the assessed zonal needs. The Planning Unit prepares a three-year plan in the manner indicated below.

1. For each zone, the additional building, furniture and equipment requirements by primary cycle, junior secondary cycle and senior secondary cycle are assessed and the expenditure required is phased over a three-year period. The zonal requirements and the phased expenditure over the three-year period forms the draft zonal plan.
2. The costs of additional requirements of the zones are aggregated to show the cost of additional requirements for the sub-district/district, under primary, junior secondary and senior secondary cycles. The sub-district/district requirements and the phased expenditure forms the draft sub-district/ district plan.
3. Using past data, the financial resources that are likely to be made available to the district during the next three years are estimated under :
   a) Ministry estimates ;
   b) decentralized budget.

As the funds available for a zone would not be sufficient to meet all the additional requirements of each cycle, it is necessary to prioritize the requirements of each cycle of each zone in a sub-district/district. The priorities of each cycle may be selected by the Planning Unit. In the case of primary and junior secondary education, priority is given to ill-served zones. The focus is on the provision of basic needs such as classrooms, classroom furniture, blackboards, water, latrines and urinals. In the case of senior secondary education, priority is to be determined in the light of zonal needs and the need for optimum use of resources.

The Planning Unit clearly indicates :

a) facilities needed, facilities available and additional facilities to be provided for the primary and secondary cycles of each zone during a three-year period ;
b) input locations and the year(s) during which the specified facilities are to be provided, i.e. names of schools and the year(s) during which the facilities are to be provided.

The items indicated under a) and b) for a zone constitute a three-year zonal investment plan. This three-year plan is a rolling plan. As one year elapses, another year is added by including some of the assessed needs which were not included in the first three-year investment period.

Having done this, the Planning Unit of the Regional Education Department has to prepare the three-year sub-district plan based on the three-year zonal investment plans. The sub-district plan would consist of :

a) all the zonal plans as components ;
b) a summary indicating the facilities needed and the facilities to be provided for the whole sub-district during a three-year period for the primary, junior and senior secondary cycles ;
c) any other proposals not included in any zonal plans but considered necessary for the educational development of the whole sub-district. In districts without sub-district divisions, there is no need for the preparation of sub-district plans.

The three-year sub-district investment plan is also a rolling plan.

Finally, the Planning Unit has to prepare the three-year district investment plan on the basis of sub-district/zonal investment plans. The district plan would have all sub-district plans as components. This plan is also a rolling plan. In districts without sub-districts, the district plan is based on the zonal plans. The three-year district plan as outlined above focusses only on the development of infrastructural facilities. A copy of the district investment plan approved by the Ministry of Education is sent to the regional director of education for implementation.

The preparation of annual estimates (capital expenditure) is based on the annual implementation programme which incorporates the first year of the three-year investment plan.

The Planning Branch of the Ministry of Education consolidates the expenditure proposals submitted by regional directors and prepares a plan. This plan is reflected in the Public Investment Programme prepared by the National Planning Division.

The Planning Branch of the Ministry of Education analyses statistical information to bring out disparities in the distribution of facilities and teachers between districts, and formulates guidelines for the allocation of funds under the capital projects and deployment of teachers. These statistics are collected in an annual school census. The arrangements for conducting the census are made by the Statistics Unit of the Planning Branch in collaboration with the district education departments. The printed census forms are sent to schools through circuit education officers.

School cluster system

One of the innovative systems of management and planning that has been introduced after the publication of the White Paper on Educational Reforms is the school cluster system. This system, which is aimed at reducing disparities in human and material resources among the country's more than 9,500 schools, is expected to make it easier for even the smallest school to be a member of a group sharing collective resources.

Each cluster is expected to function as an administrative entity to meet the educational needs of the entire area it serves. Pupil admissions, requisition of supplies, capital expenditure and allocation of teachers is expected under this system to be based on each cluster serving as one organizational unit. The smallest unit for planning, once the system becomes fully operational, is the school cluster.

The system is being tested at present on a pilot basis and it is estimated that almost 90 per cent of the pupil population will be brought under the scheme. Those left out will be the few very large schools and some isolated small schools. It is envisaged that about 3,000-5,000 pupils will belong to a single cluster.

Each cluster will comprise a number of primary schools and several secondary schools. Schools having collegiate grades may also be included. The number of different types of schools, as well as the grades and streams available within a cluster, will be such as will provide the best possible schooling to the community with the available resources.

For rationalization of the use of resources, the core school within the cluster is expected to be developed, in general, to have the best facilities. For instance, a core school will invariably have a laboratory, workshop, library, audio-visual equipment, etc., which will be shared by other schools within the cluster. The principal of the core school will function as the executive head of the cluster and the chairman of the Cluster Board, while principals of schools and representatives of school development societies will serve as the other members. The Board will deal with planning of educational activities relating to the schools within the cluster.

Higher education

Since 1978, the functions of university education and technical education have been assigned to the Ministry of Higher Education. Activities relating to university education are conducted under the purview of the University Grants Commission. The Secretary, Ministry of Higher Education is also the Chairman of the University Grants Commission.

The Ministry of Higher Education is organized in such a way that its functions are divided into eight sections under the general supervision and direction of the Secretary to the Ministry. These divisions include university education, technical education, foreign projects, administration, finance and supplies, civil works, etc. There is no special planning unit in the Ministry.

The Director of Technical Education is responsible for the general supervision and administration, design of curricula and the planning and programming of technical education. He is assisted by an additional director. There are two chief education officers, one for commerce and the other for technician and engineering crafts. These officers assist the Director in staffing, curricula development, initiation of programmes and in-service and pre-service training. The training officer is the third officer at this level. He is responsible to the Director for the placement of trainees and all activities pertaining to the in-service and pre-service programme of training. The two chief education officers are assisted by two education officers. They attend to the work relating to the selection of staff, establishment, student enquiries and transfers.

The technical education programme of the Ministry is implemented through polytechnical and junior technical institutes located in selected urban centres. As a general rule, those institutes offering courses at diploma level have been designated as polytechnical institutes. At present, there are eight polytechnical institutes, fourteen junior technical institutes and five affiliated technical units located in various urban centres.

A salient weakness of the management structure of technical education at the Ministry of Higher Education is the absence of an inspection/advisory service which could keep it informed on matters pertaining to resource allocation and uses, staffing, staff development, student enrolment and other requirements. As there is no planning unit, decisions regarding the quantitative expansion and quality improvement of technical education are taken on an *ad hoc* basis. The absence of a planning unit is also felt in the area of project implementation. There is a lack of monitoring of projects and vast allocations of resources for capital expenditure remain unspent at the end of the fiscal year.

A planning unit organized to perform the following functions could play a significant role with regard to technical education coming under the purview of the Ministry of Higher Education :

1. design of appropriate curricula in polytechnical junior technical education ;

2. implementation of such curricula in the various technical institutes concerned ;
3. direction, supervision and co-ordination of technical education programmes ;
4. identification of needs for construction and improvements to buildings required and acquisition of equipment and furniture ;
5. projection of technical manpower needs.

Another weakness of the technical education programme conducted by the Ministry of Higher Education is lack of co-ordination with technical and vocational training. For the efficient management and planning of technicians and trade craft education, co-ordination between the various ministries involved is essential if waste of resources is to be avoided.

The absence of any form of formal liaison between the Ministry of Higher Education, the Technical Directorate and Industry is also noted and found surprising in view of the obvious need at present for the education system to provide the output related to the needs of industry.

A further weakness is lack of co-ordination with technical and vocational training facilities provided by other ministries, such as the Ministries of Labour, Youth Affairs and Employment, and the Departments of Social Services, Agriculture, Telecommunications, etc. In recognition of this problem, a proposal was made in the White Paper on Education to establish a Tertiary Education Commission (TEC). The Commission is expected to guide, co-ordinate, develop and support non-university higher education, as well as technical and vocational education.

The TEC would absorb all government institutions providing in-service vocational and technical education and apprenticeship training such as polytechnical institutes, junior technical institutes, vocational skills development centres, the National Apprenticeship Board, etc. Only those institutions which train personnel for their own specific needs, such as the armed forces, the railway department, the water department, etc., would be outside its purview. The Commission would also be responsible for the education and training of technical teachers and instructors and the testing and certification corresponding to technical and vocational training courses.

University Grants Commission

Until 1978, management of general, technical and university education was the sole responsibility of the Ministry of Education. In that year, the Ministry of Higher Education was created to be in charge of the functions of development of both university and technical education. At present the co-ordination of university education and the apportionment of funds to universities come within the purview of the University Grants Commission, which was also set up in 1978. The other major functions of the Commission are the maintenance of academic standards in universities, the regulation of university administration, and the exercise, performance and discharge of such powers, duties and functions as are conferred or imposed on, or assigned to the Commission under the University Grants Commission Act of 1978.

University corporate plan

In order to fulfil in part the obligations of the University Grants Commission with regard to the planning and co-ordination of university education, a corporate five-year plan is prepared. Once the plan is prepared, it is updated annually on the lines of a five-year rolling plan.

The process of plan preparation is as follows : the Planning and Research Branch of the University Grants Commission instructs each university to prepare an individual plan for its overall development, bearing in mind its long-term objectives, the potential for expansion and anticipated expenditure. The universities are given specific guidelines by the Planning and Research Branch as to how their individual plans should be prepared. A format is sent to them to ensure uniformity. Adequate time is given for the submission of individual plans.

On receipt of these plans, meetings are held by the University Grants Commission with the respective vice chancellors and faculty deans. The individual plans are revised, if necessary, at these meetings. Other meetings are then held to discuss the final corporate plan having due regard to the new proposals made in the individual plans.

The guiding principles that underly the main proposals of the present Corporate Plan 1984-1988 are as follows :

1. a continuation of a shift away from the humanities and social sciences in undergraduate intake and increase in numbers in science-based faculties ;
2. a shift of emphasis in university education from an overwhelming concentration on undergraduate teaching to a more effective diversion of resources to postgraduate teaching and research ;
3. the emergence of centres of excellence ;
4. the establishment of new academic disciplines within the universities (e.g. computer science).

Though the Planning and Research Branch is mainly responsible for the preparation of the five-year plans, it does engage in other closely-linked functions such as preparation of the annual capital and recurrent budget, formulation of project proposals for local and foreign funding, and the appraisal of projects. These are carried out by other branches with very little co-ordination with the Planning and Research Branch.

There is also a general lack of co-ordination between general and higher education. One of the major weaknesses of co-ordination is reflected in the tenth grade school (GCEC O' Level) and university entrance grade (Advanced Level) curricula. There is a sudden break in continuity of subjects taught, which is particularly evident in the science stream.

The most serious weakness, however, is reflected in the graduate output and demand for professional skills. This is most evident in the case of arts students, where the mismatch between supply and demand has resulted in a severe problem of graduate unemployment. The problem in regard to physical sciences, particularly medicine and dental surgery, has been a shortfall. While the oversupply of arts graduates is mainly the result of the social pressures for university education, the mismatch in the physical science disciplines reflects poor manpower planning. The manpower data on which university entrance figures are determined are weak in regard to the coverage by range of occupations and the period of forecast. This is mainly due to weaknesses in the macro-economic and sectoral development forecasts. The time horizon of five years provided by the National Planning Division's macro-economic projections is also too short for manpower development, which normally has a longer gestation period.

4.   SCIENCE AND TECHNOLOGY

A large number of state-sponsored institutions in Sri Lanka are engaged in science and technology development. However, the financial resources allocated to R&D activities are about 0.2 per cent of GNP. A further problem is the absence of an effective national co-ordinating body which could help establish both inter-sectoral and intrasectoral links in science and technology, as well as determine priorities for the allocation of limited resources. To appreciate the complexity of the planning and co-ordinating problem with regard to S&T and its integration into the development process, it is necessary to take a brief look at the objectives and functions of the multifarious institutions.

S&T has been mainly concentrated in the universities, the Ceylon Institute for Scientific and Industrial Research, the National Engineering Research & Development Centre, the Atomic Energy Authority, the Appropriate Technology Research & Development Centre, and more than 20 institutes and departments dealing with agricultural research. There are also a few private sector institutions involved in technology development, but their role is marginal. A planned effort to deal with problems of S&T development will therefore have to concentrate on state-sponsored institutions.

Science and technology policy

In 1984, under a directive issued by the President, a National Science Planning and Co-ordinating Committee (NSPCC) was established in the Ministry of Plan Implementation to formulate and implement a science and technology policy for Sri Lanka. The NSPCC was represented by the various ministries and departments of the government as well as the universities.

Since the task to be performed was in the nature of an integrated strategy involving diverse scientific disciplines and different sectors, it was considered necessary to identify, as far as possible, certain areas that are common to all sectors and also those specific scientific areas relevant to each sector. For this purpose and to guide the chairmen and co-chairmen who were appointed for each sector committee, common terms of reference were drawn up. Sector committees were formed for the following areas : agriculture, forestry and fisheries, agriculture research complex, industry, electronics and computer science, energy, environment, science education, health and nutrition, and social infrastructure.

The terms of reference covered the following :

1. Situation analysis - a review of S&T of each sector (status report). Detailed discussions of the physical, technical, financial, manpower, institutional and organizational aspects in relation to S&T, R&D, etc.
2. Objectives - a statement of short- and long-term scientific objectives of study in relation to each sector. Identification of time considerations in achieving these objectives.
3. Plan of action (short- and medium- to long-term strategy) -
    i)   Short-term strategy - directed towards achieving knowledge, information, manpower, research and technology findings, training capability, etc.
    ii)   Medium- to long-term strategy - directed to identifying additional technical inputs and goals to be reached in terms of medium- to long-term scientific research and technology development.
4. Specific areas to be considered in the sectoral S&T study :
    i)   S&T planning to be complementary to economic planning.
    ii)   Need for a scientific data system and MIS. In some the necessity for setting up a data bank and documentation centre.
    iii)   Role of scientists in national planning, development and administration.
    iv)   Institutional reform in terms of duplication, underutilization and other gaps.
    v)   Recognition of research work and adequate remuneration.
    vi)   Commercial exploitation of R&D such as inventions and patents.

vii) Area of technology transfer, training and upgrading of technical skills at different levels specific to each sector.

viii) Role of the private sector in scientific development.

ix) Scientific infrastructure development.

x) Identification and development of emerging and prospective technologies in each sector.

xi) Monitoring and evaluation of S&T development in each sector.

Each sector committee, comprising on average about ten members, was made up of subject matter specialists, extension specialists, policy planners as well as others co-opted from the private sector. These committees met about eight times in the process of preparing their respective reports. Several eminent scientists, both local and foreign, were invited to address the NSPCC and participate in the various discussions, review meetings and other current issues pertaining to S&T in Sri Lanka. The NSPCC also held a special session with ministerial secretaries responsible for key sectors.

Once the sector committee reports were completed, these were discussed in workshops followed by action to revise the reports. On completion of the revised versions, two seminars were held further to review and integrate their contents into a final working document. At the seminars, high priority areas common to all sectors were identified for future action and the infrastructure required to implement a planned scientific programme was discussed. The latter discussion included the strengthening of existing institutions and the restructuration and reorganization of other scientific agencies.

The integrated S&T policy document and its companion sectoral reports take the form of a perspective plan covering all sectors of the economy. One difference is that there are no quantitative targets set either in physical or financial terms with a time horizon for implementation ; nor are there any cost estimates. It is a set of recommendations without, however, the identification of the agencies which should be called upon for their implementation. To make this S&T policy implementable in Sri Lanka's present context, it must be incorporated into the government's Five-Year Public Investment Programme.

The Agriculture Research Programme

Meanwhile, as part of the Agriculture, Food and Nutrition Strategy mentioned earlier, an Agriculture Research Policy and Programme has been worked out in great detail incorporating all the elements necessary to make it a truly implementable plan.

However, this policy, which has been prepared as an integrated project, has very little connection with the agricultural sector policy of the integrated S&T policy prepared by NSPCC.

The National Agriculture, Food and Nutrition Strategy (AFNS), which was the collective effort of thirteen line ministries, co-ordinated by the National Planning Division of the Ministry of Finance and Planning, contains three parts.

Part One deals with sector-wide strategies, cutting across ministerial lines, because they apply to the agriculture sector as a whole. Part Two is mainly a summary of the issues and strategies contained in the individual task form reports relating to crop agriculture, tea, rubber and coconut smallholdings, fisheries, live-stock, irrigation, land, forestry and nutrition. Part Three lays out a programme of investments designed to give flesh to the strategy. The investment programme of the AFNS is picked up according to priorities by the Public Investment Programme, once the detailed projects are formulated and approval procedures complete.

The Agriculture Research Project was identified in the AFNS as one of its priority areas of concern due to the role agricultural research has played and is expected to play in the development of agriculture in Sri Lanka. The AFNS recognized that "linkages between government policy-makers, producers, processors and the researchers are weak and must be strengthened". This was particularly noticed with regard to the critical linkages within the line ministries, between the policy-makers and the research stations.

The shortcomings were mostly apparent with regard to the special needs of smallholders, who play a dominant role in domestic agriculture. In order to incorporate their needs effectively into the design of research projects, it was found necessary to establish interdisciplinary, inter-institutional research ventures based on joint agro-economic and socio-economic research teams at the farm level.

With a view to strengthening these connections and to advising government on research priorities, the AFNS proposed the establishment of a Council for Agricultural Research Policy, representative of policy-makers, research scientists, producers and consumers. This recommendation was incorporated into the Agriculture Research Project, which also addressed a number of other issues such as the adequacy of research staff, support staff training, equipment, physical facilities, recurrent funding per scientist, organization and management.

The Council, which is in the process of being incorporated by Act of Parliament, will give guidance on the main areas of research priority - the agricultural research plan which will guide allocation of resources for research. The detailed research pro-gramme formulated within these guidelines will, however, be prepared by research scientists, who also need to be well informed of the particular problems of their farmer clients. To strengthen the information linkage between farmer and scientist, at present rather weak, the Agriculture Research Project aims to increase farming systems research efforts, involving technical and social scientists.

The Agricultural Research Project contains a very detailed breakdown of costs both local and foreign, by type of activity as well as by institution and implementing body. It will be funded by the government as well as by the World Bank. It is therefore

included in the 1986-1990 Public Investment Programme to be implemented from 1987.

Briefly, the following steps were taken in the preparation of
the Agriculture Research Project :

a) The first step was the convening by the National Planning
    Division of the Agricultural Research Group (ARG) and the
    formation of its sub-committee. All agriculture-related
    ministries as well as research institutes were represented.

b) The sub-committee prepared the terms of reference for a compre-
    hensive review, analysis and evaluation of the agricultural
    research system in Sri Lanka. It was discussed at the ARG and
    approved.

c) The terms of reference consisted of two broad sections. The
    first called for a description of the current situation in all
    institutions including research structure, manpower resources
    and conditions of service, administrative and financial
    structure, and priority and policy guidelines. The second
    section called for an analysis of the wide range of linkages
    between research institutions and national and international
    bodies, an assessment of how well national priorities are
    reflected in the research programmes of the various
    institutions, a comparison of alternative research structures
    and organizations, and finally, preliminary suggestions for
    projects to strengthen the agricultural research system in
    order to improve its role in the national development of agri-
    culture.

d) Thereafter, the study was carried out in several stages.
    Firstly, the sub-committee designed a questionnaire and sent it
    to all research institutions. On the basis of the responses,
    field visits were organized by sub-committee members who pre-
    pared a preliminary report to the ARG. Secondly, a team from
    the International Service for National Agricultural Research
    (ISNAR) based in the Hague visited Sri Lanka to consider
    jointly with the sub-committee the contents of the report and
    undertake the necessary analytical work, whereupon a joint
    report was prepared. Thirdly, the joint report was reviewed
    and submitted to the Committee of Development Secretaries for
    approval. Fourthly, the approved report was submitted to the
    World Bank, which sent a project identification mission. On
    the basis of a series of discussions with the World Bank, a
    project report was formulated. Fifthly, on approval being
    given by the World Bank for funding, an implementation pro-
    gramme was drawn up and in incorporated into the Public Invest-
    ment Programme for local and World Bank funding, according to
    the system of priorities drawn up in the project.

5.   CULTURAL DEVELOPMENT

Activities falling under the classification 'culture' are subsumed under the Ministry of Cultural Affairs, which controls the work of the Departments of Archaeology, of National Museums, of National Archives, and of Buddhist Affairs (reorganized under this title in 1981), succeding the former Department of Cultural Affairs.
The Ministry itself carries out certain functions grouped under two main headings :

Promotion of Publications and Literary Activities -

1.   Compilation and printing of the *Sinhala Encyclopaedia*, *Sinhala Dictionary*, *Buddhist Encyclopaedia* and the *Mahavamsa*.
2.   Translation of the Pali Buddhist Scriptures - the *Tripitaka* into Sinhala and the compilation and editing of Pali texts.
3.   Other publications, and the running of a bookshop.

Promotion of Arts and Crafts -

1.   Promotion of the performance of local and foreign drama, music recitals, opera, ballet and exhibitions of paintings, sculpture and handicrafts.
2.   Operation of district cultural councils.
3.   Research on literary works and publication of literature.

Central Cultural Fund (CCF)

This Fund was set up by Act of Parliament, approved in December 1980, with a Board of Governors consisting of seven Cabinet Ministers with the Prime Minister as Chairman. It was intended to implement expeditiously the Cultural Triangle Project jointly in-augurated from the Audience Hall in Kandy by the President of Sri Lanka and the Director-General of Unesco. The Cultural Fund has been granted concessions and the fact of its inauguration under the auspices of Unesco serves to attract funds internationally as well as nationally. The World Food Programme has provided free rations for workers on site and efforts are being made to obtain grants from academic institutions, mercantile organizations, foundations interested in cultural conservation and the Sri Lankan community in general, both overseas and domestically.
The initial estimated cost of the project was Rs. 519 million, but due to cost escalation and general inflation, as well as ex-pansion of the scope of work, it is likely to reach the figure of Rs. 1,400 million. The government commitment is to contribute 10 per cent of the total cost and Unesco, apart from lending its patronage, is not in a position to provide funds, although a small contribution of $ 80,000 was made through UNDP funding. Tourist

fees have amounted to approximately Rs. 23 million in 1984, with a target of Rs. 51 million, of which over 50 per cent was realized. Revenue dropped in 1986 due to disturbances in the flow of tourist traffic.

The ongoing work covers six projects, namely the Jetavanarama and Abhayagiri Monuments at Anuradhapura, Alahana Pirivena at Polonnaruwa, the Water Gardens at Sigiriya, the Painted Caves at Dambulla, the living Monuments of the Royal City of Kandy, and the Cultural Complex, Colombo.

The Cultural Triangle is one of the few projects to have been formulated on the classical lines of project formulation with a fair degree of clarification of cash flows, capital requirements and some concept of return on investment. The pay-back period, as scheduled by the Merchant Bank, a subsidiary of the Bank of Ceylon, begins in seven years' time and continues for 20-25 years, based entirely on resources becoming available to the CCF and contributions received. It is therefore one of the outstanding examples of project planning within the Ministry and it is desirable that this methodology be extended to other activities, not only of the Archaeological Department but also of other Departments in the Ministry of Cultural Affairs.

The significance of the programme is inherent in the fact that the ancient and medieval history of Sri Lanka hinged on the three ancient cities of the Cultural Triangle, the monuments there reflecting the civilization, engineering and associated skills which then existed. The restoration and preservation programme is undertaken for Sri Lanka, in order to give "supreme" expression to its "historical core, religious values, cultural identity and artistic creativity, for the sake of Asia as a whole as a centre of Buddhist tradition and for the sake of the world as a whole, since it forms an integral part of its indivisible heritage".

The excavation and construction of monuments within the Cultural Triangle will most likely be a continuous operation over a long period. The current programme (including a certain number and level of selected activities) are slated for completion in 1989, due to financial, human and other constraints. A programme of this dimension requiring substantial funding cannot be financed in the traditional manner from government budgetary allocations, income from tourist round tickets, local and foreign donations, etc. In this situation, a project team headed by a certified and consultant cost accountant provided by the Merchant Bank of Sri Lanka was constituted. It was concluded that supplementary sources of international financing should be found, stimulated by promotional work and the appeal by Unesco to its Member States.

Detailed cost estimates based on district work components, excavation, construction, layout, annual maintenance and other costs (treated as cost centres) were prepared separately by the project team for each item of the Cultural Triangle Project, with proportions of central and administrative overheads imputed to each item. Each of the seven component sites had a steering committee and expenditure was monitored.

Objectives of cultural development

The objectives of cultural development may be summarized comprehensively as follows :

1. Preservation of national culture.
2. Revival of national culture.
3. Enrichment of national culture.
4. Strengthening the resilience of national culture.
5. Dissemination of and channelling of culture for useful purposes.

Preservation of national culture

The national culture of any country or its cultural heritage is at the same time material and non-material.

a) The material heritage consists of monuments, outstanding architectural creations (whether religious or secular), sites of historical, scientific and aesthetic value, objects of historical, scientific, technological or aesthetic interest and craft-ware.
b) The non-material heritage includes symbols mediated through the arts, literature, language, oral tradition, mythology, customs, beliefs, folklore, value systems, rites, rituals and games.

As regards a) above, a tremendous volume of work has been carried out in Sri Lanka, dating back to the British colonial era, on the excavation, restoration and preservation of monuments and buildings of the pre-colonial culture and civilization of Sri Lanka from 2500 B.C. onwards. This task, carried on painstakingly and diligently by the Department of Archaeology, has paid handsome dividends in resurrecting the buildings and monuments of Sri Lanka's ancient hydraulic civilization, covered over, in the words of a British civil servant, by "The Jungle Tide" [4].

An equally praiseworthy record is the retrieval, preservation, dating, identification and classification of prehistoric artefacts, plant, animal, fish and insect fossils, and other work on geological and palaeontological objects as well as ethnological finds. The retrieval of objects has been, for the most part, the work of the Archaeological Department, and their preservation, identification and classification that of the Department of National Museums.

The latter Department has also to its credit the amassing of a voluminous collection of ola leaf manuscripts (corresponding to the papyri manuscripts in the Alexandria Museum in Egypt), ancient literary works, more recent publications (now out of print) and rare books which are lodged in the depository collection in Colombo.

The establishment of the CCF, set up in 1980 to implement the work plan of the joint Sri Lanka-Unesco Cultural Triangle Project described above, represents the highpoint in Sri Lanka's record of conservation of antiquities.

As regards category b) above, much remains to be done and the work so far completed is desultory and minimal. There is some literature, for example the works of scholars such as Paranavithane, M.D. Raghavan and W.A. de Silva, and R.H. Basset. The country's folklore remains a rich and rewarding field for further exploration and research.

Revival and enrichment of national culture

There is no indication that any purposeful planning exists in order to strengthen the resilience of national culture and channel it for useful purposes. Individual writers have attempted to break fresh ground by the revival of indigenous culture, e.g. the poet Alwis Perera, the novelists W.A. de Silva and Martin Wickremasinghe and the world acclaimed dramatist and academic E.R. de S. Sarathchandra. Assistance has been rendered by the Ministry of Cultural Affairs in organizing meetings of artists and poets and assisting needy artists in response to demand. But the revival of culture has been largely the work of individual writers and artists. The formation of a national council of dedicated persons who could, irrespective of parochial, political or other affiliations, devote themselves to the supreme task of bringing about a cultural renaissance is an urgent necessity.

The problems of culture and the arts

There are five prime aspects of Sri Lanka's culture which bear mention :

1. The culture of the country is composed of heterogeneous elements which include Sinhala Buddhist, Tamil, Hindu and Islamic. There has to some extent been a borrowing of cultural traditions and practices which have enriched primarily the Hindu and Buddhist cultures, as well as the Muslim culture of Sri Lanka so as to make it peculiarly Sri Lankan as opposed to the Muslim culture of the Middle East. It may be noted that this is not unusual and that countries such as the United States of America, the USSR, Yugoslavia and India are outstanding examples of countries which are culturally heterogeneous. Nevertheless, each of these countries have sought, each in its own way, to weld together disparate elements of cultures and traditions.
2. The second aspect is that the country's distinctive cultural traditions stem from the past, whether it be the physical heritage embodied in stone or the living aesthetic, religious

and literary traditions, not excluding traditional folklore. These living traditions are under threat of extinction and worse still deterioration under the impact of science, technology, modernization and commercialism.

3. It is necessary to create an environment to offset the impact of undue foreign cultural influence whilst encouraging contemporary development in the arts. Here, the state may have to play a role in setting standards in the arts and literature in the absence of a strong and dynamic private lobby for the preservation and development of indigenous culture and the arts.

4. Another problem is the democratization of culture, to ensure that caste, race, religion or economic class present no barrier to access. Progress towards this end is of course bound up with the widening of educational opportunity and the achievement of higher levels of literacy, as well as a higher quality of life for the population. The mass media must be fully utilized for this purpose, since research indicates television to be the most effective medium, followed by newspapers and the radio.

5. Finally there is the serious problem of opening up to world culture. It is not a question of whether Sri Lankan culture should open up to world culture. This is absolutely essential as all cultures have derived their dynamism from cross-cultural influences. What is at issue is the extent to which adaptation should be made. It should be recognized that there is a school of thought which believes in what is known as the 'homogenization' of world culture, implying that the latter will increasingly represent the cultural and behavioural patterns of the West and that specific characteristics peculiar to other areas, countries or regions will disappear from attention. There are thus two extremes to be avoided : complete isolation from the influence of world culture which spells stagnation, and complete and uncritical openness to those same influences, which leads to complete assimilation and even degeneration. It should be recognized that the Western model, which is sometimes held up as the product of advanced civilization, has created its own crop of problems which distinctive cultures of Asia might do well to avoid. Traditional Sri Lankan aesthetic culture still survives but languishes in neglect. The impact of modernization and rapid change may erase it completely, even in rural areas, if no determined effort is made to conserve and develop the traditional arts, crafts, folklore, dance forms, etc.

Organization of a national council

To deal with the foregoing, the best organizational forum, combining both flexibility and direct authority stemming from the political decision-making level, would seem to be a cultural co-ordinating

council presided over by the Minister of Cultural Affairs. This
council could have broad representation from universities, research
institutes, private and public cultural institutes, representatives
of the three mass media and from the principal religions, as well as
representatives from the Department of Buddhist Affairs and the
Department of Hindu and Islamic Affairs. This council could oversee
and carry out the activities listed below :

a)   to set up a Central Cultural Fund for the living arts and
     crafts and literature, similar to that created by the CCF for
     the Cultural Triangle ;

b)   to transform *Kalayatanas* (arts schools) into centres for pre-
     serving traditional art forms, linking them with higher
     education and professional schools ;

c)   to obtain advice from the Institute of Aesthetic Studies of the
     university, either directly or through its representatives on
     the council ;

d)   to elaborate and develop indigenous Sinhala dance forms as well
     as indigenous Tamil dance forms. To this end the State Dance
     Ensemble should be maintained by the government agents of the
     respective districts for the preservation and development of
     the Kandyan, Ruhuna, Saharagamuwa, Batticaloa and Jaffna dance
     forms ;

e)   to obtain technical co-operation from competent state
     institutions to improve traditional dyes and colours and to
     establish design and the use of colours referred to above ;

f)   to develop schemes to assist needy artists and to accord
     recognized artists certain privileges, now accorded to the
     higher professions, in recognition of the recommendations of
     the General Conference of Unesco held in 1980 at Belgrade
     regarding the status of artists ;

g)   to reactivate the *Sahitya mandalayas* (literary academies) ;

h)   to provide opportunities throughout the educational system for
     Sinhala students to learn Sinhala as a second language. This
     has been tried before unsuccessfully and its successful im-
     plementation is possible only after some degree of accord has
     been reached between the two communities ;

i)   to translate classical modern literature as well as leading
     religious texts of the main religions of Sri Lanka into Sinhala
     and Tamil where such texts have not been translated ;

j)   to establish a network of cultural centres with one national
     culture centre to provide for theatre halls, art galleries,
     exhibition rooms, rooms for readers' clubs, lecture halls,
     libraries for the arts, culture and literature, etc.
     Kalyatanas should be closely associated with such a programme
     and even be accommodated at this centre where feasible ;

k)   to provide avenues for training in cultural administration for
     those responsible for implementing schemes related to culture
     under the Ministries of State and Cultural Affairs ;

l)   to explore possibilities of encouraging the private sector to
     participate in and contribute to the promotion of the country's
     national cultural policy as determined by the cultural co-
     ordinating council.

Cultural planning

In any country, culture is considered an offshoot or epiphenomenon which arises from other more basic and material activities. In the view of some philosophers, culture is the superstructure over a material base. Consequently, planning in the field of culture, in the best instance, is restricted to planning of projects within the restricted resources available for cultural development. A corollary that follows is that the Ministry of Cultural Affairs will have to spell out the fundamental objectives of cultural development in line with state policy and formulate practical and practicable strategies for achieving them. Programmes and projects formulated within the scope of the strategy should be selected for implementation with a clear statement of priorities to indicate which projects could be dropped or deferred, if there is lack of resources.

Further, no less important is the imperative for the plan to relate to plans in other connected sectors, in particular education and communications. In all areas of overall activities spanning many sectors such as culture and environment, it is important to be conscious of the possibilities of overlap in activities and equally the possibilities of counter-productive activity by different agencies. It is therefore necessary for the Ministry of Culture to consider not only the individual projects under different departments of the Ministry but also under other related ministries as a whole.

6. COMMUNICATIONS IN SRI LANKA

The Ministry of State is in charge of the information and publicity functions of the government, namely :

1. to hold periodic news conferences and provide press releases on behalf of the government, when important matters are in the foreground or agitating the public ;
2. to release regular information bulletins on Cabinet decisions of importance.

Among the departments and public/private institutions coming directly or indirectly under the purview of the Ministry and active in communications are :

1. The Information Department ;
2. The Sri Lanka Broadcasting Corporation (SLBC) ;
3. The Rupavahini Corporation (RC) ;
4. The Independent Television Network (ITN) ;
5. The State Film Corporation (SFC) ;

6. The Government Press Department ;
7. The State Printing Corporation (SPC) ;
8. The Department of Wild Life ;
9. The Department of Zoological Gardens ;
10. The Government Publications Bureau ;
11. The National News Agency 'Lanka Puwath' ;
12. The Press ;
13. The Sri Lanka Press Council ;
14. The Family Planning Communications Project ;
15. The National Film Corporation (NCF) ;
16. The Tourist Board.

It will thus be noted that this Ministry has a very broad span of coverage as regards influence and control over the transmission of information domestically and overseas.

For all media, general guidelines, stated to be Ministry policy, are :

a) to retain credibility ;
b) to maintain good public relations ;
c) to project news and information, not on a generalized or over-all basis, but with the accent on its effect on the individual.

General observations

'Knowledge is Power' has been a hackneyed expression ever since man learned to transmit knowledge - from person to person, group to group, family to family and finally nation to nation. Commun-ications is important in the relations between "governments and governed as between enterprises that generate, manage and process information and the individuals and societies whose lives may be influenced in various ways because they do not always possess the means of exercising their intelligence or judgment freely". In such a situation, the power to influence becomes a monopoly which fortifies the power of the information-generating enterprises and enables them to exercise "enormous cultural power which, in the final analysis exerts control over the political and the economic forces - undermining the traditional conception of the separation of powers". Further, "information can be, and often has been, used to perpetuate preconceived ideas, to reinforce ignorance and contempt - even intolerance - for others". Equally it can be "a fertile source of mutual understanding and respect" [5].

The enormous power for good or ill wielded by the generators of information needs to be understood. "In a single major industrial-ized country... the communications market ... amounted to 21.3 thousand million dollars..." and this market is expected to expand to "103.1 thousand million dollars in 1990" [6]. This is a 490 per cent increase in eight years ! Additionally, this balloon-ing volume of information (some of it flowing in excess, indigest-ible, and styled as 'information overload') has created inequalities between a minority engaged in transmitting messages and the majority who are "at the receiving end" as "passive receivers" [7]. This is true both between and within nations. And so the necessity arises for communication to be democratized so that there may be greater participation by the underprivileged sectors, again both among nations and within nations. This applies with greater force to the rural segments (normally very large) in developing nations.

Unesco has recommended five principles aimed at the democratization of information :

1. Communication is a fundamental right both of the individual and the community ; it is also a major means to ensure participation of citizens in the management of public institutions and projects.
2. It is necessary to preserve the rights and remove imbalances, inequalities and distortions now affecting communication within and between countries, both in respect of structures and the flow of news and knowledge and programmes for such transmission.
3. Solutions must be found to "match needs and values" of different peoples in programmes, implying respect for cultural identities without disruption of national unity. This implies the inculcation of tolerance.
4. There should be implementation of coherent national communication policies, integrated into general development activities.
5. The possible bases upon which a New World Information and Communication Order can be built should be explored to achieve balanced information flows.

Studies on the impact of the press on development

The Marga Institute has carried out the only significant study on the Sri Lankan press and development. Some of the findings of the study as well as its plan are mentioned below. The projected 30-year period of study from 1948 to 1979 was divided into three sub-periods : a) 1948 to 1960 ; b) 1960 to 1973 ; and c) 1973 to 1978.

The criteria of assessment under two main headings (news, and opinion and comment) are summarized below :

News :

1. The assessment of the space devoted to development information relative to other items and the emphasis given (front page display, lead stories).
2. How far the press initiates development news and assesses development information on its own.
3. Is reporting independent and objective ? Are sources purely official or are other sources used as checks ?

4. Are any observed failings in objectivity, inaccuracies and imbalances attributable to political partiality (private press) or state control (state press) ?

5. How far are different viewpoints on controversial matters on development fairly represented and has the reporting of defects and shortcomings in development made any impact on government policy ?

6. What concepts of development feature prominently and is the reporting informative, intelligible, interesting and readable to the average reader ?

Opinion and comments

1. What proportion of editorials, documentaries and feature articles devoted to development matters such as news, opinion or comments is independent, objective and fair ?

2. Is observed lack of objectivity or unfairness related to political partiality or state control ?

3. How far are different points of view on controversial development matters reflected, and has critical comment been able to make an impact on government action ?

4. Are any commentaries of the concepts or philosophy of development carried by the press ?

5. Is such investigative information intelligible and readable to the general reader ?

It was found that even in the earliest period where there was uniformity and homogeneity in the general outlook on development with a "close relationship of political outlook between the principal newspaper groups and the government in power" at the time, it does not follow that the press was 'free' because it was private and free of state control ; it was not "free of political circumstances", but these were circumstances of its own choosing following from political choices made by the newspaper management. At that time, only the *Ceylon Daily News* "projected coherent views of what forms development should take" and their features and documentaries advocated "a faithful adoption of the Western model, that is mechanized large-scale industry, mechanized agriculture, procurement of the newest Western technology through import of skills, attraction of foreign investment and aid". But this did not preclude at times some criticism of government development purposes. On the matter of subsidy, it has been found that the newspapers from time to time reflected the twists and turns of government policy with regard to expansion or contraction of subsidies without any critical standpoint of their own.

It was also found that opposition opinion on development conclusions was inadequately represented except for skimpy reports of Parliament and public meetings. Opposition opinion on controversial development matters got hardly any coverage.

The post-1966 period brought about a change in the government/press relationship in that the two main newspaper groups were no longer linked in political loyalty to the government in power. Potentially, this was a healthy situation. Between 1957 and 1960, the daily news, documentaries and features in the *Economic Research Staff* sharply criticized the lack of coherent economic policy by the government in power. Research would show, however, that the objective was not actively to help development activities but to capitalize on contradictions. It is also found that a great majority of development news sources were solidly slanted against current policy. Another related feature was that the press, while concentrating on divisive tendencies, did not "generally help to build up a consciousness of unity" with the result that the Sinhala- and Tamil-owned press adhered to "a parochial, racial conscious- ness", while the English press maintained a benign neutrality as it was addressing a mixed public. The general conclusion seems to be that neutrality of press coverage cannot be expected either from a private or state press as both have their own masters to satisfy. This situation is, however, not hopeless as the important thing is that every government in power, whatever its political complexion, has much more interest than the press in satisfying a very large spectrum of the population that it serves. The problem then is not to try to think of elusive objectivity and neutrality but to plan through related agencies - Ministry of State, Department of Inform- ation, Press Council, Lankapuvath, and the other media - to ensure not only an exposure of accepted development policies but also a mode of presentation of news and views which would secure more active participation in development activities than in the past.

Broadcasting and development : the Mahaweli Community Radio (MCR)

News studios and a broadcasting complex have been set up in Anuradhapura and connected to the main network programme transmitted via Anuradhapura for about four hours every day. Studios at Jaffna and Kandy are being planned as part of the expansion programme.

The Mahaweli Community Radio has become justly famous, not only locally, as an innovation in broadcasting with a strong development accent. The MCR is the only grassroots broadcasting institution in the country. It was inaugurated in collaboration with Unesco, with equipment and training assistance from the Danish International Development Agency (DANIDA). The MCR is as elemental and down-to- earth as its potential audience. It has no control room, recording studios or sophisticated computers. It has a staff of 30 workers with three production teams and a mobile open-air studio carrying tape recorders, mixer and monitoring equipment designed for field work. All equipment is carried in boxes that also operate as stands and the only additional equipment is a folding table. The entire outfit takes fifteen minutes to assemble at any location. All programmes are, however, previously planned and are recorded for rural listeners in their own language and idioms, with villagers participating in the programme. The team normally spends three days in the village. The recordings themselves are spontaneous but the words and music are recorded largely in the field and then edited at the Peradeniya radio centre before being broadcast over the Rajarata Sevaya and the Mahanuwara Sevaya as well as over the main Colombo Station.

Programmes are developed on the basis of feedback received by the programme divisions from the listener research division. The pattern of broadcasting is that there are fixed points such as the news bulletins and religious broadcasts at regular times and intervals. Over and above this, 60 per cent of the broadcasts over the national service consist of musical items, listeners' requests, birthday greetings, etc. 40 per cent of the programmes have a direct development role over and above the normal programmes which also have development dimensions. These special programmes cover the main line ministries such as Mahaweli, Housing and Construction, Agriculture, Industries and Fisheries. Some of these ministries have units attached to the Sri Lanka Broadcasting Corporation studies and the officers in these units are responsible to their ministries for the formulation and content of programmes.

Apart from these special programmes, others are broadcast with the objective of socio-economic development in rural areas and 90 per cent of these general programmes are development-oriented and are suggested by the ministries.

Television and development

The Rupavahini Corporation (RC) was established in parallel with another organization, the Independent Television Network (ITN), at a cost of Rs. 306 million, a gift from the Government of Japan. Construction work commenced in October 1979 with the building of studios in Colombo. The studios were to transmit programmes via 'micro wave' to the transmitting station located at Pidurutalagala mountain (2500 m.). Two reporter stations amplified the television beams from Kandy and Kokuvil, thus covering 85 per cent of the island's population. A national television centre was set up to prepare programme material. National television operates daily two services lasting five hours, except on Sundays and holidays when the duration is increased. All the country's significant development activities have been featured in one or other programme.

The growth of Rupavahini has been phenomenal, as also its success in incorporating development material. Many foreign news services have noted that Sri Lanka has witnessed "remarkable growth in its television services with 52 per cent of local material in its two-year old television network". The Rupavahini expansion programme proposes to make an extra channel operational by late 1987 or early 1988. Television producers have been completing training abroad, the majority at Radio Free Berlin (SFB) Television Training Centre (TTC), which has been specially designed to help developing countries improve their programme production and transmission through the optimization of available resources.

The grassroots television programme (parallel with MCR of the SLBC) has produced, apart from its several local programmes, a most outstanding teledrama - *Dimuthu Muthu*, the first long series with 26 episodes directed by Nihalsinghe, an acclaimed local film director. The head of the RC has stated that more are in preparation and RC will continue to produce items with the development theme uppermost even though production is somewhat expensive. The entire series will display a way of life true of any village in Sri Lanka and reflect current concerns, including the pressures operating on village people to drift to the towns. However, the temptation to broadcast less expensive programmes from outside sources is great, unless costs can be substantially reduced. Rupavahini has set up an Audience Survey and Research Unit which has already completed several studies bearing in mind that the main objective of intro-ducing television to Sri Lanka was to carry the development message to the rural masses. The Unit measured the effectiveness of these programmes.

The total number of licences issued for television sets is estimated at 271,759. It is expected that this figure will reach about 750,000 and then level off, as cost will become prohibitive at this point. The present coverage with approximately 270,000 sets is estimated to correspond to an audience of 5 million at peak times, with one out of three persons, on average, having access to a tele-vision set.

The statistical analysis for programme time for 1983 and 1984 shows that out of 1607 hours and 1760 hours of total transmission respectively, 492 hours (30.6 per cent) and 499 hours (28.3 per cent) respectively were devoted to telecast programmes on develop-ment including current affairs and documentaries. In 1985, out of a total telecasting time of 1888 hours, 577 hours (30.6 per cent) were devoted to development programmes. The 52 per cent estimated there-fore has to include programmes which indirectly embodies development or educational elements. The surprising result of the survey, figuring 300 randomly selected households, of which 93.7 per cent responded, revealed that only 12.1 per cent of selected respondents actually viewed programmes on development. Category preference of the respondents in this survey clearly indicates that the vast majority (63.4 per cent) watched only dramas, while 7.6 per cent watched non-formal educational programmes, 5 per cent watched doc-umentaries, and most surprising of all, 3.2 per cent watched the news, 2.5 per cent watched musical programmes, 0.7 per cent watched children's programmes, 0.4 per cent sports and religious programmes, and only 5 per cent watched development programmes. A further study showed that knowledge of even the existence of development projects was quite limited, and that out of ten listed development projects, around 50 per cent of the respondents were aware of all the projects. The source of information of correspondents concerning development projects has been equally interesting. The majority responded that most of the development projects were known to them through television, while newspapers were the second most important source of information, with radio ranking third. It is also reveal-ing that political meetings had a very low rating as a source of development information.

The Independent Television Network (ITN) started its trans-missions in 1980. It was intended to be a commercial television network and the first experimental broadcasts in late 1979 covered only a radius of 30 miles from Colombo. The private entrepreneurs who were in charge of the project could not work together and consequently a Competent Authority was appointed under the Government-Owned Business Undertaking (GOBU) Act to take over and run the company.

The ITN had an initial equity of Rs. 5 million and was viable financially, acquiring a site of about 21 acres at Jayawardanapura, where the terrain is situated 120 ft. above sea level, transmission being from a tower 240 ft. high. A transmission level of 360 ft. was thus achieved. There are however many areas where reception is difficult because of obstruction, as the ITN does not have the advantage of transmitting from the highpoint of the island. It will ne necessary both to have one highpoint transmission south of the central massif and another highpoint north. At present, coverage is 40 to 60 miles, depending on level of obstruction. The proposed expansion plan foresees the installation of boosters at Enselwatte in Deniyaya and at Matale (in the central hills), in order to achieve an island-wide coverage of target populated areas. The ITN is also due to negotiate for foreign assistance in this expansion programme.

As regards development coverage, half an hour out of a total of four-and-a-half hours' transmission consists of local programmes in Sinhala and Enlgish with the news in three languages replicated from the Rupavahini broadcast. The rest of the nearly four hour programme is made up of costly imported material. The bulk of programmes are supplied by foreign television companies such as the BBC, Thames, Granada, Scottish Television, Yorkshire Television, Arthur Rank from the United Kingdom, and Paramount, CBS, Columbia and Warner Bros. from the USA.

Communications and the development message

It will be seen from the preceding study of the various executive arms of the Ministry of State that this Ministry has control of the means of transmission over the bulk of communications media. This represents an ideal opportunity to put across or project the development message and to secure active participation of the populace. At present, there is a lack of co-ordinated programming across the various media controlled by this Ministry, as well as programming down to the last minute within each of the communications institutions, more particularly the Information Department, SLBC and Rupavahini. This situation can lead to overlap and waste of programme projection time.

Media methodology embraces three types of message transmission, be they development messages or plain advertisements. These are :

1. The didactic or 'direct' method which is the least credible, has the least impact and could at times even be counterproductive. Usually ceremonials, anniversaries, special

occasions presided over by leading personages or political figures are covered by SLBC and TV. Here the message comes across direct in a manner which is the least persuasive. Research has shown, as indicated earlier, that the degree of learning even from speeches at political meetings is minimal.

2. The documentary or 'oblique' method, under which programmes are presented against a cultural, scenic or even historical background, where although the message is explicit, it is left to be learnt by implication rather than through a direct effort to convince. In a documentary, it is the cleverness of the setting against which the message is conveyed that is effective.

3. The last method can be termed 'integral', as it is woven into the texture of the presentation. Here the method of delivery is more specific, is targeted to certain groups for which the message is intended but is implanted organically within a screenplay, teledrama or a radio feature programme.

The ministry in charge of communications therefore has a strong opportunity to put across the development message effectively. But this must be carried out with clarity, with the targeted audience in mind, and the manner in which the message is conveyed must be clearly thought out ahead of time.

In closing, it is opportune to emphasize that, as for culture, various government departments and agencies which have specific messages to put across have very limited funds at their disposal and overall communications expenditure does not rank high in government budgetary allocations. It is therefore imperative that a rule, which has normally been applied to business enterprises, should be applied even more rigorously to the practice of communications in conveying the development message and in securing fuller participation, namely that there should be maximum output (and impact) from minimum input. This means that communications as well as cultural development expenditure cannot escape the rule of cost-effectiveness.

7. CONCLUSIONS

In the preceding sections, we have discussed the system of national planning currently in operation in Sri Lanka against the background of past experiences and of planning adopted in the areas of competence of Unesco. The rolling five-year Public Investment Programme was described in detail to indicate both the methodology adopted in its preparation and the central role it plays in the planning system.

After several years of experimentation with different types of planning, the rolling five-year plan method of the Public Investment Programme has come to stay as a pragmatic and effective method of dealing with the problems of economic and social development in Sri Lanka. It has proved to be pragmatic because it takes into account the administrative and planning constraints inherent in centralized comprehensive planning.

Many developing countries have, and are still engaged in comprehensive planning arising out of the need to deal in an integrated way with the interwoven problems of economic and social development. While theoretically it provides a neat optimal solution to problems of harnessing and exploiting national resources in order to achieve the multiple objectives of a society by integrating "all activities at all operational levels" (including the private sector), in practice, it is hard to realise. The multitude of decisions that have to be taken, covering large numbers of producers, suppliers and consumers both in the productive and the service sectors, becomes an insurmountable problem. Even in the most advanced countries supported by modern information technology it is not possible to organize the timely flow of all the necessary data. An integrated approach to planning therefore has to be achieved through a combination of pragmatism and effectiveness.

In the Sri Lankan context, the Public Investment Programme has become effective because it deals with resource allocations which have far-reaching effects. Public investment deals with only about 55 per cent of total investment in the economy, but its influence covers a much wider area, because of its impact on private sector activity. Further, the resource allocations envisaged in the Public Investment Programme are closely interwoven with the Budget. While the five-year programme helps maintain a medium-term perspective all the time, the rolling plan technique allows the flexibility that is required in a country which is affected by the uncertainties of a predominantly agricultural structure and a changing international environment.

The areas of education, science and technology, communication and culture are predominantly government activities or are heavily influenced by them. The Public Investment Programme therefore offers an effective means of dealing with those areas in an integrated way. But for this purpose, their planning must be made consistent with the inter-sectoral and intra-sectoral priorities upon which resource allocations in the Public Investment Programme are based.

As indicated in the section on sectoral planning, however, it was only in respect of the Agricultural Research Project that procedures were followed which help integration into the Public Investment Programme. To recapitulate, we observed that the objectives of the project and its roles were defined in the process of formulating the Agriculture, Food and Nutrition Strategy. The project was therefore a part of an overall package of policies directed towards developing agriculture. In its formulation, all the relevant organizations participated, including the National Planning Division, which is responsible for the final preparation of the Public Investment Programme. The project identified costs of individual items and priorities and procedures for implementation.

The science and technology policy prepared by the NSPCC, however, does not arise out of an overall economic and social development strategy, even though it takes into account very broadly the objectives of development. A science and technology policy must be an integral part of an economic development strategy and must therefore relate to sectoral and sub-sectoral strategies.

In fact, the Agricultural Research Project must be an integral component of overall S&T policy. Similarly, S&T policies in other areas such as industry, transport, telecommunications, etc., must arise out of sectoral strategies developed with regard to them. The task ahead for planners in Sri Lanka is therefore to review the National Science Policy formulated by the NSPCC in the light of the sectoral strategies being developed in transport, telecommunications, power and energy, manufacturing industries and health.

It is also proposed to formulate an integrated strategy for education which will cover general, tertiary and higher education as well as regional dispersal issues. This will provide an opportunity to incorporate elements of S&T, communications (particularly in regard to distance education) and culture.

An area which needs strengthening is communications for development. *Ad hoc* methods of using communications must be replaced by a planned approach which can weave communications into the development strategy. This, however, requires development of better tools of analysis with regard to costs and benefits of communication. A good example is the use of communication technology in preventive health care. Large amounts of resources are allocated by the state every year for curative services. If it is possible to estimate the reduction of spending on curative services that could be achieved as a result of primary health care, particularly through the promotion of public awareness, the task of determining priorities in the allocation of resources would become easier and integration of health and communication would be achieved. Surveys in certain areas have, in fact, established the strong connection between public awareness of hygiene through communication and the reduction of diarrhoeal diseases. Integration of communication, however, as well as other sectors such as education, culture, science and technology, etc., into the Public Investment Programme, that is into the resource allocation process, is difficult unless costs can be related to benefits in some quantifiable form, so that planners will be able to deal with their basic concern of priorities in the allocation of scarce resources.

NOTES

1   The Ten Year Plan, The National Planning Council, Colombo, 1959, p. 460.

2   The Development Programme 1966-67. Ministry of Planning and Economic Affairs, July 1966.

3   The Five Year Plan, Ministry of Finance and Employment, p. 109.

4   John Still, *The Jungle Tide*.

5   Unesco's Draft Medium-Term Plan (1984-1989), para. 3003.

6   *Ibid.*, para. 3014.

7   *Ibid.*, para. 3013.